American Psychological Association • Washington, DC

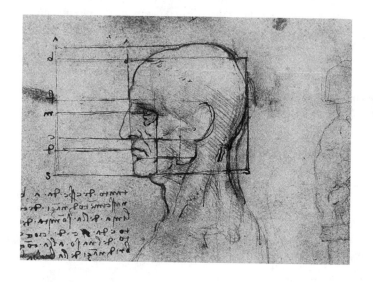

Interpretative Guide

to the

Millon
Clinical
Multiaxial
Inventory

JAMES P. CHOCA
LUKE A. SHANLEY
ERIC VAN DENBURG

Third printing September 1993

Published by
American Psychological Association
750 First Street, NE
Washington, DC 20002

Copies may be ordered from
APA Order Department
P.O. Box 2710
Hyattsville, MD 20784

In the UK and Europe, copies may be ordered from
American Psychological Association
3 Henrietta Street
Covent Garden, London
WC2E 8LU England

Typeset in Futura and New Baskerville by TAPSCO, Inc., Akron, PA.

Printer: BookCrafters, Inc., Chelsea, MI
Designer and Typographer: Enigma Concepts, Inc., Silver Spring, MD
Technical/Production Editor: Christine P. Landry

Library of Congress Cataloging-in-Publication Data
Choca, James, 1945—
    Interpretative guide to the Millon Clinical Multiaxial Inventory/
James P. Choca, Luke A. Shanley, Eric Van Denburg.
        p. cm.
    Includes bibliographical references and index.
    ISBN 1-55798-146-9 (acid-free paper)
    1. Millon Clinical Multiaxial Inventory. 2. Personality
disorders—Diagnosis. I. Shanley, Luke A., 1943-   . II. Van
Denburg, Eric J. (Eric James) III. Title
        (DNLM: 1. Personality Disorders-diagnosis. 2. Personality
Disorders—pszychology. 3. Personality Inventory. WM 141 C545i)
    RC473.M47C48 1991
616.89'075-dc20
DNLM/DLC
for Library of Congress

British Library Cataloguing in Publication Data   91-26205
A CIP record is available from the British Library   CIP

Contents

Foreword

Professor Choca has begun his preface to this exemplary book by offering a brief glimpse into the origins of his professional career. Perhaps I can be permitted to sketch the early events that gave rise to the professional career of the Millon Clinical Multiaxial Inventory (MCMI).

A year or two after the publication in 1969 of my *Modern Psychopathology* text, I began, with some regularity, to receive letters and phone calls from graduate students who read the book and thought it provided ideas that could aid them in formulating their dissertations. Most inquired about the availability of an "operational" measure they could use to assess or diagnose the pathologies of personality that were generated by the text's theoretical model. Regretfully, I said that there was no such tool available. Nevertheless, I encouraged them to pursue whatever lines of interest they may have had in the subject. Some were sufficiently motivated to state that they would attempt to develop their own "Millon" instrument as part of the dissertation enterprise. At first, I was pleased to see the appeal of my work and considered such aspirations to be not only ambitious but highly commendable.

As the number of these potential Millon progenies grew into the teens, however, my concern grew proportionately regarding both the diversity and adequacy of these representations of the theory. To establish a measure of instrumental uniformity for future investigators, as well as to assure at least a modicum of psychometric quality among tools that ostensibly reflected the theory's constructs, I was prompted (perhaps "driven" is a more accurate word) to consider undertaking the test-construction task myself. At that time, in early 1971, I fortunately was directing a research supervision group composed of psychologists- and psychiatrists-in-training during their internship and residency periods. All of them had read *Modern Psychopathology* and found my proposal of working together to develop instruments to identify and quantify the test's personality constructs to be both worthy and challenging.

I set as our initial task that of exploring alternate methods for gathering relevant clinical data. About 11 or 12 of us were involved in that early phase. Some were asked to analyze the possibilities of identifying new indexes from well-established projective tests, such as the Rorschach and the Thematic Apperception Test; others were to investigate whether we could compose relevant scales from existing objective inventories, such as the Sixteen Factor Personality Questionnaire (16PF) and the Minnesota Multiphasic Personality Inventory (MMPI). Another group examined the potential inherent in developing a new and original structured interview. After 4 or 5 months of weekly discussions, the group concluded that an entirely new instrument would be required if we were to represent the full scope of the theory, especially its diverse and then-novel pathological personality patterns (our work, it should be recalled, preceded by several years that undertaken by the DSM–III Task Force). It was judged further that we would attempt to construct both a self-report inventory and a semistructured interview schedule.

Naively, we assumed that both construction tasks could be completed in about 18 months, a time period that would allow several members of the research group to participate on a continuing basis. Despite the fact that we "postponed" developing the interview schedule after a brief initial period, the "more limited" task of the inventory took almost 7 years to complete. The framework and preliminary item selections of the inventory were well underway, however, by the end of the first full year of our work and was described briefly in a book I coauthored in 1972: *Research Methods in Psychopathology*. The initial forms of the clinical instrument were entitled the *Millon-Illinois Self-Report Inventory;* it was at this early phase that Jim Choca became acquainted with the test-construction project, although he was by then quite knowledgeable about the theory and its personality derivations. Since then, he has remained one among a small group of very early adherents who has not only followed the development of the test but has continued to contribute to its further progress. For his diligence and creative efforts, he, and his younger colleagues, have both my respect and admiration.

In this book, Choca, Shanley, and Van Denburg join that growing list of psychologists and psychiatrists who demonstrate that valid personality assessments are neither impertinent nor grandiose fantasies of an arrogant and inchoate science. As I have written elsewhere, psychodiagnostic procedures in the past contained more than their share of mystique. Not only were assessments often an exercise in oracular craft and intuitive artistry, but they typically were clothed in obscure and esoteric jargon. A change in the character of personality theory and assessment began to brew in the late 1960s. Slow though these advances might have been, there were clear signs that new ideas would soon emerge. Projective techniques such as the Rorschach began to be analyzed quantitatively and were increasingly anchored to the empirical domain. The so-called objective inventories, such as the 16PF and MMPI, were being interpreted increasingly in terms of configural profiles. No longer approached as sets of separate scales, these formerly segmented instruments were now being analyzed as holistic integrations that possessed clinical significance only as gestalt composites. In addition, the former insistence that diagnostic interpretation be "objective," that is, anchored solely to empirical correlates, gave way to clinical syntheses, including the "dynamics" of the previously maligned projectives. Although part-function instruments, oriented toward one expressive form of pathology or another (e.g., anxiety or depression), are still popular, the newest tools moved increasingly toward composite structures, (i.e., "whole" personalities). These personality formulations were not conceived of as random sets or discrete attributes (i.e., scales) that must be individually deduced and then pieced together but as integrated configurations from the start. Hence, we have seen the development of various tools explicitly designed to diagnose, for example, the "borderline" personality. The MCMI represents the most recent trend in holistic personality scales, going one step beyond most techniques by including all of the *Diagnostic and Statistical Manual (DSM)* personality disorders in a single inventory. Holism is not limited to inventories alone. New structured interview schedules and clinical rating scales have been developed to provide another rich source of data. Not to be overlooked is the sound psychometric manner in which most of these newer tools have been constructed, thereby wedding the empirical and quantitative features that were the major strength of the structured objective inventories with the dynamic and integrative qualities that characterized the more intuitive projective techniques. It is in bridging the quantitative and integrative that Choca, Shanley, and Van Denburg make their special contribution in this book.

We should also not overlook the very special status assigned the personality syndromes in the *DSM*. With the advent of the third edition of this official classification, personality disorders not only gained a place of consequence among syndromal categories but became central to its multiaxial schema. The logic for assigning personality its own special status is more than a matter of differentiating syndromes of a more acute and dramatic form from those of a longstanding and prosaic character. More relevant to this partitioning decision was the assertion that personality can serve usefully as a dynamic substrate from which clinicians can better grasp the significance and meaning of their patients' transient and florid disorders. In the *DSM*, then, personality disorders not only attained a nosological status of prominence in their own right but were assigned a contextual role that made them fundamental to the understanding and interpretation of all other psychopathologies. Here, again, Choca, Shanley, and Van Denburg have provided readers with an opportunity to examine the various ways in which the MCMI demonstrates the interrelationships between Axis I and Axis II.

As Choca notes in his preface, the approach he and his colleagues have taken in the text differs in certain respects from my most recent formulations; they remain truer to my early notions than I have. Hence, I am hesitant to endorse their entire thesis; for example, I do not share the confidence they show in drawing certain distinctions among their profile interpretations, nor do I believe that the MCMI personality "disorder" scales are best conceived of as personality "styles." This latter point reflects matters of a pragmatic rather than of a conceptual nature. Although the issue deserves a full explication on my part, the foreword to a book is not the place to expand on contentions of this sort. To be brief, I have judged it best to opt in favor of focusing an inventory on target rather than broad-based populations; hence, the MCMI is oriented toward matters of import among adult mental health patients, the MAPI centers attention on adolescent clinical populations, the MBHI focuses on those whose primary ailments are of a medical or physical nature, and the forthcoming MPSI (Millon Personality Style Inventory) addresses traits among nonclinical or so-called normal adults (as can be seen, I, too, have chosen the "style" terminology, but only for people who do not evince discernable psychic pathology).

Despite differences such as these, I consider this book to be the product of research clinicians of the highest order, and I am delighted by the thoroughness and balance they have shown in presenting the strengths and limitations of the MCMI. I continue to learn much from them, as no doubt will readers of this book.

Perhaps the text's greatest value to its readers is an implicit one, namely, that the growing appeal of the MCMI lies in its heuristic fertility. The inventory is more than another "objective" tool in the diagnostician's assessment kit. It provides clinicians with a theoretical schema for mastering the realm of personality pathology, a means for understanding the processes that underlie their patient's overtly dysfunctional behaviors, thoughts, and feelings. Moreover, the openness of the theory not only illuminates the patient's personal life but encourages the clinician to uncover insights beyond those on which the MCMI's interpretative model has been grounded.

Finally, let me congratulate the authors on being the first to provide the profession with a full text on the instrument. Although several other MCMI volumes are "in the pipeline," few will be as informed and as carefully reasoned as theirs.

Theodore Millon

Preface

My first clinical supervisor, Dr. James Morton, was all smiles when he saw me carrying my abnormal psychology textbook. He knew that it was my first time in a psychiatric ward and joked about my need for a "security blanket." I tried to defend the value of my textbook by stating that I may have to look up some of the information before properly classifying any client with whom I was asked to work.

It was at that point that Dr. Morton pointed to the door opening into the hallway and bet me a Coca-Cola that the next patient to pass by would be schizophrenic. In retrospect, I think many of the patients I met during that year might have also suffered from an organic mental disorder. At the time, however, schizophrenia was the fashionable diagnosis, at least at that institution for chronic psychiatric patients, and its definition was ambiguous enough that practically all inpatients had that diagnosis. The explanation of such facts of life, unfortunately, only led to another uninformed statement on my part: "Oh, so they are all the same."

After supervising students for a few years, I tend to react to that kind of naïveté unenthusiastically. If Dr. Morton felt any discouragement at having to start at such a low level with his new student, he certainly hid it well. He patiently explained that, in fact, every person was different. With time, he was able to impress on me his notion that the clinical syndromes reflected only the different ways in which people react when they are no longer able to cope with life. To understand why the patient is unable to cope, or to understand what makes the individual unique, he held that clinicians had to discover many aspects of the person, particularly the individual's life-style.

My interactions with Dr. Morton eventually led to my learning the Adlerian concept of life-style (Adler, 1956), the methods that could be used to uncover the characteristics of that life-style, and the way in which the life-style affects the clinical picture. Dr. Morton would have argued that, the same way that Georgia O'Keefe did not have to sign her paintings for others to recognize them as her work, personality styles often leave a clearly identifiable imprint in many things a person may do. One goal in writing this book was to continue Dr. Morton's work and help clinicians develop more of an appreciation for the importance of the person's life-style.

Many developments in the mental health field during the intervening years made the appreciation for the importance of the personality style a bit less rare. One such important development was the publication of Theodore Millon's *Modern Psychopathology: A Biosocial Approach to Maladaptive Learning and Functioning* in 1969. I was so delighted with the eight personality prototypes that the book described that I contacted Millon and was eventually able to meet him and another member of his group, Robert Meagher. As a courtesy to a would-be researcher, I was given copies of the mimeographed true–false inventory they were working on, an inventory that was designed to measure the kind of personality characteristics that we were all interested in.

By the time I became a staff psychologist at Lakeside, this inventory had been upgraded with a name (the Millon Illinois Self-Report Inventory [MISRI]) and had been printed. Some time thereafter, the inventory was renamed to the Millon Multiaxial Clinical Inventory (MMCI) when the Millon group left Illinois. Eventually, this name was altered again to the test's current name: the Millon Clinical Multiaxial Inventory (MCMI). A second goal in writing this book was to share what we have learned through years of using the different versions of this test.

In our work with the MCMI, Luke Shanley, Eric Van Denburg, and I have developed our own ways of thinking about the test that we feel are somewhat different from Millon's. For one thing, we have remained loyal to the original eight personality prototypes that Millon proposed in 1969. For another, we think of these prototypes as personality *styles* rather than personality *disorders*. Through the present work we hope to offer a slightly different representation of what the scores mean that would be offered by the Millon narratives.

This work is intended to be an interpretative guide. Although there are several such books to help clinicians interpret the Minnesota Multiphasic Personality Inventory, nothing of the kind is available for the MCMI. Although this book should help the clinical psychologist better understand the National Computer System automated computer narratives, we aim to do more than that. We offer the narratives that we have used in describing different personality styles; we also describe the test in a way that we hope will lead readers into developing their own sense of what the scores mean so that they, in turn, can produce their own descriptions.

Finally, our task is to review all of the available literature, pointing out the strengths as well as the weaknesses of the MCMI. In this way, this book is different from the test manual in that the latter cannot be expected to be very critical of the test whose use it is designed to propagate. We attempt to take all of the inventory's critics into consideration and make the reader aware of the way in which the test may falter. In spite of our belief that the MCMI is the best measure of personality styles that is currently available, we try to be as fair as possible.

Acknowledgments

We would like to thank all of those who have research in the growing field of personality styles and whose work will often be cited in this book. High on that list, of course, are Theodore Millon and Robert Meagher. Dr. Meagher's death, coinciding with the day we received the page proofs for this book, is a personal and professional loss that will be impossible to replace.

This book contains the contributions of many other individuals. Most obvious is the influence of our research associates and past or present members of the staff at Lakeside. The list of such people includes Gene Alexander, Linda Bresolin, Michael Bresolin, Diane Cohen, Kenneth Cohen, Kay Cooper, William Davis, Rodney Eiger, Richard Ferm, Dan Garside, Zachary Gavriel, John Gerber, Jonathan Goldman, John Gottlieb, Evelyn Graham, Jerry Grant, Richard Greenblatt, Marlene Grupp, David Gutmann, Mort Hammer, Barry Hoffman, Joan Hong, Walter Kitt, Russell Le Blanc, Margaret Loomis, Elie Mangoubi, Althea Mason, Kun Ki Min, Sidney Moragne, Jeri Morris, Andrew Mouton, Ann Newman, John Nihizer, Anna Okonek, David Ostrow, Charles Peterson, Kathy Pietschmann, Leonard Porter, Colleen Ryan, Jesús Sánchez, Lee Schwartz, Fred Stulp, Judith Silverman, Roberta Thompson, David Tobin, Linda Topping, and Lila Uskokovic. The input of professionals at other hospitals where we work, especially Rose Gomez, has also been greatly appreciated.

We are indebted for the support that our professional projects have always received from the hospital administration, especially Ira Lawrence, Ken Khuans, Irwin Singer, and our director, Joseph Moore. There is no doubt that the energy for our production came, in great part, from the enthusiasm and encouragement of Edward Sheridan, the chairman of the Division of Psychology at the Northwestern Medical School at the time this book was being written. Because, in his eyes, every one of our modest contributions was wonderful, our contacts with him always left us eager to work even more energetically in the next project.

The help of Martha O'Malley, who typed much of the manuscript and helped with the preparatory work, was invaluable. We are indebted to Christy Robinson for the administration and processing of many inventories. Our librarian, Cheryl Kinnaird, consistently provided us with the many necessary references in a competent and effective manner.

Finally, we would like to thank the staff of the Book Acquisitions and Development of the American Psychological Association, particularly Julia Frank-McNeil and Mary Lynn Skutley. The book was tremendously improved by the changes and suggestions made by our editors, Deanna D'Errico and Christine P. Landry.

James P. Choca

Introduction

This book was written to help professionals in the mental health fields, particularly clinical psychologists, understand and interpret the Millon Clinical Multiaxial Inventory (MCMI). To appreciate all sections of the book, readers will need to be acquainted with the basic concepts in the field of psychological testing and statistics. Knowledge of psychopathology and the revised third edition of the *Diagnostic and Statistical Manual of Mental Disorders (DSM–III–R;* American Psychiatric Association, 1987), the psychiatric classification system, will also be necessary.

The book is divided into two parts: The first part discusses the design, development, and operating characteristics of the test, and the second part is dedicated to the more pragmatic issues of clinical use.

In chapter 1, we discuss the basics of personality style theory and the model that provides the theoretical underpinning for the MCMI. We continue by relating how the test was designed and organized (chap. 2). A brief description of the kinds of items used for each of the clinical scales is also included in chapter 2. In chapter 3 we discuss the process used to standardize the test and the statistical properties of the instrument. Finally, in the last 2 chapters in Part I, we explore extraneous variables that may affect the validity of the instrument, both in terms of response sets used by the subject taking the test (chap. 4) and particular subject variables (chap. 5).

In Part II, we share our ideas about how the MCMI can be used in the assessment of personality styles (chap. 6) and provide our own narratives. The use of the test in the assessment of personality disorders and clinical syndromes is discussed in chapter 7. In order to further aid in the clinical use of the test, we provide five case reports from our own practice in chapter 8. In chapter 9, we explore the use of the MCMI with other psychological tests. Finally, we conclude with a discussion of how the MCMI may aid in treatment planning and psychotherapy.

The MCMI is available in two versions: the original (the MCMI-I) and the second and most current edition, which is referred to as the *MCMI-II*. Throughout this work, we use the label *MCMI* when the issue being discussed applies to both versions of the test. Otherwise, we note whether we are referring to the MCMI-I or the MCMI-II.

PART I

Design, Development, and Operating Characteristics of the MCMI

1 Personality Theory

Although Millon is a social learning theorist, the MCMI is not intrinsically tied to any of the traditional schools of psychology and can be used by clinicians professing very different views. The reason for this eclecticism is that the test itself was designed to measure fairly covert traits or symptoms but not etiology. It would seem that the different schools of psychology are mostly distinguished by the assumptions they hold regarding what makes people think, feel, or behave in a particular way. Thus, when a clinical tool is not bound to a theory of causative factors, it will tend to be acceptable to a wider variety of professionals.

This is not to say that the MCMI does not have a theoretical basis. Millon's theoretical writings have covered the entire gamut: He has hypothesized how personality traits may relate to one another (1969, 1973, 1981; Millon & Millon, 1974), what the etiology of particular personality styles may be (1969, 1973, 1990), and even how the adaptive potential of the personality style may fit into evolutionary theory (1990). As opposed to the empirically derived Minnesota Multiphasic Personality Inventory (MMPI), the structure of the test is obviously tied to a way of looking at the individual.

In this chapter we discuss personality style theory and the prototypes that Millon (1969) has proposed. We believe that the strength of the MCMI is that it provides a measure of the personality style; as a result, it is important for the reader to develop some appreciation for the importance of this concept in understanding a person.

As Endler and his co-workers have suggested (Endler & Edwards, 1988), personality issues are best understood from a systemic, or interactional, view. According to this view, as the individual relates to his or her environment, a certain amount of conflict often occurs. Dohrenwend and Dohrenwend (1981) showed that stressful life situations typically have significant effects on any individual's well-being. Different individuals, however, react differently to a particular life stressor, depending on the psychological meaning that the specific event may have for them (Endler & Magnusson, 1976). A threshold can be postulated, which is thought to vary from one person to the next, below which the friction is tolerated and causes no further difficulties, even if it is experienced as tension or discomfort.

In order to avoid the discomfort resulting from friction between people and their environments, people use defense mechanisms. To the extent that these defenses lower the level of tension and do not cause additional problems, they are adaptive and allow people to function better than they would without them. When excessive, however, either the tension or the defenses can become a problem that the individual has to face, in addition to whatever difficulty was originally causing the friction. By then, the friction, or the defensive structure, has become maladjustive and can be thought to be psychopathological.

Much of the friction that is generated between an individual and the environment is attributable to incompatibility. Consider, for instance, a man who has a great need to please others and has a tendency to be uncomfortable in situations in which decisions have to be made without consultations with others. As an entry-level employee, he may be placed under the tutelage of an older, more knowledgeable individual who is willing to teach the "tricks of the trade." Under this supervisor's mentorship, the employee performs quite well: The situation represents a good fit that benefits this hypothetical worker, his supervisor, and the company.

Such a treasured employee is prone to eventually be promoted to head a particular section of the company. Depending on the circumstances, the compatibility may leave much to be desired at this point. If he is not given much guidance in his new position and is expected to exert authority over disgruntled or problematic employees, he may be poorly equipped to do the job and may start experiencing a great deal of tension, unhappiness, or even psychopathology.

Although it may occur often enough, this scenario is not the most typical situation that can be discussed with regard to the compatibility between an individual and the environment. Most people are not lucky enough to have such a perfect fit with their surroundings that there is absolutely no friction. On the other hand, when the goodness of fit is awful, most individuals escape the situation altogether. As a result, in the great majority of the cases that one encounters, the fit between the individual and the environment includes complementary areas as well as difficulties.

In order to understand the relationship between an individual and the environment, many elements have to be considered. Aspects of the environment, for instance, have to be understood, including the social and occupational situations in which the person may be involved. There are also many aspects that the individual brings into this equation, including the person's stage in life and his or her abilities, expectations, and goals. Throughout this book we hope to make the reader more aware of the contribution of yet another factor: the individual's personality style.

Personality Style Theory

By *personality style* we mean the psychological essence of the person, regardless of pathology or ability to cope. The definition offered by the *DSM–III–R* is that of an "enduring" pattern of "perceiving, relating to, and thinking about the environment and oneself" that is "exhibited in a wide range of important social and personal contexts" (American Psychiatric Association, 1987, p. 335). In other words, a personality style is the set of life-long assumptions that the person holds about the self and the world, together with the typical ways of thinking and feeling, and the behavioral patterns associated with those assumptions.

The area to be emphasized in our definition is that the personality style involves life-long assumptions about oneself and others. This particular quality is what best sets the personality style apart from most other clinical constructs. From the basic assumptions people have about themselves and the world typically emanate patterns of thinking, ways of feeling, and behaviors that are compatible with those assumptions of the world. For example, people who see themselves as being less capable than other people usually feel inadequate and behave in a cooperative and submissive manner.

The personality style can also be seen as a conglomerate of personality traits that tend to cluster together (Buss, 1989). As is the case with most human attributes, personality traits are not always distributed in a way that makes logical sense or that is internally consistent. One may encounter a disorganized, overemotional, and easily distractible individual who, nevertheless, keeps an impeccable office in which every file is labeled and every piece of paper is in the right place. There may be an inadequate–dependent man who becomes a tyrant at home after he has had a few drinks, and so on. These are, however, the exceptions rather than the rule. It should be noted that there are personality theorists who hold to a "situation-specific" rather than "trait" conceptualization of the personality (e.g., Mischel, 1968, 1973). As Buss (1989) argued, however, the debate over the relative power of the situation (or experimental manipulation) and the traits is unproductive; what needs to be studied is the way that traits and situations interact to produce a particular feeling or behavior. The majority of the theorists would hold that most individuals who are orderly are also careful, clean, meticulous, disciplined, and punctual. It is these clusters of traits that tend to go together that we refer to as a personality style.

As conceived here, personality styles are nonpathological entities. They involve assumptions about life that are intrinsically neutral and that invariably have more than a grain of truth in terms of depicting what is real in a person and the world around him or her. For instance, an individual who comes to assume that he or she is more capable or appealing than others can obviously validate that assumption by emphasizing his or her positive attributes and the deficiencies or limitations that others may present. In other words, the fact that people have some positive attributes and that other people are less fortunate in some ways is true of absolutely every human being, but it is emphasized only by those who have come to view themselves as superior.

For the sake of logic and simplicity, in this book we assume that no personality style is necessarily better than any other. This is a controversial issue because both Millon (1981) and the *DSM–III–R* speak of personality styles that are presumed to be more adaptive. Moreover, Strack, Lorr, and Campbell (1989) have been able to show that psychiatric patients, in general, tended to score higher than normal individuals on the Schizoid, Avoidant, and Negativistic scales of the MCMI and on the Personality Adjective Checklist. Normal individuals, on the other hand, were inclined to score higher on the Histrionic and Narcissistic scales of the MCMI. Their findings, therefore, argue for an association between personality traits involving internalized and inhibited behaviors and maladjustment. Other researchers have similarly shown "healthy correlates" of histrionic, narcissistic, antisocial, and compulsive personality inclinations (Leaf et al., 1990); others have found that the treatment response of patients with personality disorders judged to be less dysfunctional was considerably better than the response of patients with the more dysfunctional personality types (Vaglum et al., 1990).

The research design problems with regard to whether some personality styles are better than others are so complex that it makes the question very difficult to research.[1] Moreover, even if there is some advantage to particular personality styles, it is undeniable that well-functioning people can be found with any one of the personality clusters that we refer to as personality

---

[1] An attempt can be made to show that different personality styles may be associated with different types of clinical syndromes (Axis I psychopathology) or with the severity of those syndromes, but this does not really answer the question of whether different personality styles are more or less functional in and of themselves. It is also of little value to compare individuals with different personality styles without taking into account the severity of their particular style because extreme and inflexible styles—regardless of the type—can be expected to be less functional than those that are less extreme or more flexible. To answer the question, one would have to, for instance, match individuals with different personality styles on the basis of the severity of their style, without taking into account their level of adjustment. Then, one would have to find a way to measure success or adjustment in a way that is not biased against one or more of the personality styles. Self-report measures would not be acceptable because they can be expected to lead to narcissists, for instance, seeing themselves as more successful than dependent individuals. Similarly, many markers of success in American society can be expected to be related to traits such as self-confidence; one thing to avoid in this project is a circular definition between success or adjustment and narcissism. Further complicating the task is the fact that most personality styles represent a combination of more than one of the "pure" styles so that the number of different groups necessary to do the work with accuracy becomes astronomical.

styles. Conversely, groups of very dysfunctional psychiatric patients have been found to have personality styles that are thought to be healthier (e.g., Craig & Olson, 1990).

We assume, therefore, that every personality style will give its bearer some advantages and some disadvantages. The orderly and disciplined individual, for example, will tend to perform better when the task demands meticulousness and careful attention to detail. This individual, however, may have difficulty with change or with situations in which a particular way of behaving cannot be prepared beforehand. In other words, the same character traits that can help a person become a good accountant may be a liability if the person wanted to become a stunt person.

Unfortunately, none of the ways of defining a personality style will allow the clear and unequivocal differentiation of this construct from other clinical entities. One must be aware that these definitions represent the human attempts to conceive reality and not reality itself (Schwartz, Wiggins, & Norko, 1989). There is actually no clear-cut distinction between what we are calling the personality style and the other psychological aspects of the individual. Widiger (1989) pointed out that the boundaries between personality and clinical syndromes are often quite unclear. The borderline personality disorder, for instance, is partly characterized by mood instability or fluctuations resembling affective disorders; the schizoid, avoidant, and schizotypal personalities have much in common with schizophrenia. When all is said and done, one needs to develop an intuitive feeling for where to draw the line in what will be considered a personality style and what may be better conceived of as abilities, psychopathology, motivated behavior, or other human attributes. The idea of personality styles is, at best, a conceptual framework that can be used to understand the vicissitudes of human nature rather than a tangible entity that one may be able to see in an indisputable manner.

Historical Perspective

Primitive descriptions of personality styles can be traced back to the Greeks. In his book, *The Sacred Disease,* Hippocrates (original date of publication unknown/1950) proposed that there were four "humors" in the human body and that the balance of these humors led to the person being either "quiet, depressed, and oblivious" or "excited, noisy, and mischievous." It is of interest that even Hippocrates's etiological concepts have survived the passage of time: Researchers are still trying to find some chemical explanation for personality characteristics (e.g., Choca, Okonek, Ferm, & Ostrow, 1982; Shaughnessy, Dorus, Pandey, & Davis, 1980).

Several of the founding fathers in the field of psychopathology wrote about particular personality styles. Freud and Abraham, for example, described the "oral-receptive character," which was the precursor of the dependent personality style (Abraham, 1924/1927). W. Reich (1949), another early psychoanalyst, also addressed the vicissitudes of character formation and the consistent patterning of defenses within a given personality. Perhaps the first person to emphasize the role of the underlying personality as a general aspect of all human beings was Alfred Adler (1956). The Adlerian approach is to describe the client's life-style on the basis of his or her history, attempting to conceptualize what it is that makes that person "tick." After a thorough evaluation of a client, a man may be described, for instance, as being angry at his mother for abandoning him when he was 1 year old and dedicating his life to finding women who have problems with commitments so that they can be punished for their disloyalty. Done in this manner, the person's life-style has the potential for being true to the uniqueness and individuality of the human being because such a description would not apply to many other individuals.

The Adlerian approach, however, can be problematic in several ways. The issue of the validity and reliability in such a diagnostic system seems paramount: The chances that another clinician would arrive at the same statement regarding a person's life-style are going to be extremely poor. In fact, it may be that even the same clinician, on seeing the patient on a different occasion, may arrive at a somewhat different conceptualization of the person's psychological essence. There is also the issue of how much of the conceptualized life-style is a product of what the client is actually presenting, as opposed to being an imaginative fabrication on the part of the clinician, or a transference of his or her own psychological issues.

Thus, in spite of the appeal that the Adlerian system has, it would seem that in order to use the concept of personality style productively, a model or system is needed. In allowing the clinician to classify or group individuals, such a model would offer great advantages: One can then compare or contrast one person with another or apply data collected from a group of individuals (e.g., histrionics) to a single person who is thought to be a member of that group.

Any time a system of classification is developed, one must accept the fact that individuals need to be bent to fit the model and therefore that the sense of uniqueness that the individual presents must be forfeited to some degree. If researchers were unwilling to do so, they would have to resign themselves to having very little say about the individual in addition to what the person says about himself or herself or to have the same set of psychodynamics for everyone.

One method that has been followed in developing a valid and reliable system for assessing personality styles is totally empirical and nontheoretical. Cattell (1946, 1965) factor-analyzed all of the words pertaining to the personality that could be found in the English language. This search for the basic personality traits culminated in the creation of the Sixteen Personality Factor Questionnaire (16PF) and its recent revision (Cattell, 1986).

Cattell's approach obviously enjoys a scientific purity and psychometric simplicity that is difficult to match. Nevertheless, it has never had wide appeal. One possible reason for its lack of popularity may be that it relies on single traits and does not offer a systematic way of integrating those traits into one personality style. In other words, the approach does not easily capture the essence of the person as a whole but instead focuses too much on the individual traits. The same criticism can be raised about the Edwards Personal Preference Schedule (Edwards, 1959), which measures needs and motives.

In the 1950s, Timothy Leary proposed a circumplex model that defines interpersonal personality styles on the basis of a circle in which the two axes represent continua of control and affiliation (Leary, 1957; Leary & Coffey, 1955). The circle is divided to yield eight basic personality styles: managerial–autocratic, responsible–hypernormal, cooperative–conventional, docile–independent, self-effacing–masochistic, rebellious–distrustful, aggressive–sadistic, and competitive–narcissistic. Benjamin (1974, 1984) expanded the model into the three dimensions—focus, affiliation, and interdependence—that allow consideration of intrapsychic phenomena.

Kiesler (1983) has also done a great deal of work on his circumplex model of personality functioning, devising what he called the "interpersonal circle." He posited two central relationship issues for all people: how friendly or hostile they will be with each other and how much in charge or control each will be in their relationships.

Leary's (1957) circumplex continues to have a following and has been shown to have commonalities with the *DSM–III* (American Psychiatric Association, 1980) and the Millon system (DeJong, van den Brink, Jansen, & Schippers, 1989; Morey, 1985; Widiger & Kelso, 1983; Wiggins, 1982). Nevertheless, the model has not been widely accepted. The problem may lie in the fact that the intricacies of the model are more than most people can easily master. The lack of acceptance may also be related to the fact that psychiatric nosology is usually based on prototypes rather than the kind of continua that Leary proposed (Schwartz et al., 1989); in other words, none of the different editions of the *DSM* have allowed for an individual to be "a little" schizophrenic or have ever recognized that psychological traits are a matter of degree. Because clinicians are accustomed to thinking that an individual is either schizophrenic or not, in an all-or-none fashion, a system that calls for continua seems foreign and unduly complex. Finally, and perhaps most important, Leary's circumplex did not lead to labels such as "schizoid" or "dependent" that are easily recognizable by the majority of the professionals in the field.

Millon's Typology

Like Leary, Millon (1969) proposed a system based on personality prototypes rather than on single traits. He described what—in theory—would be the prototypes of particular personality styles and left the job of determining how close to that prototype a particular individual is to the diagnosing clinician or the psychometric instrument. He arrived at his eight basic styles by borrowing from the descriptions that had been previously used for personality disorders. The eight basic personality styles are schizoid, avoidant, dependent, histrionic, narcissistic, antisocial, compulsive, and negativistic. In so doing, he generated a system that benefited from the wisdom of many years of clinical practice. Moreover, Millon's typology seemed very familiar to the practitioners in the field because it retained trait clusters that were well known to clinicians.

By molding his personality styles in the image of the personality disorders, Millon (1969) was postulating that there were similarities between the way "normal" individuals function and the kind of pathology characterized by the personality disorders. Supporting this hypothesis is the work of Strack and his associates (Strack et al., 1989), who were able to show that the factorial structure of two personality instruments—the MCMI and the Personality Adjective Check List—were virtually identical for normal individuals and psychiatric patients.

Even though the Millon styles are single prototypes that have no intrinsic logical relation to one another, Millon has suggested schemata that can be used to organize these personality styles. One such model fits all of the personality styles in a circle in which the vertical axis represents affiliation, with poles of autonomy versus enmeshment, and the horizontal axis deals with the level of emotionality, with the poles being expressiveness and impassiveness. This circular representation of the personality disorders has been shown to have an empirical basis (Sim & Romney, 1990; Strack, Lorr, & Campbell, 1990). In his most recent theoretical work, however, Millon (1990) proposed the use of three polarities (pleasure–pain, active–passive, and self–other), which he saw as having roots in the evolution of humankind and from which the personality prototypes are derived. The usefulness of these three polarities in the understanding of personality patterns was supported by the data gathered from undergraduate students by Pincus and Wiggins (1990). Finally, attempts to fit the Millon personality styles into the five-factor model have also been made (Costa & McCrae, 1990). The five factors that can be allegedly used to explain all important personality aspects according to this model are Extraversion, Agreeableness, Neuroticism, Openness to Experience, and Conscientiousness.

Basically, Millon's model first examines whether the person is inclined to form strong relationships with others. For those who do not form strong relationships, the model then distinguishes between individuals who are loners by design, having little interest in interpersonal relationships (schizoids), and individuals who isolate themselves as a defensive maneuver against the possibility of rejection (avoidants). If the person ordinarily forms strong interpersonal relationships, the model then examines the type of relationship formed in terms of the assumptions the individual makes about the self and the other people in the environment.

Some of the people who form strong relationships with others tend to need others in order to feel safe and comfortable. Of these, the dependent style characterizes a person who believes that others know best. Such people typically establish submissive relationships in which the other person takes responsibility for any decision that is made. In contrast, the histrionic style is not as clearly submissive but frequently needs the attention of others.

Some individuals form relationships with others in which they play the stronger or more dominant role. The first of these two styles is the inverse of the dependent, in that it typifies a person who believes himself or herself to be more capable, gifted, or appealing than other people. Instead of behaving submissively, the narcissistic individual is inclined to tell other people what to do. The second independent personality style defines a person who sees the world as a competitive situation in which those who do well achieve their goals by being dominant and strong, even if it is at the cost of being unkind or hurtful toward others (antisocial).

Millon acknowledged that there are two other personality styles that have been widely recognized and proposed a way of fitting them into the general scheme. In the model, these two other personality styles are conceived of as people who relate in a way that is neither dependent nor independent, a way that Millon labels *ambivalent*. The first of these two styles is not very ambivalent in the usual sense of the word but does relate to other people in a way that is not consistently dependent or independent. For the compulsive individual, the world is a hierarchical structure in which a person either has a higher or a lower rank than another. Using this hierarchical view, compulsive individuals relate in a dependent or compliant manner toward those perceived to have a higher status and in an independent or authoritative fashion with those having a lesser rank.

Finally, the last style is characterized by individuals who see themselves as inadequate and in need of support but who are very cynical about the abilities of others and are uninclined to put others on a pedestal. As a result, they behave in a fairly conflictual way toward others in terms of the dependence–independence parameter. The most prevalent style of relating for these negativistic individuals is the passive–aggressive substyle in which the person is able to be overtly compliant while venting his or her conflictual feelings in a covert manner. An explosive substyle involving a cycle of hostile eruptions followed by periods of contrition can also be found.

From our viewpoint, not all of the recognized personality disorders can be easily depathologized into describing a personality style. Take, for instance, the borderline personality disorder. This syndrome involves a pattern of unstable moods accompanied by impulsive acting-out, self-damaging acts, identity confusion, and chronic boredom or emptiness (American Psychiatric Association, 1987). The feature that is always present in individuals diagnosed as having this disorder seems to be impulsiveness. In contrast to the personality styles already described, it is difficult to conceive the core of this disorder as resulting from a basic assumption of life (Clarkin,

Widiger, Frances, Hurt, & Gilmore, 1983). The disorder has been seen theoretically as resulting from a failure of integration in the basic personality (Door, Barley, Gard, & Webb, 1983; Kernberg, 1975). In contrast to the personality styles in which some advantages can be seen for individuals having that particular style, the borderline pattern seems intrinsically problematic and disadvantageous.

It obviously becomes a matter of judgment whether a recognized personality pattern has enough of the qualities that one would like to see in a personality style to be considered such. In his original writings, Millon (1969) only recognized the eight personality styles that we recognize in this book. We accept the borderline, paranoid, and schizotypal personality disorders as personality disorders, but we feel that these three patterns of behavior are not found in individuals who do not have an emotional disorder.

In the MCMI-II (Millon, 1987), two additional personality styles were added: the sadistic and the self-defeating. In this book, we also treat those two additional entities as pathological patterns and not basic personality styles.

It should be noted that the sadistic and self-defeating prototypes were being discussed as additional personality disorders by the work group revising the *DSM–III* when the MCMI-I was being revised. These discussions were surrounded by a great deal of controversy because the inclusion of those two categories was vehemently opposed by certain segments of the population. In the end, those disorders were relegated to the appendix of the *DSM–III–R* as proposed categories "needing further study" (American Psychiatric Association, 1987, p. 367). This unfortunately left the MCMI-II with two categories that may never become part of the official nomenclature.

In addition to the historical issues, we have trouble visualizing how either the sadistic or the self-defeating disorders can be conceptualized as a personality style that offers some advantage to the individuals who bear those traits. Moreover, both of these styles appear to include one of the basic eight personality styles: The sadistic personality is probably a variant of the negativistic or the antisocial style, whereas the masochistic or the self-defeating personality probably involves dependent or avoidant elements.

The eight prototypes that we are referring to as personality styles are not mutually exclusive of one another. In fact, most individuals we encounter fit more than one prototype. The interpretative system that we use considers the three highest personality style elevations in describing the personality style of one individual. This approach adds considerable complexity to the interpretations but has the advantage of returning some of the uniqueness that a particular individual presents, as well as describing with greater fidelity the way the individual is prone to think, feel, and behave.

Personality Styles and Personality Disorders

Personality disorders are defined by the *DSM–III–R* as life-long pathological personality patterns. The *DSM–III–R* adds that "it is only when personality traits are inflexible and maladaptive and cause either significant functional impairment or subjective distress that they constitute personality disorders" (American Psychiatric Association, 1987, p. 335). In other words, not only does the clinician have to attend to the kind of personality that his or her subject may have, but the diagnosis of the character structure is further complicated by the issue of the functionality of the personality pattern.

After looking at Charlie Brown, one could decide that he typifies the dependent personality style. The figure that emerges from Charles Schultz's famous cartoon is one of an individual who tends to feel less capable than others and blames his lack of leadership for the frequent loss of baseball games. A cooperative person, he never gets angry and is inclined to try to follow the advice or recommendations of others.

The fact that this fictitious figure fits nicely the dependent prototype, however, does not mean that Charlie Brown suffers from a personality disorder. Even though he has dependent traits, Charlie Brown does not meet criteria for the dependent personality disorder of the *DSM–III–R* because he is able to function well in spite (or because) of his dependency. In fact, in many ways the success of the figure of Charlie Brown may be due to his being a typical "normal" neighborhood kid with whom everyone can identify.

In contrast, the figure of Oblomov portrayed by Ivan Goncharov in the short story by the same name is one of an individual who is constantly comparing himself unfavorably with others. Oblomov feels so inadequate that his life is restricted to the mere essentials, with his ability to function leaving much to be desired. Accordingly, one would see Charlie Brown as having a dependent personality style and Oblomov as suffering from a dependent personality disorder.

What makes a personality style dysfunctional? At a concrete level, the issue can be answered for a particular individual by determining whether the person meets the *DSM–III–R* criteria for any of the specific personality disorders. In some ways, however, this approach avoids the real question by relying on what the *DSM–III–R* experts could agree on as signs of pathology.

Using a statistical notion of normality, it could be argued that the extremity of the traits that compose the personality structure can lead to maladjustment (Kiesler, 1983; Leary, 1957; Sim & Romney, 1990). From this viewpoint, the difference between Charlie Brown and Oblomov is that the feelings of inadequacy that Charlie Brown harbors are mild, whereas Oblomov feels so inadequate that he cannot get himself to do any of the things that "others" can do.

More typically, the concept clinicians use to explain the difference between functional and dysfunctional personality structures is that of adaptive flexibility (Kiesler, 1986a; Leary, 1957; Sim & Romney, 1990). Niccolo Machiavelli already had very definite ideas about this issue in the 16th century. In his book, *The Prince,* Machiavelli (1532/1931) explained that a person "may be seen happy today and ruined tomorrow" without having changed his or her disposition or behavior. This early political scientist believed that the person who adapts to the environment tends to prosper; those who "clash with the times" do not (Machiavelli, 1532/1931, pp. 204–205). Machiavelli also conceded that adaptability is difficult because when people have always prospered by proceeding one way, they find it hard to change. Nevertheless, using our terminology, histrionic individuals who are by nature spontaneous and disorganized could make good pilots only if they learned to check the aircraft very compulsively before flying. Individuals with antisocial tendencies will need to drop their guarded competitiveness to some degree if they are to establish intimate relationships in life. Philosopher Jan Patocka claimed that the real test is not how well people can play the role they invented for themselves but how well they play the role that destiny brings them (Terry, 1990). If individuals are able to behave in a flexible manner and use personality traits that are not part of their nature in response to specific situations, the results are likely to be more positive than in the case of people who can only behave in the manner that is most egosyntonic.

Inflexibility could also be postulated to lead to the kind of vicious circles that Millon (1981) talked about as leading to psychopathology. When compulsive individuals inappropriately persist in using compulsive defenses to deal with difficulties that they are facing, the inadaptive persistence is likely to intensify their problems, which, in turn, could lead to the application of the compulsive mechanisms with further vehemence.

Leary (1957) also postulated that maladjustment could also result from a discrepancy between the person's self-perception and the way he or she is perceived by others. Sim and Romney (1990) were able to support that contention by showing that such discrepancies were significantly larger for a group with personality disorders than they were for a nonpsychiatric control group.

Finally, maladjustment could also result from a poor fit between the individual and the environment. If, in the view of the clinician, the maladjustment is mostly attributable to incompatibility, then the person should not be seen as having a personality disorder because the symptoms would be expected to be temporary. Because the issue of the goodness of fit is present with everyone, and because the environment could possibly be accommodated so that even people with obvious personality disorders would be able to function, this issue constitutes another gray area that is often a matter of clinical judgment. In order to decide, however, the clinician needs to look at the life of the client longitudinally and determine whether the person has continually had characterological difficulties regardless of the situation he or she was facing.

Personality Styles in a Social Context

As we have already noted, the complexities of defining and understanding an individual's personality style are further complicated by the fact that personality styles do not exist in a vacuum. People partly define themselves through their social relationships: they are more inclined to feel adequate or even grandiose when they are relating to people who feel inadequate so that, as the Spanish saying goes, "in the land of the blind, the one-eyed is king."

In order to illustrate the depth of understanding that the concept of personality styles can bring into the assessment of interpersonal relationships, we can turn to Ibsen's (1879) play, *A Doll's House*. At the beginning of the play, Ibsen portrays an overadequate–underadequate marital relationship. Torvald Helmer is a compulsive–narcissist who carries himself with an air of self-importance and who sets all of the rules for the family. In contrast, the histrionic Nora is a submissive social butterfly. They were seemingly happy until someone attempted to blackmail them. We then learn that when Torvald was seriously ill (in other words, at a time when Nora did not have the kind of support she needed in order to be able to cope well with her environment), she forged her father's signature on a document. On learning about the forgery, Torvald decides not to take the blame for this crime and is not willing to protect his wife in that particular situation instead of assuming the role that Nora expected him to take.

The decision not to take the blame is consistent with Torvald's own personality style because the perfectionistic attitude of the obsessive–compulsive and the emphasis on an unblemished status of the narcissist made it particularly difficult for him to be generous at the time. For Nora, however, the husband's decision meant that he was undependable and that, when the chips are down, she might be left to fend for herself. This realization made her so uncomfortable that, even after the threat has miraculously disappeared, she is not able to regain her composure or return to the kind of relationship that they once had. The play ends with Nora leaving the home in order to "find herself." It is clear at that point that the trauma has catalyzed changes in Nora so that she is bound to be a less trusting and more self-sufficient woman in the future.

One could fantasize as to the kind of relationship the marriage of Torvald and Nora may become if a more assertive Nora were to return to the marriage. Faced with the positive changes that might have taken place in Nora's case, Torvald could also become a more enhanced and healthy individual by giving up some of his obsessive controls and his narcissistic need to place others at a lower level than himself. The marriage may then eventually become less of an overadequate–underadequate relationship and more of an equal relationship. Realistically, before such a development is finalized, one would have to expect a period of unrest. We could envision, for instance, the marriage turning, at least for a period of time, into a conflictual relationship in which Torvald attempts to reestablish the kind of dominance he once had while dismissing the fact that the changes in Nora will not permit the relationship to return to what it was.

Ibsen's play illustrates how personality styles complement or clash with each other and how the changes in one personality style affect the entire relationship. We feel that this kind of analysis can be helpful, not only in looking at the kinds of relationships that patients establish in their lives but at the kind of relationship they will establish with clinicians in the therapeutic setting.

Our interpretation of Ibsen's play was based entirely on his descriptions of the protagonists and the way they behave as the drama unfolds. Possibly someone else could read the same work and conceptualize the main characters in a completely different way. Moreover, in our clinical work we encounter many individuals who would have difficulty describing themselves with the clarity and insight that Ibsen offers in his work. As a result, it is extremely helpful to have an instrument that allows patients to reveal themselves in a way that permits a formulation of their particular personality style. In the chapters that follow, we describe how the MCMI is organized and how well it performs that function.

2 Overview of the MCMI

The MCMI is a 175-item, true–false self-report psychological inventory intended to be used with psychiatric patients. By now the MCMI is one of the most popular instruments of its kind (Piotrowski & Keller, 1989; Piotrowski & Lubin, 1989, 1990). The success of this inventory is highlighted by the test being used in other countries and having been translated into other languages (Luteijn, 1990; Simonsen & Mortensen, 1990).

In contrast to the empirical-keying method used for the MMPI (Hathaway & McKinley, 1967), the MCMI items were chosen on a theoretical basis, following the concepts and ideas developed by Millon prior to the creation of the inventory. The MCMI-I has 20 clinical scales and the MCMI-II has 22. In either case, the scales are clustered into three groups: personality scales, severe personality patterns, and clinical syndromes. Additionally, both versions of the test have an adjustment factor and a Validity scale; the MCMI-II has two other scales measuring subjects response tendencies.

In this chapter we discuss how the test is administered and scored. We then review what kinds of items the different scales contain. Finally, we present the criticisms that the test has received with regard to the overall design and scoring.

Administration

The MCMI is administered by means of a well-designed form sold by National Computer Systems (NCS). Subjects answer the items on the same paper on which the items are presented. Subjects should complete the inventory alone in a comfortable setting; the room should be well lit and quiet. The procedure should be explained well and the subject checked with, using the first few items, to ensure that the instructions have been understood.

One issue that comes up repeatedly during the administration of the MCMI is the subject's difficulty in deciding whether the item is mostly true or false. Some individuals object to statements that have the word *always* or *never* in them, pointing out that such statements are invariably an exaggeration and, strictly speaking, could never be true or false; in such cases, we are likely to agree with the subject but encourage him or her to decide whether it is "mostly" true or false and mark the form accordingly.

Some of the substance abuse items raise questions among nonsubstance abusers who feel that certain items imply that they have a problem in that area, regardless of their answer. In those cases, we are inclined to reassure the subject that, for instance, admitting "success" in drinking a minimal amount of alcohol does not imply that drinking was a problem at one time. With any other question that the subject may have, the examiner should encourage the subject to complete the inventory in the most accurate way possible, without ever suggesting what the answer should be.

Subjects should be encouraged to answer all items and, if some are blank at the end, the examiner should have the subject read the items again and try to arrive at a decision.

Scoring

Once a completed MCMI has been obtained, the test must be scored. For the MCMI-I, the raw scores are arrived at by simply counting the number of items for a given scale that were marked in a given direction. In the case of the MCMI-II, an item may add one, two, or three points toward the raw score of a particular scale, depending on how central to the concept of that particular clinical entity the item is theoretically thought to be.

For the MCMI-I, the raw score can be computed manually using the scoring templates sold by NCS. The templates for the MCMI-II were being designed at the time this book was written but were not yet available. For either form of the test, the user can process the data through one of three systems offered by NCS: The test blank can be mailed to the company in Minneapolis for scoring, it can be entered through a telephone modem using the NCS Arion system, or it can be processed on an IBM-compatible personal computer using NCS software and decoding equipment. In any case, the user must purchase the appropriate materials or services from NCS prior to administering the test.

Once the scores are computed, they have to be converted into a standardized score. The MCMI-I uses different conversion tables for men and women, the general population, and Black and Hispanic individuals. Although similar tables are offered in the MCMI-II manual, only the general tables for men and women are being used by NCS to convert the raw scores into standardized scores because there was concern that the tables for minorities were based on samples that were too small.

The standard score used by the MCMI is the Base Rate (BR) score. The BR score was developed in lieu of the *T* Score often used by previous tests, such as the MMPI, and has been praised as a significant psychometric advance (Wetzler, 1990). The problem with the *T* Score is that it assumes a normal distribution of the characteristics being measured, an assumption that obviously does not hold because psychiatric disorders are not normally distributed. The end result is that the same *T* elevation defines different percentiles of the population for the different scales; in other words, a *T* Score of 80 on the Depression scale of the original MMPI is associated with a different percentile rank than the same *T* value on the Schizophrenic scale. This effect is undesirable because it takes away the meaning for the relative elevations of the different scales.

To avoid this problem, the BR score takes into account the prevalence of the particular characteristic within the standardizing population so that the same BR score would place an individual in the same relative position in the standardizing population as one moves from one scale to the next. In order to bring this about, Millon used four anchor points: A BR score of 35 was defined as the median score for the normal or nonpsychiatric population; a BR score of 60 was set as the median for psychiatric patients; a BR score of 75 served as the anchor point for the definite presence of the particular characteristic being measured; and a BR score of 85 was defined as the point at which the characteristic in question is the most predominant characteristic for the individual.

In addition to placing the individual in the same position relative to the standardizing population, the BR score takes into account the prevalence of the particular characteristic in the population. As Meehl and Rosen (1955) indicated, the base rate score involves an adjustment to the cutoff point to maximize correct classification by considering the effect of the base rate on the frequency of valid and false-positives. Thus, psychiatric disorders with high base rates will need lower cutoff points and psychiatric disorders with low base rates will need relatively higher cutoff points (Millon, 1977). It has been argued that using rates that take into account prevalence improve the effectiveness of the diagnostic system (Finn, 1982; Meehl & Rosen, 1955; Widiger, Hurt, Frances, Clarkin, & Gilmore, 1984; Widiger & Kelso, 1983). In fact, Duthie and Vincent (1986) demonstrated that the hit rate of the Diagnostic Inventory of Personality and Symptoms jumped from 44% to 70% when base rates were used instead of the *T* Score.

One can think of the BR score as indicating the probability that the subject has the particular characteristics being measured rather than the simple placement that he or she occupies in the normal distribution. As a result, a low BR score does not indicate anything about the subject, as opposed to a low *T* Score, which implies an absence of the characteristic being measured. That aspect of the BR score serves to add simplicity to the process of interpreting the scores because the user needs only to attend to the elevations obtained and the low scores can be mostly disregarded.

After the BR score is computed for each scale, these scores are adjusted to take into consideration the subject's response set or answering biases. The MCMI-I adjusted the BR score of some of the scales in accordance to a "weight factor" designed to indicate whether the subject was likely to deny emotional traits or inflate them. Some scores were also adjusted when particular personality scales were predominantly elevated; this adjustment was based on the assumption that some personality styles include a tendency to exaggerate or minimize the presence of emotional problems. In addition to both of these adjustments, the MCMI-II introduced adjustments for subjects appearing to be depressed or anxious, adjustments based on the results obtained on the Desirability and Debasement scales of the inventory, and adjustments for subjects who were in an inpatient psychiatric unit at the time they completed the test. For further information on how the adjustments are made, refer to the test manual.

In the sections that follow, the scales of the MCMI are clustered into four groups: scales that measure personality styles, scales measuring severe personality patterns, the symptom formation scales designed to tap Axis I disorders superimposed on the personality structure, and the modifier or response set indexes assessing the validity with which the subject responded to the test. Because our own approach is to depathologize the personality scales and talk about them as measuring styles that are seen in the normal population, we group the two new scales of the MCMI-II (the Self-Defeating and the Aggressive scales) with the severe personality patterns.

In the rest of this section, we offer our own characterization of the kinds of items that are included in the different scales. We describe only the MCMI-II because it is the most current version of the test. Through the years, the labels used for the different scales have changed, a fact that occasionally creates some confusion. We note the different names used in this chapter but subsequently use only the name given in italics in the sections below.

Personality Style Scales

The first of the personality scales is the *Schizoid scale* (Scale 1). This scale is associated with an asocial personality style; by far the most common issue reflected on the items included in this scale is that of social isolation. Other important aspects that the scale was designed to measure are emotional blandness and apathy; as a result, items involving passivity, suppression of one's own feelings, and being sexually inhibited are well represented. Items that contribute in a lesser way deal with not receiving enough recognition, being unadventurous, doubting oneself, resisting someone else's guidance, being perfectionistic, or having somatic complaints.

The *Avoidant scale* (Scale 2) measures a style that, like the Schizoid scale, is marked by social detachment. Avoidant individuals, however, face an approach–avoidance conflict: They would like to relate to others but feel such apprehension in social settings that they avoid interpersonal situations in order to decrease their anxiety. The items of this scale typically deal with mistrust and suspiciousness of others, feelings of worthlessness, and having a desire to isolate oneself. Low self-esteem, a tendency to suppress one's feelings, and sexual inhibition are also major issues.

The next two scales represent personality styles characterized by a need for strong relationships with people who are supportive and reassuring. The items of the *Dependent scale,* or Cooperative scale (Scale 3), underscore low self-confidence, a submissive attitude, and a desire to obtain nurturing and protection from someone else. Other significant issues include a high regard for authority, social passivity, and the suppression of "bad" feelings such as anger.

The most obvious features found in the *Histrionic scale,* or Dramatic scale (Scale 4), are gregariousness, a search for attention, and an inclination toward impulsivity. A need for nurturing and a tendency to become easily bored or frustrated are also significant aspects. Items dealing with mood swings and guilt feelings are also included.

Next are the two "independent" scales. The personality styles that these scales were designed to measure are characterized by self-sufficiency in the person's relationships with others. A feeling of superiority, a strong belief in oneself, and a dislike of being externally controlled are the highlights of the *Narcissistic scale,* or Self-Confident scale (Scale 5). These traits are followed closely by items that represent an inclination to be sociable and outgoing, a tendency to present oneself in a self-protective or defensive manner, a propensity for showing one's anger or disappointment, and a lack of empathy toward others.

The underlying theme of the antisocial style in Millon's system is the view of the world as a competitive place. The predominant items of the *Antisocial scale,* or Competitive scale (Scale 6A), deal with a need to be self-confident and not to depend on others, a resentment of authority, and a dislike for being controlled. Impulsivity and mistrust are well represented. Other items deal with a tendency to shy away from emotional involvement, a lack of empathy toward others, and a tendency to use people for one's own purpose.

The last two personality styles describe people who relate in a way that is neither dependent or independent. A compliant attitude toward authority and a tendency to be controlling with everyone else are prevailing aspects of the *Compulsive scale,* or Disciplined scale (Scale 7). Other prevalent issues are a moralistic attitude and a belief in following the rules. Keeping one's emotions in check, being orderly and meticulous, and feeling that "my way is the only way" are important features of this scale, as are an emphasis on the importance of predictability and a tendency to be socially cautious. Self-righteousness and sexual inhibitions contribute in a minor way to the total score.

Finally, the *Negativistic scale,* or Passive-Aggressive/Explosive scale (Scale 8A), demonstrates an intense dislike of being controlled and a resentful attitude toward authority. Items dealing with moodiness and guilt or remorseful feelings will be observed, along with items reflecting a mistrust of others, a desire to hurt oneself or others, and a desire to receive more appreciation and recognition. To a lesser degree, there are items dealing with having a critical attitude toward others or betraying a belief that one is undeserving or indicating self-doubt.

Severe Personality Scales

The two personality scales that were added for the MCMI-II are grouped in this book with three other scales designed to measure severe personality patterns. In our way of thinking, the eight scales already discussed do not measure a personality "disorder" but a personality "style," which may or may not constitute a personality disorder. In contrast, the five scales to be considered at this time are more clearly associated with a pathological way of functioning. It is noteworthy, for instance, that four of these five scales have been found to yield higher scores with psychiatric patients than they do with normal people (Strack et al., 1989).

The new *Aggressive/Sadistic scale* (Scale 6B) is probably a more pathological variant of the antisocial personality style. This scale was designed to measure a tendency to be at least aggressive if not hostile in the person's interactions with others. Judging from the items included, an elevation on this scale describes an individual who tends to emphasize the ability to remain independent and who is not inclined to do what others tell him or her to do. Competitive by nature, such an individual may be seen as behaving in a callous manner in the struggle to get ahead of everyone else. He or she is likely to be distrusting, to question the motives that others may have for their actions, and to assume that a person has to be vigilant and on guard in order to protect oneself. Projection is typically used as a defense so that individuals obtaining elevations on this scale would be inclined to blame others for anything that goes wrong. Such a person is likely to be interpersonally "touchy": Excitable and irritable, he or she may have a history of treating others in a rough or mean manner and of angrily "flying off the handle" whenever he or she is confronted or opposed.

The *Self-Defeating scale* (Scale 8B), on the other hand, is considered to be a more pathological variant of the negativistic personality style. Judging from the items contained in this scale, individuals obtaining elevated scores can be expected to have a very poor self-image and believe that they need the help of others in order to make ends meet. Typically their self-images are so poor that they are uncomfortable when they are treated nicely and seem to seek out situations in which they will be hurt or rejected. It is as if

they have come to expect mistreatment and routinely have, almost by design, the type of interpersonal interactions that would be expected to bring
about the abuse. This depressive outcome of interpersonal interactions is
often accomplished with the help of the resentment that such people commonly harbor. Even though such an individual is inclined to put himself or
herself down, some of the items deal with the likelihood that he or she will
additionally devalue others. Other items relate to demonstrations of resentment in an insulting or even hostile way and the derivation of some pleasure
from humiliating others. This tendency can be expected to create illwill
from others, which then activates the person's own resentment in an angry
and frustrating vicious cycle.

Considered possibly a pathological variant of the schizoid and avoidant
personality styles, the *Schizotypal scale* (Scale S) was designed to measure a
fear of human contact, suspicion and mistrust of others, and a preference
for a life of passive isolation with very few real relationships. Predominant
among the items are those dealing with being somewhat eccentric and having habits that others may find peculiar. Judging from other items, individuals obtaining elevations on this scale may have a rich fantasy life and mix
their own personal idiosyncrasies with other material in their conversations.
They may appear anxious and apprehensive or may demonstrate a flatten-
ing of affect. Finally, they may have feelings of depersonalization, feelings
of emptiness, or ideas of reference.

The *Borderline scale* (Scale C) appears to measure a pervasive pattern of
instability in terms of moods, interpersonal relationships, and self-image.
Elevations on this scale would indicate that the subject typically responds in
an impulsive and overemotional way and that his or her affective response
tends to be labile, at times showing apathy and numbness and demonstrating an excessive amount of intensity or involvement at other times. Sadness,
hopelessness, and aimlessness are often underlying the more obvious emotional response. Such individuals may have significant problems with authority and resent any control placed on them. They can be aggressive,
angry, or even cruel and are plagued by destructive ideas, which may be
directed toward themselves or others. The anger may be temporarily dis-
placed by bothersome feelings of guilt or remorse. Their self-images may
also be problematic because there are also items relating to feeling worthless and being encumbered by self-doubt, along with feeling used by others.

Because the conceptualization of the borderline syndrome in the literature is a "booming confusion" (Blatt & Auerbach, 1988, p. 199), it requires
a few additional comments. Blatt and Auerbach provided a framework for
making sense of the many ways in which borderline patients have been
talked about. They argued that there are three types of syndromes for which
this label has been used. When used in the sense of borderline schizophrenia, the term describes an "unstable" condition marked by "social role
dysfunction, eccentricity, social withdrawal, attenuated psychotic symptoms, and multiple, bizarre, neurotic symptoms" (Blatt & Auerbach, 1988,

p. 199). Under stressful conditions, these patients may develop a temporary psychotic state. It would seem that this type of "borderline schizophrenia" does not fit the *DSM–III–R* conceptualization of the borderline patient and may be better labeled a schizotypal personality disorder. On the MCMI, perhaps an elevation of the Schizotypal scale should be expected. Accompanying that elevation, one may find elevations on the scales that measure social detachment (the Schizoid and the Avoidant) and possibly in the psychotic scales if the patient takes the test during a period of regression.

Blatt and Auerbach (1988) also talked about two other definitions of the borderline patient that refer to a "relatively stable character pathology" (p. 199). The first of these personality disorders, which the authors called the "anaclitic" type, is characterized by "profound feelings of dependence and loneliness, fears of abandonment, and great affective lability in response to rejection or object loss" (p. 199). This is the type of borderline patient that is described by the *DSM–III–R* criteria (American Psychiatric Association, 1987, p. 347). Although the Borderline scale of the MCMI was not originally designed to measure the borderline syndrome as it is known today, the MCMI-II version was substantially revised and appears to be much more in line with the *DSM–III–R* criteria.

Basically, the *DSM–III–R* borderline patient is a very impulsive and emotionally labile person. Because these attributes are also an important aspect of several personality styles, an elevation on at least one of the basic personality scales is to be expected. In fact, many of the theoreticians who have written on the topic of the borderline disorder (e.g., Kernberg, 1975) have distinguished between different styles of borderline patient, such as the hysterical patient, or the narcissistic borderline patient. Stone (1980) offered a three-dimensional diagnostic cube that allows the categorization of several of the Millon personality styles at the borderline "psychostructural level" (p. 36). In our experience, individuals meeting criteria for the *DSM–III–R* borderline personality disorder are likely to have elevated scores on either the Histrionic or the Negativistic scales of the MCMI.

As always, distinguishing between the different personality styles can add much to the understanding of the basic inclinations that patients have. In the case of histrionic borderline patients, for instance, much of the mood fluctuations and instability is likely to be designed to gain the needed attention from others. Therefore, helping the patients understand and deal with the attentional needs can be expected to be therapeutic. In contrast, conflictual/passive-aggressive borderline patients can be expected to benefit from exploring how they deal with their anger; the impulsive acting-out in that case can often be best understood as angry disappointments in relating to others.

A suspicious and mistrustful attitude and a feeling of superiority are the most pronounced features measured by the *Paranoid scale* (Scale P). Other important factors deal with resenting authority and criticism, being insensitive to other people, and feeling emotionally and physically unconnected.

Individuals with elevations on this scale may express a fear of losing autonomy and may be very resistant to any attempt by others to control their lives. A tendency to be perfectionistic and well organized, to be moralistic, to have little patience, and to be short-tempered may be present, along with a somewhat competitive attitude.

Clinical Symptom Scales

The remaining clinical scales were designed to measure symptoms that are superimposed on the personality style. Typically, these symptoms are more closely associated with the patient's presenting complaints than are the personality scales and lead to diagnoses in Axis I of the *DSM–III–R*.

An elevation on the *Anxiety scale* (Scale A) should be related to the experience of a great deal of apprehension, phobic reactions, indecisiveness, tension, restlessness, and physical discomforts of the kind associated with tension. Other items deal with feeling confused, having a perceived inability to "do things right," and a diminished self-confidence. Adding in a lesser way to this scale are feelings of being unwanted and unappreciated, having a tendency to break into tears or become angry for no apparent reason, being dependent on someone else, and feeling depressed. This scale has been praised as "the most sensitive of the MCMI scales as a measure of psychological distress and disturbance" (Smith, Carroll, & Fuller, 1988, p. 172).

The *Somatic Preoccupation scale* (Scale H) is characterized by complaints of fatigue, weakness, tension, jumpiness, inordinate sweating, aches, pains, and physical discomforts. To a lesser degree, the scale contains items dealing with a lack of self-confidence, being dependent on others, feeling mentally confused and unable to sort out one's thoughts, being easily provoked to the point of tears, having difficulty sleeping, or needing to be the center of attention.

The *Mania scale,* or Hypomania scale (Scale N), was designed to measure restlessness, overactivity, elevated moods, pressured speech, impulsiveness, and irritability. Other contributing items deal with being gregarious and seeking attention, experiencing intense emotions, demonstrating jumpy and erratic behavior and moods, feeling superior to others, and being psychologically insensitive. A few items referring to a heightened sensitivity to sounds and a tendency toward alcohol abuse are also present.

An apathetic and dejected mood; feelings of discouragement, guilt, or hopelessness; and a lack of personal initiative are the cardinal issues reflected by the items of the *Dysthymia scale* (Scale D). Physical and emotional exhaustion, difficulty sleeping, low self-confidence, and self-destructive thoughts or actions may also be present, along with a tendency to break into tears or become angry at the slightest provocation. Judging by the items included, a distrust of others and a somewhat perfectionistic attitude may also be present.

The *Alcohol Abuse scale* (Scale B) is characterized by a history of excessive drinking that has produced problems in both the home and the work situations. Items dealing with diminished self-confidence and impulsivity are also evident, as is an aversion to being controlled and feeling tense, tired, sweaty, lonely, empty, and hopeless. A wish to be sociable and the experience of guilt feelings or mood swings affect this scale in a lesser way, as well as respect for authority and lack of trust.

Similarly, the *Drug Abuse scale* (Scale T) is characterized by a history of drug use pronounced enough to cause difficulties in either the home or the work situation. Items highlight impulsivity, a tendency to hurt oneself or others, a propensity for using others, a resentment of authority, and an aversion to being controlled. Other contributing issues include suspiciousness, unexplained mood swings, feelings of guilt and remorse, professing to having no clear-cut goals and feeling aimless, being angry, feeling jumpy or tense, having a low self-esteem, and behaving in a competitive manner.

The last three symptom formation scales are segregated by Millon into another group, this one of psychotic disorders. We feel that such a distinction is not consistent with the *DSM–III–R*. Moreover, the traditional contention that "psychotic" disorders are more dysfunctional regardless of severity is widely disputed so that there may be no wisdom in viewing these scales as being drastically different from the rest.

The first of these scales is the *Psychotic Thinking scale* (Scale SS). This scale was designed to select individuals suffering from confusion and disorganization of their thought processes, inappropriate affect, and unsystematized delusions or hallucinations. Contributing items also question the subject about being suspicious and mistrustful, desiring isolation, concern about being used by others, and experiencing sensations of physical or mental imbalance. Low self-esteem, a desire to hurt oneself and others, feeling unwanted and disliked, emotional constriction, and ideas of reference are also factors affecting this scale. Finally, a tendency to be rigid in one's thinking may also be present.

In addition to the Mania and the Dysthymia scales described earlier, the MCMI contains a *Psychotic Depression scale* (CC) that measures a more severe affective disorder. Such a disorder would be characterized by a depressed mood of such magnitude that it prevents the individual from functioning. This depressed mood may be accompanied by difficulty in sleeping, feelings of hopelessness, a fear of the future, agitation, and psychomotor retardation. Other features include feeling physically drained, becoming angry or tearful with little provocation, feeling unworthy or undeserving, engaging in self-destructive behaviors, being socially withdrawn or sexually overinhibited, feeling tense, and experiencing diminished self-confidence or confusion.

Finally, the *Psychotic Delusion scale* (Scale PP) assesses the presence of irrational ideas, particularly persecutory or grandiose ones. Feelings of superiority and fears of being used by others are markedly noticeable. Minor items that add to this particular scale include being moralistic, believing that some unknown entity is able to interfere with one's life, feeling emotionally detached, being rigid, feeling confused, and being somewhat perfectionistic.

Response Set Scales

Millon (1987) noted that some subjects approach a self-report inventory with a response set that alters the clinical picture that will emerge from the test. For conscious or unconscious reasons, certain individuals are inclined to put their best foot forward and to deny characteristics that are not socially desirable. On the other side of the coin are people invested in portraying themselves as being more severely dysfunctional than they actually are. The last 3 scales were designed to assess such response sets, as well as to flag those individuals who are unwilling or unable to read, understand, and complete the inventory appropriately. Millon called these scales "modifier indices" because they are used to adjust the weighted scores of some of the clinical scales. It should be noted that the first modifier index, the Disclosure Index (X), is not a scale in the usual sense of the word but a composite score computed from the personality scales.

The *Desirability scale* (Scale Y) measures the tendency to portray oneself in a good light. Items that make the subject look confident or gregarious and allege a regard for authority and a respect for the rules of society are the most prominent. Other items would indicate that the subject is efficient and organized, avoids confrontation, has a moralistic but fun-loving attitude, experiences elevated moods, and denies the presence of alcohol abuse.

The *Debasement scale* (Scale Z), on the other hand, was designed to tap an attempt to look bad on the inventory. The most prominent items speak of feeling physically and emotionally empty, having low self-esteem, and becoming angry or tearful at the slightest provocation. Feelings of being unwanted and disliked may be present, along with possible self-destructive behaviors, feeling tense, being uncomfortable around others, or feeling guilty and depressed. Slightly less important are erratic moods, a desire to hurt people, a suspicious attitude, and mental confusion.

Finally, the *Validity scale* (Scale V) contains four items that are so absurd that all of them should be marked false by any subject able to read and understand the items appropriately.

Special Scales

Retzlaff and Gibertini (1990) developed eight factor-based special scales for the MCMI-I. This recent contribution is built on two of their earlier factor-analytic studies (Gibertini & Retzlaff, 1988a; Retzlaff & Gibertini, 1987). The three personality scales derived in that manner were labeled *Aloof/Social, Submissive/Aggressive,* and *Labile/Restrained.* These scales were said to reflect the dimensions that Widiger and his associates have proposed as underlying the *DSM–III* personality disorders (Widiger, Frances, Spitzer, & Williams, 1988).

The factor analyses of the symptom formation MCMI scales led to five factor-analytic scales: Detached, Submissive, Suspicious, High Social Energy, and Generalized Distress. We include a table with the items that load on the different scales as well as the means and standard deviations for each of the scales. The reader therefore has all of the information that would be needed to score and interpret these scales.

Those five scales are still considered experimental. Only one study that we are aware of has used these scales (Adams & Clopton, 1990). The scales, however, are partially supported by our own work in this area (Choca, Greenblatt, Tobin, Shanley, & Van Denburg, 1989). Using a sample of more than 2,000 psychiatric inpatients, we uncovered 17 factors, some of which look similar to the eight scales offered by Retzlaff and Gibertini (1987, 1990).

Using the clients of a Vietnam Vet Center connected with our facility, we have tried to develop a scale to measure posttraumatic stress syndrome (PTSD). Through empirical keying, we were able to pick 17 items that significantly differentiated between the clients who had been diagnosed with PTSD and those who had not. When this scale was tested on a second sample for cross-validation, however, the means and standard deviations of the PTSD and non-PTSD groups were so close that they were practically indistinguishable. This was unfortunately the case even though the differences were statistically significant (Choca, Shanley, Peterson, & Hong, 1987).

Critical Assessment of the Overall Design and Scoring

As a self-report questionnaire, the MCMI is likely to be most productive and revealing when the subject taking the test is reasonably intelligent, has no difficulty reading English, knows himself or herself well enough to answer the questions accurately, and is willing to share what he or she knows in an open and nondefensive manner. In other words, the ideal subject is one who can become an active collaborator in the diagnostic process and has the necessary skills to be an effective contributor in this enterprise. Unfortunately, clinicians are often called on to test people who are not optimal subjects and who, for one reason or another, do not meet all of the requirements. The less ideal the subject is, of course, the less meaningful the results are bound to be. In extreme cases, such results should be seen as invalid and should be disregarded but, in any case, the limitations of having a self-report inventory should be kept in mind.

Moving on to the issue of the type of subject who may take the MCMI, it was noted that Millon (1982, 1983, 1987) has repeatedly warned against using the inventory with people who are not psychiatric patients. His argument is that the test was designed for and standardized with a psychiatric population and that the test norms may not be valid if the subject does not fit the standardizing group. In spite of the obvious weight of that argument, MCMI users have often disregarded that caveat so that there are even published studies (e.g., Repko & Cooper, 1985) that were carried out with a nonpsychiatric population.

Part of the problem is the issue of what constitutes a psychiatric patient. The chronically psychotic individual who has multiple admissions to psychiatric wards is obviously a psychiatric patient, but what about a college student who uses the counseling service at the university when he is feeling depressed because his girlfriend left him? Is he a psychiatric patient? Or the high-functioning female lawyer who has become anxious and uncomfortable while having to compete in a male-dominated law firm? In spite of the specific criteria used in the *DSM–III–R*, the present nosology still avoids to a great extent the issue of where the boundary is between normality and psychopathology (Kendell, 1983; Sabshin, 1989). Moreover, clinicians are occasionally asked to test a subject to decide on precisely whether the person has a diagnosable psychiatric disorder; if clinicians decide that it is inappropriate to use an instrument designed for psychiatric patients, they may be creating an unsolvable dilemma.

We feel that there is nothing intrinsically wrong with using the MCMI to test "normal" people, as long as the examiner is aware that the instrument was designed for and standardized with a psychiatric population. In such cases, the user will have to make the appropriate adjustments. For one thing, the narratives often have to be altered: Instead of talking of "obsessions" and "compulsions," one may discuss the subject's orderly nature and preference for well-established patterns of behavior.

In terms of the scoring, the controversial issue appears to be the differential weighting of the raw scores for the MCMI-II. Although the differential weights make sense from a theoretical viewpoint, it has been shown to add no real advantage: Streiner and Miller (1989) showed through mathematical logic that the differential weighting could not be expected to have a significant effect, a fact that was shown empirically by Retzlaff, Sheehan, and Lorr (in press). The latter article revealed a nearly perfect correlation between the weighted and the unweighted raw scores.

Some critics of the MCMI have noted that, whereas the BR score approach is an overdue and psychometrically valid innovation, the fact that it is unfamiliar requires more explanation. It is likely, for instance, that many practitioners will want to use the MCMI with hospitalized patients and others may want to use it for outpatient screening (Hess, 1985). There is the very real possibility that two such different patient samples with potentially very different base rates, when subjected to the same cutting scores, would produce classification accuracy rates that are substantially different from those in the test manual. Although the test manual presented base-rate syndrome data for standardizing samples, it did not provide separate sample base rates for different groups.

Unfortunately, the cutoff scores included in the test manual will not result in optimally accurate diagnoses if the local base rates differ from those produced by Millon's (1977, 1982) normative samples (Butcher & Owen, 1978). Meehl and Rosen (1955) cautioned against the use of "inflexible cutting scores" for any psychometric device. Widiger (1985) suggested that "the MCMI would be improved by employing alternative cutoff points that varied according to the local base rate" (p. 709). Clinicians have long been urged to systematically collect local clinic prevalence data that could then be used in estimating pretest probabilities (Meehl & Rosen, 1955). In order to determine adequately whether the MCMI and other instruments contribute to or take away from the accuracy of clinical decision making, long-standing pleas for the collection of local prevalence or base-rate data appear as relevant today as they were 35 years ago (Gibertini, Brandenburg, & Retzlaff, 1986).

Psychometric
3 Characteristics

In this chapter we summarize the procedures that were followed in the development of the MCMI, as well as the standardization data offered in the test manuals (Millon, 1977, 1987). We also review investigations by other authors that have examined the validity, reliability, or factorial structure of the test. However, studies dealing with the concurrent validity of the MCMI with other tests are covered in chapter 9.

Item Development

MCMI-I

Three successive steps were used for the initial (theoretical) test construction of the MCMI-I. In the first step, more than 3,500 items were written on the basis of Millon's ideas (as expounded in Millon, 1969). These items were then grouped into a set of 20 scales. In the second step, the item pool was edited to reduce redundancy and increase relevance and simplicity (Millon, 1982, 1983). Empirical procedures were then used to further reduce the item pool. Such procedures included asking patients to judge the clarity and difficulty level of the items and having clinicians group the items blindly into the scales of the inventory (Millon, 1982, 1983).

Two provisional research forms, each containing 556 items, were administered to a "diverse clinical sample" of over 200 patients. Item analyses were then carried out using item–scale intercorrelation and item endorsement frequencies. Such item analyses allowed further reduction of the item pool.

The Research Form was then developed and contained 289 items. This inventory was subsequently validated by 167 mental health clinicians from

31

various locations in the United States and Great Britain who blindly rated 682 patients on the 20 clinical entities represented by the MCMI-I scales.

Comparisons of endorsement frequencies for the 20 clinical criterion groups were then used to eliminate items and to make decisions on scale overlap. The 289 items of the MCMI-I Research Form were reduced to 150, 4 of which were correction items.

Analysis of the first external validation study resulted in the decision to drop three clinical syndrome scales—Sociopathy, Hypochondriasis, and Obsession-Compulsion—because they were deemed to lack clinical utility. In their place, three new clinical scales were developed: Drug Abuse, Alcohol Abuse, and Hypomania. These scales were developed following the same procedures described earlier, and the new items were added to the 150 items for the MCMI-I Research Form.

The newly expanded form was administered to criterion groups such as patients in alcohol and drug treatment programs and patients with a history of manic episodes. Comparison groups were 64 "general psychiatric" patients and a group of 33 nonpsychiatric subjects.

The task at this point was to identify scale configurations that would be externally valid or empirically based. Modifications of these configurations were made to bring them closer to the internal structure, dynamic relationships, and substantive hypotheses of Millon's (1969) theory of personality. To keep the number of profiles at a reasonable level, the initial decision was made to construct profile patterns only from the subsection with the eight personality styles and to limit profiles to two scale high-point pairs. Once the basic two-point configuration had been established, high scores from pathological personality scales (S, C, P) and from symptom disorder sections (A through PP) were added only as separate elaborations or as modifiers of the basic two-point configural pattern. Homologous or equivalent configurations were selected when the theoretical considerations were combined with data showing that clinicians assessed differing high-point pairs as representing similar or identical diagnostic entities. The external criteria against which valid profile configurations were assessed were the profiles that clinicians had constructed when asked to make multiple diagnoses and to quantify assessments of their patients' basic personality and pathological patterns (Millon, 1982).

 One problem that has been cited frequently with regard to the MCMI is the high interscale correlation (Choca, Bresolin, Okonek, & Ostrow, 1988; Choca, Peterson, & Shanley, 1986a; Wiggins, 1982). Using Guilford's (1936) formula, the covariation ranged from −.46 (for the Antisocial-Aggressive and Dependent-Submissive scales) to +.65 (for the Borderline-Cycloid and Dysthymia scales) for the MCMI-I. Millon believed that the intercorrelations and clustering of the scales mirrored his theoretical position and clinical realities (Millon, 1982). However, as Wiggins (1982) noted, "when 20 scales averaging 37 items per scale are scored from a common pool of only 171 items, the psychometric consequences of such a high degree of scale redundancy will almost certainly be unfavorable" (p. 211).

Standardization work was also done with the correction scores (Weight Factor, Adjustment Score, and Validity Index) of the MCMI-I in order to ensure that these measures detect tendencies in response distortion. Data were collected from 75 nonclinical respondents who were instructed to "fake good," "fake bad," and respond randomly in the inventory; the results are contained in the manual.

Finally, the issue of how accurate the individual cutoff scores (BR 75 and BR 85) were in making diagnostic decisions with the MCMI-I was examined. A cross-validation sample of 256 patients closely matching the construction sample was used. For "presence of syndrome" (BR 75), the percentage of correct classifications ranged from 77 to 95. For "most prominent syndrome in category" (BR 85), the percentage of correct classifications ranged from 82 to 98.

MCMI-II

The revision of the MCMI-I was stimulated by several factors. The proposal of two new personality disorders—the sadistic or aggressive personality and the masochistic or self-defeating personality—encouraged the plan to expand the MCMI-I to include those personalities. Additional theoretical developments pointed to the need to modify descriptions of the borderline and antisocial personalities and to revise the characterization of the clinical syndrome of major depression. A third factor involved the desire to bring the inventory's scales into a closer coordination with the official nosology of the *DSM–III* (American Psychiatric Association, 1980) and its successor, the *DSM–III–R* (American Psychiatric Association, 1987). Enhancement of individual scale validity and the reduction of spurious scale overlap were additional goals that stimulated revision.

Studies undertaken after the original standardization of the MCMI-I led to the finding that 40–50 items were expendable. MCMI-II item replacement studies were aimed at generating items for two new personality scales. MCMI-I Scale 8 (Negativistic) was divided into separate scales: Scale 8A (Negativistic) and 8B (Self-Defeating). MCMI-I Scale 6 (Antisocial-Aggressive) was divided into separate scales: Scale 6A (Antisocial) and 6B (Aggressive/Sadistic). A pool of 364 new items was reduced to 193 in a series of editing stages and after a consensus study of best fit for the two new scales done by eight clinician judges. These 193 new items were added to the set of 175 MCMI-I items to constitute a new and "substantively valid" MCMI-II Provisional Form of 368 items, coordinated with both *DSM–III* and preliminary *DSM–III–R* criteria as well as theoretically based attributes (Millon, 1987).

A sample of 108 patients was given the MCMI-II Provisional Form.

New items were reduced to 111 using a variety of criteria. A population of 184 patients was then given the MCMI-II Research Form by clinicians who diagnosed the patients on both axes of the *DSM–III–R* in accordance with the published drafts of diagnostic criteria then in development (American Psychiatric Association, 1985). Correspondence between items and their criterion groups were evaluated by the same procedures used in the external validation studies for the original MCMI-I. The extent to which an item differentiated relevant criterion groups from the population of "general psychiatric patients" was the most important issue in determining selection of final items. The decision to retain or drop an item was not based on any particular cutoff score or fixed level of diagnostic efficiency. The new 111 items were reduced to a final group of 45 items on the basis of the data obtained. These 45 new items replaced 45 of the original MCMI-I items that had been found in previous item-evaluation studies to be expendable. Thus, the final MCMI-II consisted of 175 items, the same number of items contained in MCMI-I (Millon, 1987).

Standardization

MCMI-I

MCMI-I norms are based on numerous clinical groups and nonclinical samples. Drawn from industrial plants, colleges, and personnel offices, the 297 nonclinical subjects ranged in age from 18 to 62 and included 153 (52%) women and 144 (48%) men. Although the MCMI-I was not designed for use with nonpatient respondents, this group of normal subjects served to anchor base rate scores: The median scores for this group were arbitrarily assigned a BR score of 35 on all scales except for the Hypomania scale (Millon, 1982).

Patient populations whose test data provided the basis for MCMI-I norms included 1,591 clinical subjects from the construction phases of test development. Patient test protocols were obtained through the auspices of 108 hospitals and outpatient centers with 233 clinicians participating in these settings throughout the United States and Great Britain. The patient group included 669 (42%) women and 922 (58%) men; 468 (29%) were inpatients and 1,123 (71%) were outpatients. The matching cross-validation patient population of 256 clinical subjects included 111 (43%) women and 145 (57%) men; 77 (30%) were inpatients and 179 (70%) were outpatients. Of the male patients, 15% were aged 18–25, 27% were 26–35, 27% were 36–45, 23% were 46–55, and 8% were 56+. Of the female patients, 12% were aged 18–25, 25% were 26–35, 29% were 36–45, 24% were 46–55, and 10% were 56+. On the basis of estimates from samples of test settings, the percentage of the patient sample that belonged to various ethnic–racial groups was as follows: 81% White, 14% Black, 3% Latino, 1% Asian, and 1%

other-mixed. By geographic–regional location, the sample broke down as follows: 13% New England, 23% Mid-Atlantic, 28% Midwest, 10% Southeast, 10% North and South Central, 13% West Coast, and 3% Great Britain. Hollingshead's (1975) socioeconomic class distribution by percentage, estimated from a sample of test settings, was 2.5% in Class I (major business and professional); 10% in Class II (medium business, minor professional, technical); 23% in Class III (skilled craftspeople, clerical, sales workers); 43.5% in Class IV (machine operators, semiskilled workers); and 21% in Class V (unskilled laborers, menial service workers). The distribution of primary diagnoses, which was abstracted from overlapping diagnoses and which was based on a total sample of 979, was as follows: 15% neurosis, excluding neurotic depression; 11% personality disorders, excluding alcohol and drug disorders and paranoid and schizoid personalities; 16% alcohol and drug; 24% affective disorders, including neurotic depression and manic states; 19% schizophrenic, excluding paranoid schizophrenia and including schizoid personalities; 11% paranoid, including paranoid personalities and paranoid schizophrenia; 2% adjustment disorders; and 2% other (Millon, 1982).

Raw scores were converted to BR scores on the basis of known prevalence data. Cutting lines, determined by calculating optimal valid-positive: false-positive ratios, were designed to assure the maximum degree of correct diagnostic classifications (Millon, 1982). A BR score of 74 was selected as the cutting line or the point on all MCMI-I scales beyond which scale percentages would correspond to the clinically judged prevalence rate for the presence of a personality feature or symptom. A BR score of 84 was selected as the cutting line for all scales beyond which scale percentages would correspond to the clinically judged prevalence rate for the most prominent personality or symptom syndrome. With the exception of the Hypomania scale, all MCMI-I scales were assigned the BR score of 60 to designate the raw score median for all patients in the test-construction studies. Because there were differences in prevalence rates and median raw scores between male and female subjects on several MCMI-I scales, cutting lines for BR scores of 35, 60, 75, and 85 did differ slightly for men and women on those scales. The manual indicated that the percentile of correct classifications ranged from 77 to 98 using a BR score of 85 and the cross-validation sample (Millon, 1982, p. 59).

A review of the data on percentage of valid- and false-positives and correct classifications for the validation samples indicated that most false-positive cases were found among "overlapping" clinical syndromes or personality patterns. As an illustration, both the Narcissistic and the Histrionic scales tapped personality features that were often clinically demonstrated in the same patient. Such personality features often came up high on their respective MCMI-I scales even when they were not judged by clinicians to be concurrently present. Consequently, one of these would be scored as a false-positive. On the other hand, scales measuring traits or syndromes that are viewed as theoretically and clinically disparate seemed to produce far fewer false-positives. As an illustration, there were almost no false-positive cases between the Histrionic scale and the Schizoid-Asocial scale. Because these two scales do not measure theoretically overlapping traits or syndromes, patients who scored highest on one of them rarely scored high on the other.

Further review of the valid- and false-positive data revealed problems or weaknesses with regard to the usefulness of certain aspects of the MCMI-I in differential diagnosis. First, the Compulsive-Conforming scale (Scale 7) appears to be the least effective of the MCMI-I scales in terms of the ratio of valid-positives:false-positives and in terms of correct classification percentage. Thus, clinicians should be very cautious about the significance of the results of Scale 7, especially if this is not corroborated by clinical observation or other test data. Second, there is a problem within the subsection of the three pathological personality disorder scales (Schizotypal-Schizoid, Borderline-Cycloid, and Paranoid). The majority of false-positives on this subsection of the scales appeared to represent cases in which clinician–judges did not rate a concurrent presence of personality disorders but in which the patient produced overlapping high MCMI-I scores. It appears that when a patient has a marked degree of severity in a personality area measured by any one of these three scales, that "dimension of severity may occasionally overpower and blur the differential diagnostic efficiency of the scales" (Millon, 1982, p. 17).

Although the data just discussed on raw score–BR score conversions and cutting lines on the MCMI-I were contained in the original manual (Millon, 1977), notable revisions soon followed. In 1981, the data for 43,218 patients on the MCMI-I were reviewed, resulting in the recalculation and adjustment of the transformation of raw scores to BR scores. This patient population included 23,296 (54%) women and 19,922 (46%) men, of whom 16% were inpatients and 84% were outpatients. On the basis of numerous selected subsamples, BR scores between the major cutting lines of 85, 75, 60, and 35 were smoothed proportionately to represent each scale's raw score patient-frequency distribution. In order to determine the BR 20 point, the 10th percentile for patients on each basic personality scale was used. The 30th percentile among patients on each basic personality scale was used to determine the BR 40 point (Millon, 1982).

MCMI-II

The standardization of the MCMI-II was done with a sample of 1,292 patients. Of those subjects, 49.8% were men and 50.2% were women. The age ranges were as follows: 18–25, 15.5%; 26–35, 25.8%; 36–45, 35.7%; 46–55, 16.9%; and 56+, 6.1%. Patient status and testing settings included outpatient, 81.9%; inpatient, 9.9%; correctional, 2.4%; college center, 2.1%; and other, 3.8%. Marital status included 30.1% never married; 31.2%

first marriage; 13.5% remarried; 6.6% separated; 15.1% divorced; 1.1% widowed; 1.6% cohabiting; and 0.8% other. By religion, subjects were 43.7% Protestant, 28% Catholic, 5.9% Jewish, and 22.4% other. The breakdown for ethnic–racial membership was 87.7% White, 6.9% Black, 4.3% Hispanic, and 1.1% other. Regarding duration of recent episode, 20.4% were less than 1 week, 21.7% were 1–4 weeks, 12.7% were 1–3 months, 11.8% were 3–12 months, 5.1% were periodic 1–3 years, 6.2% were continuous 1–3 years, 2.6% were periodic 3–7 years, 2.3% were continuous 3–7 years, 5.5% were less than 7 years, and 11.7% were cannot classify. With regard to the patient's stated major problem, 30.8% were marital/family, 17.1% were job/school work, 16.8% were self-confidence, 10.9% were moodiness, 6.0% were ill/tired, 5.4% were loneliness, 4.3% were sexual problem, 3.8% were alcohol, 2.7% were antisocial behavior, and 2.2% were drugs (Millon, 1987).

Validity

MCMI-I

Three different types of test validity are commonly recognized. The issue of face validity was discussed previously in the descriptions of how the test was developed. *Concurrent validity* refers to correlations of one test with other tests measuring similar constructs when taken by the same individuals at approximately the same time. Although such correlations can be used to reassure oneself that the test is measuring what it is supposed to measure, the correlations also reveal the relation between the two tests in question. In this book we discuss the concurrent validity studies in chapter 5, emphasizing what the data disclose about the two instruments. In this section, we review only data showing the validity of the MCMI against external nontest criteria.

Gibertini et al. (1986) reexamined the normative data of the MCMI-I to determine the sensitivity, specificity, positive predictive power (PPP), and negative predictive power (NPP) of the test. *Sensitivity* (the proportion of true-positives) refers to the probability that the test score will be elevated when the disorder is actually present. *Specificity* (the proportion of true-negatives) refers to the probability that the test score will not be elevated when the disorder is absent. In order to examine how powerful the test is, one has to take into account the prevalence of a particular disorder because, to be useful, an instrument has to achieve greater accuracy than would be achieved by educated guesses. As Gibertini et al. explained,

> Sensitivity and specificity are usually thought of as characteristics of the test that are independent of the prevalence characteristics of the population; that is, the test should identify the same proportion of disordered cases across

populations irrespective of the number of actual disordered cases in each of the populations. Positive predictive power is defined as the probability that the disorder is present given the test is positive and is calculated as the proportion of test-positive cases with the disorder across all test-positive cases. Clinicians will recognize this index as providing the answer to the question they ask while interpreting a clinically significant test score, namely: What is the likelihood that this patient has the disorder now that I know that the test was positive? Negative predictive power is defined as the probability that the disorder is absent given the test is negative. It is the proportion of test-negative cases without the disorder across all test-negative cases. (1986, p. 556)

The indexes of PPP and NPP are influenced by the magnitude of the sensitivity and specificity of the test and the prevalence of the disorder in the population. When the sensitivity and specificity of the test are very high (e.g., 90%), the PPP and the NPP indexes are optimal. However, as prevalence decreases, so does PPP. In populations with very few disordered cases, even tests with high specificity and sensitivity can have low predictive power. Overall diagnostic power, an index representing the proportion of correct classifications, also varies in its usefulness as disorder prevalence rates vary.

Millon (1983) presented data on the generally high sensitivity and specificity and of the MCMI-I scales. Gibertini et al. (1986) found that the MCMI-I scales varied widely in their usefulness for assigning diagnostic labels to individual patients. PPPs ranged from 19% to 84%. Defining a good scale as one with a PPP of 70% or more, a fair scale as having a PPP of 50%–69%, and a poor scale as having a PPP below 50%, they rated each scale for its ability to predict "presence of a syndrome": Eight were good (Avoidant, Dependent, Histrionic, Negativistic, Borderline, Anxiety, Dysthymia, and Drug Abuse); 9 were fair (Schizoid, Narcissistic, Antisocial, Compulsive, Schizotypal, Paranoid, Somatoform, Hypomania, and Alcohol Abuse); and 3 were poor (Psychotic Thinking, Psychotic Depression, and Psychotic Delusions). They also rated each scale for its ability to predict the "most prominent syndrome": Five were good (Avoidant, Schizotypal, Paranoid, Anxiety, and Dysthymia); 11 were fair (Schizoid, Dependent, Histrionic, Narcissistic, Antisocial, Compulsive, Negativistic, Borderline, Hypomania, Alcohol Abuse, and Drug Abuse); and 4 were poor (Somatoform, Psychotic Thinking, Psychotic Depression, and Psychotic Delusions).

The MCMI-I scales were also found to have generally high NPPs. Thus, negative test scores will rarely be false-negatives and, in addition, patients who are actually free of a given disorder will tend not to score in the clinical range for presence of that disorder.

A third finding discussed by Gibertini et al. (1986) has to do with the generally high overall diagnostic power of the MCMI-I and the factors that one must consider in interpreting the value of this global index. Figures for the overall diagnostic power of the inventory for correctly classifying patients regarding the presence or absence of a trait or disorder range from 82% to 94% for presence of syndrome and from 86% to 97% for the most prominent syndrome (Millon, 1983). Crucial to understanding the meaning of the overall diagnostic power index is an awareness that, especially when prevalence is low, the index can be misleading because it is possible to have high overall diagnostic power even when the actual number of false-positives and false-negatives is greater than the number of true-positives.

One area of controversy with the MCMI has been over how validly the instrument measures the psychiatric disorders and syndromes of the *DSM–III*. The NCS printout for the MCMI-I was identified as a *"DSM–III* report" and provided Axis I and Axis II diagnoses (Millon, 1983, p. 25; Widiger, Williams, Spitzer, & Frances, 1985). All 11 personality scales of the MCMI-I were given titles of an Axis II diagnosis from the *DSM–III*. The remaining syndrome or symptom scales of the MCMI-I were titled to closely resemble the *DSM–III* diagnoses on Axis I. Instructions in the manuals for the MCMI-I (Millon, 1977, 1982, 1983) explained that elevations on the scales were to be interpreted as indicating the presence of *DSM–III* disorders. The test author had described a variety of efforts to coordinate the MCMI-I as closely as possible to the *DSM–III*, writing that "no other diagnostic instrument currently available, other than the MCMI, is fully consonant with the nosological format and conceptual terminology of this official system" (Millon, 1983, p. 1).

Critics have objected to the contention that the MCMI-I was a measure of *DSM–III* disorders (J. Reich, 1985; Widiger & Frances, 1987; Widiger et al., 1985; Widiger, Williams, Spitzer, & Frances, 1986; Widiger & Sanderson, 1987). They argued that there had been no published research to support the alleged correspondence between the MCMI-I and the *DSM–III*. Furthermore, it was noted that the derivation and cross-validation research for the MCMI-I scales had used Millon's (1969) taxonomy and not that of the *DSM–III*. After detailing differences between the *DSM–III* diagnostic criteria for numerous personality disorders and the criteria that Millon had written as initial drafts for these personality disorders, Widiger et al. (1985) supported their contention with an evaluation of content validity, conducted by eight graduate student judges, of the Aggressive and Gregarious scales of the MCMI-I. These critics did acknowledge that an analysis of the content validity of the MCMI-I was not necessarily relevant to its predictive validity and observed that Millon's personality types represented, in many cases, marked improvements over the *DSM–III* categories. Moreover, some scales were observed to be very similar to *DSM–III* categories and one was even essentially synonymous with a psychiatric disorder described in Axis II of the *DSM–III*.

Millon (1985, 1986) answered his critics by noting that the original MCMI was altered in the later stages of its development to improve its usefulness to clinicians. Millon (1985) argued that the real issue is whether the MCMI's conceptual and trait-oriented criteria are at least as good as the biographical and behavioral criteria of the *DSM–III* in "achieving high concordance with independently derived clinical assessments" (p. 380).

The controversy continued with an article by Widiger and Sanderson (1987), who examined the effectiveness of four of the personality scales against the findings of the Personality Interview Questions, a semistructured interview that was conducted by a college senior. The findings demonstrated good convergent validity for the Avoidant and Dependent scales; the Antisocial and Negativistic scales, on the other hand, were judged to be much less successful. These findings were seen as consistent with Widiger and Sanderson's contention that the MCMI is more congruent with the *DSM–III* for those disorders for which Millon's typology coincides with the *DSM–III* prototype.

Similarly, Torgersen and Alnaes (1990) reported a good correspondence between the *DSM–III* personality disorders, as measured by the Structured Clinical Interview (SCID), and the Avoidant and Dependent scales of the MCMI-I. A fair correspondence was found for the Schizotypal, Histrionic, Borderline, Narcissistic, and Paranoid scales, whereas the Schizoid, Negativistic, and Compulsive scales showed poor correspondence.

In other studies, however, the MCMI-I has not fared as well. Piersma (1987) compared MCMI findings with the *DSM–III* diagnoses at the time of discharge. He noted that an elevation of a personality scale was obtained in 98% of the patients, whereas only 40% of the sample had received the diagnosis of a personality disorder from the clinician. Moreover, the MCMI diagnosis was consistent with the clinician only 20% of the time with regard to the particular type of personality disorder.

Wetzler and Dubro (1990) reported the MCMI-I as having a very high sensitivity, so that almost 75% of the patients with a personality disorder were identified, but the test tended to err by classifying many patients judged not to have a personality disorder as having such (false-positives). The PPP of the test in this study was shown to be .49; because the BR for the presence of a personality disorder was .51, the effectiveness of the test was seen as poor. Wetzler and Dubro pointed out that the poor concordance with the MCMI has been obtained in studies using diagnoses generated in standard clinical practice as the criterion measure; they noted that the MCMI has looked better when a semistructured interview was used. This observation opens to question whether it is the MCMI-I that is deficient or the clinical diagnosis used as criterion measure.

The validity of the symptom formation scales of the MCMI-I has also come to the attention of researchers. In our work with people with affective disorders, the Dysthymia and Hypomania scales seemed useful diagnostically because they correctly classified 65% and 56% of the patients in a depressed and manic state, respectively (Choca et al., 1988). Similar support for the Dysthymia scale has been cited by other researchers (Goldberg,

Shaw, & Segal, 1987; Wetzler, Kahn, Strauman, & Dubro, 1989), although Flynn and McMahon (1983) found only modest correlations between the scale and three items dealing with depression and suicidality from an unstandardized survey.

With our patients with affective disorders, the Cycloid scale seemed to be affected by a depressed mood but appeared to be fairly insensitive to mood elevations. As a result, we felt that the Cycloid scale was somewhat redundant with the Dysthymia scale (Choca et al., 1988). It is noteworthy that this scale has now been changed to the Borderline scale in the MCMI-II.

The Psychotic Depression scale was so seldom elevated in any of the samples available that it was felt to be of little clinical utility (Choca et al., 1988; Goldberg et al., 1987; Wetzler et al., 1989). Flynn and McMahon (1983) also reported a modest correlation between this scale and their three items dealing with depression and suicidality. Goldberg et al. (1987) factor-analyzed the items of the Major Depression scale and discovered three factors: Mood Disturbance, Suicide Ideation, and Dependency Conflicts. They felt that the problem with this scale was that it neglected the vegetative symptoms of depression.

The substance abuse scales have also received the attention of researchers. Jaffe and Archer (1987) compared five different scales on their ability to predict drug use among college students. The two MCMI-I substance abuse scales performed well: The discriminant functions used one or both of these scales to predict each of the 12 different categories of substance use except tobacco. The intercorrelation between the two MCMI substance abuse scales was reported to be .65, and the authors noted that the scales have 15 items in common. Accordingly, they questioned whether both of the scales were needed. In their own work, Jaffe and Archer found the Alcohol Abuse scale to be more useful than the Drug Abuse scale, even when the drug use being predicted was not alcohol.

Using a psychiatric population, Bryer, Martines, and Dignan (1990) investigated the effectiveness of the MCMI-I substance abuse scales in distinguishing between substance abusers and the rest of the patients. Using the cutoff BR score of 75, both of these scales were found to correctly classify 79% of the sample. The Alcohol scale had 43% valid-positives and 52% false-positives, whereas the Drug Abuse scale yielded 49% valid-positives and 64% false-positives. Bryer et al. (1990) questioned the utility of the scales as screening instruments in a psychiatric population because, with their data, "subjects scoring above [the] cutoff, more often than not, did not have the substance abuse history that the particular scale had predicted" (p. 440).

The performance of the MCMI-I substance abuse scales may also leave something to be desired when they are used with a substance-abusing population. Gibertini and Retzlaff (1988b) found that only 17% of their sample from an inpatient alcohol rehabilitation program had elevated scores on the

Alcohol Abuse scale. The same problem was found by H. R. Miller and Streiner (1990), who reported that the Alcohol scale identified only 33%–43% of the alcoholics. Gibertini and Retzlaff (1988b) complained that the scale unfortunately tends to measure only severe and prolonged substance abuse so that there are few false-positives but that it tends to miss many of the problem drinkers. Similarly, over half of the former opiate addicts studied by Marsh and her co-workers failed to have elevated scores on the MCMI-I Drug Abuse scale (Marsh, Stile, Stoughton, & Trout-Landen, 1988). It has been noted that very few of the items that make up these substance abuse scales actually address substance abuse. Because there is little evidence for a generic addictive personality, it has been argued that the MCMI-I substance abuse scales can be expected to perform fairly poorly (Bryer et al., 1990; Marsh et al., 1988). Calsyn, Saxon, and Daisy (1990) found that 60.6% of drug-abusing patients scored below the clinical relevance cutoff point on the MCMI-I Drug Abuse scale (Scale T) and concluded that the true-positive rate was so low for drug abusers that it was useless.

To some extent, the practical question to ask is how effective the MCMI scales are compared with other available assessment instruments. The issue is relevant because even the MMPI, the traditional standard in this area, has significant limitations in its ability to predict the clinical diagnoses (e.g., Pancoast, Archer, & Gordon, 1988).

In a recent article, Dubro, Wetzler, and Kahn (1988) compared the efficiency of the MCMI-I, the MMPI Psychopathic Deviate (*Pd*) scale, and the Personality Diagnostic Questionnaire (PDQ). The Structured Interview for the DSM–III Personality Disorders (SIDP) was used as the measure against which the other instruments were examined. Dubro et al. found the MCMI to have "excellent sensitivity" when used as a screening instrument, to be a "fair" predictor of the cluster of personality disorders in which the patient would fall, and to be "fairly successful" at identifying the four personality disorders that enjoyed enough representation in the sample to make statistics meaningful (p. 261). Of the three instruments, only the PDQ was occasionally more effective than the MCMI-I. Because the PDQ consists of items taken directly from the *DSM–III* personality disorder criteria from where the SIDP is also taken, the finding that the MCMI-I was generally as successful as this instrument provided strong support for the test's validity. Another study that compared different assessment techniques showed the MCMI scales to have a greater relation with diagnostician ratings than the personality scales developed by Morey, Waugh, and Blashfield (1985) from the MMPI (Morey, 1986).

Three studies compared the usefulness of the MCMI-I and the MMPI with two very different patient populations. Patrick (1988) administered both tests to 103 psychiatric inpatients and found that two MCMI-I clinical syndrome scales (Psychotic Thinking and Psychotic Depression) were "grossly inaccurate" according to the criterion of concordance with final chart diagnosis. A third clinical syndrome scale, Psychotic Delusions, did identify one of two paranoid disorders in the sample, but this was offset by its relatively high false-positive rate. The true-positive rate was found to be lower than that reported by Millon (1983) for psychotic disorders despite a high prevalence of schizophrenia in the sample. The MMPI was found to be more accurate than the MCMI-I in the identification of both schizophrenia and major depression. Using a similar psychiatric population, Helmes and Barilko (1988) reported that the MCMI-I could only diagnose 1 of 10 symptoms recovered from the patient's chart; the MMPI was not much more effective because it was only able to discriminate 2 of the 10 symptoms.

Uomoto, Turner, and Herron (1988) compared the MCMI-I and the MMPI in predictions of surgical outcome in lumbar laminectomy patients. Neither instrument was found to be markedly superior to the other for this purpose. If one must choose only one personality measure, the authors suggested the MMPI because only three MMPI scales (*Hs, L,* and *K*) plus two demographic variables (age and financial compensation) were needed to obtain a reasonably good hit rate for predicting outcome of lumbar laminectomy. Uomoto et al. also noted that they used the MCMI-I with a normal (nonpsychiatric) population even though the test author advised against this. They also noted another methodological limitation in that both patient and surgeon bias might have influenced results because outcome ratings were made by the surgeon. Finally, they noted that although psychological factors are important, physiological variables such as presence versus absence of disk herniation play a crucial role in deciding surgical outcome.

MCMI-II

In developing the MCMI-II, clinician judges made the diagnostic assignments on the basis of the criteria from the draft of the *DSM–III–R.* This was done in an effort to satisfy objections to the claim that the MCMI-I was a measure of *DSM–III* syndromes. For the external validity of the MCMI-II, Millon (1987) reported that the sensitivity of the scales ranged from 50% to 79%, the specificity ranged from 91% to 99%, the PPP ranged from 58% to 80%, the NPP ranged from 93% to 98%, and the overall diagnostic power ranged from 88% to 97%.

Because the MCMI-II has not been available for long, there is almost no literature outside of the standardization data. In a recent article, McCann (1990) found support for the convergent validity of the MCMI-II clinical syndrome scales using a multitrait–multimethod factor analysis and the MMPI. Poor discriminant validity was found for the Alcohol Abuse, Drug Abuse, and Paranoid scales. The sample included only 85 psychiatric inpatients, however, something that suggests caution in accepting the findings.

In another recent study, Piersma (1991) examined the effectiveness with which the Dysthymia and Major Depression scales of the MCMI-II distinguish between a major depression and another type of depression. Using a cutoff BR score of 75, he reported that the Major Depression scale missed 39% of the individuals in his sample. Otherwise, however, his data generally supported the validity of the scales.

Reliability

MCMI-I

Test–retest studies for the MCMI-I involved more than 140 patients and yielded reliability coefficients ranging from the low 60s to the low 90s. Most of the basic personality scales were in the 80s, the pathological personality scales were in the high 70s, and the clinical syndrome scales were in the mid-60s (Millon, 1982).

Because the MCMI is designed to differentiate among enduring personality characteristics and more transient clinical symptoms, the scales would be expected to perform differently in test–retest studies. The findings reported are consistent with the theoretical expectation in that the basic and pathological personality scales showed a higher stability than the symptoms scales.

The Millon (1982) findings have been supported for the MCMI-I by data gathered by McMahon, Flynn, and Davidson (1985a) from three different clinical samples. Like Millon, those authors found higher stability estimates for basic personality scales when compared with stability estimates found for symptom scales. In one of their samples, for example, the median reliability coefficients for the basic personality scales and the symptom scales were .66 and .57, respectively.

Another report on the stability of the MCMI-I for psychiatric inpatients was offered by Piersma (1986a). In that study, reliability coefficients for basic personality scales ranged from .48 to .75, the pathological personality scales ranged from .27 to .57, and the symptom scales ranged from .21 to .75. Again, Piersma's results supported previous MCMI-I findings in that the basic personality scales did evidence a greater stability across time than did the symptoms scales. Piersma's data for his inpatient sample showed lower overall stability coefficients on the MCMI-I than did the other samples from previous research. This finding held true for both the basic personality scales and the symptom scales. Piersma suggested a number of reasons that might account for the finding that his overall stability coefficients were lower than those found in the other samples, including that his patients were tested at the very beginning of treatment when they were in the most distress and then just prior to discharge when, presumably, their symptoms had abated. In contrast, the data reported by Millon (1982) and McMahon et al. (1985a) were gathered at the beginning and middle points in the treatment.

In what appears to be the longest interval between test and retest dates, Overholser (1989) computed Pearson product-moment correlations for 25 psychiatric inpatients who were given first and second administrations of the test in successive hospitalizations. Hospitalizations were separated by time intervals ranging from 112 to 1,160 days, with the mean interval being 379 days. Correlation coefficients for the MCMI-I personality scales were as follows: Schizoid, .71; Avoidant, .76; Dependent, .67; Histrionic, .80; Narcissistic, .87; Antisocial, .85; Compulsive, .44; Negativistic, .61; Schizotypal, .75; Borderline, .64; and Paranoid, .51. The average correlation across the personality scales was .69, and the average correlation across clinical symptoms scales was .67. Despite certain methodological limitations, these findings do lend some slight support to the assertion that MCMI-I scores are relatively consistent across separate hospitalizations for psychiatric inpatients. With this increased test–retest interval, however, support was not found for the notion that personality scales as a group are more stable than clinical symptoms scales as a group.

J. Reich (1989) reported the following 8-week test–retest reliabilities in 73 treated psychiatric patients: Passive-Aggressive scale, .66; Compulsive, .64; Dependent, .88; Avoidant, .82; Borderline, .89; Antisocial, .79; Narcissistic, .75; Histrionic, .75; Schizotypal, .76; Schizoid, .75; and Paranoid, .60. He stated that patients were first tested in the "clinically ill state" and then retested in the "recovered state."

Finally, Piersma (1987) examined changes in the MCMI-I personality diagnosis that a psychiatric inpatient would receive on admission as opposed to that received at the time of discharge. He reported that only 27% of the sample would have received the same diagnosis in terms of the patient's elevations on the MCMI. The poor showing was blamed on the emotional state influencing the measurement of personality variables at a time when the patients were acutely disturbed.

Internal consistency data for the MCMI-I scales are presented in the manual for the test (Millon, 1982). Kuder-Richardson coefficients ranged from a low of .58 for the Psychotic Delusion scale to a high of .95 for the Borderline scale. With the exception of the Psychotic Delusion scale, all scales had coefficients at or above .70.

The retest stability of high-point scale profiles is important because of the increasing use of such configurations in clinical interpretation. The data Millon (1987) presented were based on results from 421 psychiatric patients who had been tested at a variety of points in their treatment course. Millon reported that patients had the same first or second highest scale on two administrations in about 70% of the MCMI-I cases. In addition, approximately 50% of the patients had the same highest two-point code in either the same or reverse order.

In summary, studies on the test–retest stability of the MCMI-I provide support for the assertion that the instrument reliably assesses the presence of both enduring personality traits and transient symptom states. Reliability figures, of course, vary depending on the population studied, the length of interval between first and second testings, and the timing of testing sessions at first or second admission, midphase, or discharge points. Test–retest stability is higher for personality style scales as a group than it is for clinical symptoms scales as a group; this situation is entirely consistent with the underlying theory and intent of these instruments. The highest stability results for personality scales as well as for symptoms scales were found for nonpatient subjects who were introduced to no clinical interventions. The theoretically expected pattern of relatively high reliability for personality scales and relatively low reliability for symptoms scales appeared most clearly in those studies in which both inpatients and outpatients were tested shortly after entering treatment and shortly before leaving treatment.

MCMI-II

Stability coefficients for the MCMI-II scales for a variety of populations are reported in the manual (Millon, 1987). Test–retest intervals ranged from 3 to 5 weeks. Coefficients for 91 nonclinical subjects were both high and fairly consistent; as one might expect with this population, personality scales did not appear significantly more stable than clinical symptom scales. The basic personality scales had stability coefficients that ranged from .80 to .89; for the personality aberration scales, the range was 79–89, and for the nine clinical syndrome scales, the range was 79–91. The high stability coefficients attained for this nonclinical control group represent solid evidence for the test–retest reliability of the MCMI-II scales and also provide a basic frame of reference against which data from other groups can be compared. That the nonclinical group obtained the highest stability coefficients among all samples studied was interpreted to be a function of the fact that they had not been subjected to any intervention aimed at changing their psychic state as well as being a function of the ease with which nonclinical subjects can respond consistently to test items that represent extremes in emotionality and social behaviors.

The lowest stability coefficients were found in a group of 47 heterogeneous psychiatric inpatients who were tested at intake and again at discharge. The stability coefficients ranged from .59 to .75 for basic personality scales, from .49 to .72 for personality aberration scales, and from .43 to .66 for the clinical symptoms scales (Millon, 1987). These findings were supported by Piersma (1989), except that the coefficients reported by the latter were somewhat lower than Millon's. Piersma was also able to demonstrate that the MCMI-II yielded higher stability coefficients than the original version of the test.

Stability data for the two scale, high-point profiles of the MCMI-II are also presented in the manual (Millon, 1987). On the basis of 168 heterogeneous psychiatric inpatients and outpatients who were retested at intervals of 3–5 weeks, almost 65% had the same first or second highest MCMI-II scale on both administrations. Forty-five percent of patients had the same highest two-scale profiles, either in the same or the reverse order. These are impressive reliability figures, especially because the number of scales involved has increased from the MCMI-I to the MCMI-II. In addition, the latest stability data for the two-point profiles on the MCMI-II include more cases that were tested at intake and at discharge, an arrangement that is seen as the most stringent gauge of reliability (Millon, 1987).

Psychometric Structure

MCMI-I

Factor-analytic techniques have been used with the Millon instruments even though the application of such techniques to the MCMI-I and to the MCMI-II is fraught with difficulties and limitations. Perhaps the most basic problem is that the Millon instruments are, by design, essentially nonfactorial: The underlying structural model calls for built-in scale overlaps and considerable item redundancy (Millon, 1982). An illustration of the difficulties that such overlap presents for the execution and interpretation of factorial solutions by scales is found in the first of two analyses reported in the manual (Millon, 1982). "Scales 8, C, A, H, D, and CC load .892 or better on Factor 1," Hess (1985) observed, "yet all but 4 of Scale A's 37 items appear on at least one of the other five scales" (p. 985). Certainly the real meanings of such loadings by scales are highly questionable when 89% of Scale A's items are shared. The impact of item overlap and resultant high interscale correlation on an overdetermined factor structure has been repeatedly cited in the literature (Choca, Peterson, & Shanley, 1986a; Gibertini & Retzlaff, 1988a; Hess, 1985; Widiger, 1985).

As Guilford (1952) noted, factor-analyzing a group of scales that share items may be inappropriate. The reason for this was explained by Gibertini and Retzlaff (1988a) in the following manner:

> When two or more scales share items they become linearly dependent to an extent proportional to the percentile of the item-overlap. This essentially guarantees that the correlation matrix to be factored has some degree of structure not provided by the subject response patterns. Some part of the resulting factor pattern, in other words, will be artificial. This artificial structure will be constant across populations. If this effect is large relative to that of the subject response patterns, then the artificial structure will "drive" the factor analysis and create very stable factors which have little to do with subject responses. (pp. 4–5)

It should be noted that the same problem has been cited with regard to the MMPI (Shure & Rogers, 1965).

Beyond the essentially nonfactorial structure of the Millon tests, there are important additional conceptual and methodological difficulties. For instance, the selection of a factor method and choosing a solution to summarize the covariation matrix involve complex methodological questions. There are also the issues of weighing, for various sample populations, the influence of differences in demographic features and clinical homogeneity (Millon, 1982).

More than 15 factor-analytic studies have been reported to date for the Millon instruments. Researchers have examined populations of general psychiatric patients (Choca, Peterson, & Shanley, 1986a; Choca, Shanley, Peterson, & Van Denburg, 1990; Choca et al., 1989; Greenblatt, Mozdzierz, Murphy, & Trimakas, 1986; Lorr, Retzlaff, & Tarr, 1989; Millon, 1982, 1987; Piersma, 1986b), alcohol abusers (Gibertini & Retzlaff, 1988a; Lorr et al., 1989; McMahon & Davidson, 1988; McMahon, Gersh, & Davidson, 1989b), drug abusers (Flynn & McMahon, 1984), substance abusers (Millon, 1982), and Air Force trainees (Gibertini & Retzlaff, 1988a; Retzlaff & Gibertini, 1987). Retzlaff, Lorr, and Hyer (1989) obtained data for male and female college students and reported on a sample of male veterans in PTSD, alcohol, and psychiatry programs.

Despite differences in the subject population used, the studies just mentioned have reported a strong similarity among the factorial solutions available. The factor for paranoia, for example, was found in 9 of the applicable studies, lability and schizoid detachment were labeled in 8, passive-submission-aggression was noted in 7, whereas both psychoticism and general maladjustment were found in at least 4 of the investigations. Table 1 shows a sample of the different studies available in the literature and the factors that emerged from those studies.

Researchers have reported that results of their factor-analytic studies lend support to the Millon instruments in terms of the underlying theory, a fairly stable factorial structure, the arrangement of and relation among component personality and symptoms scales, and their clinical usefulness with patient populations. Piersma (1986b), for instance, concluded that his results give further support to Millon's goal of constructing "an instrument that is capable of assessing both presenting symptomatology and more enduring, long-term personality traits and characteristics" (p. 584). McMahon and Davidson (1988) contended that their results suggest that the original MCMI-I may provide a "more differentiated classification" of substance abusers than has been found in various MMPI studies.

A combined factor analysis of the MCMI-I and the MMPI in a male criminal offender population of 2,245 subjects was conducted by Ownby, Wallbrown, Carmin, and Barnett (1990). Results indicated that there were important areas of overlap for the two instruments in terms of measuring the same aspects of subject functioning. Results also indicated that each of those instruments contains unique sources of variance. The authors recommended the use of both instruments as complementary components within an objective assessment battery. They also argued cogently that the consis-

Table 1

Sample of the Available Factor Analyses of the Millon Clinical Multiaxial Inventory Using all Scales

First author	Year	Subjects	# of factors	Factors
Choca	1986	Psychiatric	3	Maladjustment Labile Acting-Out Psychoticism
Flynn	1984	Drug abusers	4	Negativism Detachment Passive-Submissiveness Paranoid
Gibertini	1988a	Air Force trainees	4	Distress Social Acting-Out Suspiciousness Submissive-Aggressiveness
Gibertini	1988a	Alcohol abusers	4	Distress Social Acting-Out Suspiciousness Submissive-Aggressiveness
Greenblatt	1986	Psychiatric	3[a]	Detachment Impulsiveness Psychoticism
Lewis	1990	Psychiatric	3	General Maladjustment Acting-out Avoidant-Schizoid
McMahon	1988	Alcohol abusers (two samples)	4	Schizoid-Avoidant Anxious-Depressed Lability of Mood Paranoid-Delusional
McMahon	1989	Alcohol abusers	4	Schizoid-Avoidant Somatoform Drug Abuse-Hypomania Paranoid-Delusional
Millon	1977	Psychiatric	4	Lability Paranoia Schizoid Social Restraint
Millon	1977	Substance abusers	4	Lability Paranoia General Pathology Lability-Schizoid
Piersma	1986	Psychiatric	5	Interpersonal Withdrawal Emotional Distress Impulsivity-Negativism Paranoid Distrust Dependency-Submission

[a] Nonmetric multidimensional scaling was used.

tently found factor structures for the MCMI-I and the MMPI reflect clinical realities and not just test artifact attributable to overlapping items and scales.

McMahon, Applegate, Kouzekanani, and Davidson (1990) examined the factor structure of the MCMI-I in a well-defined alcoholic population using the stringent standards of confirmatory factor analysis. Results were inconclusive for an initial analysis based on all 20 scales of the test. However, a second analysis, which was based only on the first 8 personality scales of the test, produced a good fit between a two-factor model and the test data. Retzlaff et al. (1989) reported that the factors they found were highly consistent with the scale keyings of the newly published MCMI-II scales.

Similarities and Contrasts in Factorial Solutions

In this section we present a more detailed discussion of a number of studies that illustrate similarities and contrasts in factorial solutions, that provide insight into the utility of Millon instruments for special patient populations, or that constitute methodological and conceptual innovations for MCMI-I and MCMI-II factor-analytic investigations. We conclude with a review and summary of findings with implications for future research.

Most factor-analytic studies of the Millon instruments have been based on the scores subjects obtained on the 20 clinical scales; as already noted, item overlap and interscale correlation can produce an artificially stable factor structure. Some investigators have attempted to deal with the overlap problem by using correlations of shared and unshared scale items (Lumsden, 1986, 1988). Others have performed a factor analysis on the matrix of the item-overlap coefficients (Gibertini & Retzlaff, 1988a). Finally, others have sought to avoid the issue of scale overlap by working with the subjects' answers to the individual items of the inventory.

For instance, we collected 2,129 MCMI-I protocols from male patients hospitalized on acute care psychiatric units at two different Veterans Administration (VA) medical centers. The patients' responses were then subjected to a principal-components analysis and a varimax rotation. Seventeen interpretable factors emerged from that analysis, accounting for 41% of the total variance: Depression, Schizoid, Hypomania, Dependent, Narcissistic, Alcohol, Conflictual, Compulsive, Histrionic, Drug Abuse, Suicidal, Paranoid, Tearfulness, Validity, Somaticism, Tiredness, and Changeability (Choca et al., 1989).

This item-based analysis, then, yielded considerably more factors than scale-based factor analyses. Of the 17 interpretable factors that emerged, 14 contained loadings that made them resemble scales from the MCMI-I. Support was found for 6 of Millon's basic personality scales, 1 of his pathological personality disorder scales, and 5 of his clinical symptom syndrome scales. Three of the factors (Suicidality, Tearfulness, and Tiredness) appeared to be part of a depression cluster but emerged as separate factors. There was one factor—Changeability—that loaded on items dealing with changing one's opinion or feelings and that could be seen as being associated with the MCMI-I Borderline scale. The Avoidant and the Competitive-Antisocial scales were not represented in this factorial solution. The MCMI-I scales most poorly represented in the factor structure were those assessing psychoticism and severely maladaptive personality scales, a surprising finding in a sample of acute care psychiatric inpatients. Also, in contrast to scale-based factor analyses, no general maladjustment factor emerged.

In a second item-based factorial study, Lorr et al. (1989) analyzed MCMI-I data from a sample of 253 psychiatric outpatients and 185 inpatient alcoholics. Although the findings have to be interpreted with caution because of the small sample used, we include the results here because they seem to support some of our own findings. Six personality factors emerged that were interpreted as follows: Social Introversion–Extraversion, Dependency on Others, Verbal Hostility, Need to Please Others, Self-Dramatization, and Orderliness. The five symptom factors that emerged were named Depression, Manic Excitement, Drug Abuse, Alcoholic Misuse, and Suicidal Ideation. Of the six interpretable personality factors, five could be seen to correspond well to Millon's (1969) personality disorders. The Social Introversion-Extraversion factor is similar at one pole to the Avoidant and Schizoid scales and at the opposite pole is similar to the Histrionic scale. The factors Dependency on Others and Need to Please Others appear similar to Millon's Dependent scale. The factor for Self-Dramatization appears to represent aspects of Millon's Histrionic scale. The Orderliness factor corresponds well with Millon's Compulsive scale. The Verbal Hostility factor represents much of Millon's Antisocial scale. In this analysis, no dimensions separated out that would correspond closely to Millon's Narcissistic or Negativistic scales.

Factor-analytic studies of the MCMI-I at the item level represent an important methodological refinement in that they manage to avoid the problem of item overlap. Such studies allow for the ascertainment, without influence by the scale keys, of latent variables that underlie the individual items. In marked contrast to scale-based factor analyses that typically have yielded three to five factors for the MCMI-I, these studies have demonstrated a factor structure for Millon's test that is at once more diverse, more differentiated and well defined, and lends support to the stability of the underlying personality theory's structural model. The authors (Choca et al., 1989; Lorr et al., 1989) of the two item-based factor analyses have produced highly similar results. They also, interestingly enough, offered similar recommendations: Develop nonredundant scales, add missing scales, and enlarge those scales that need a greater number of items for their definition.

MCMI-II

For the MCMI-II, the scale-based factor analysis produced a broader range of factors than did the previous scale-based studies for the MCMI-I (Millon,

1987). On the basis of 769 cases from the normative psychiatric population, the results of the varimax-rotated factor matrix for the MCMI-II were reported in that test's manual and are summarized briefly here.

Factor 1, which might be called "Maladjustment," accounted for 31% of the variance. Dominant themes included low self-esteem, limited and poor interpersonal relationships, peculiarities of cognition and behavior, and depressed affect. High positive loadings were found on the Avoidant, Self-Defeating, Schizotypal, Thought Disorder, and Major Depression scales. Moderately high positive loadings were found on the Negativistic, Schizoid, and Borderline scales. Factor 2, which might be called "Acting-Out/Self-Indulgent," accounted for 29% of the variance. Dominant themes included stimulus-seeking, self-indulgent and acting-out pathologies associated with interpersonal hostility, abrasive self-confidence, and manic temperament. High positive loadings were found on the Histrionic, Narcissistic, Hypomania, and Drug Dependent scales. Relatively high positive loadings were found on the Antisocial, Aggressive-Sadistic, and Paranoid scales. Factor 3, which might be called "Anxious and Depressed Somatization," accounted for 13% of the variance. Dominant themes included covarying symptomatology of the classic triad with moderate severity. High positive loadings were found on the Anxiety, Dysthymia, and Somatoform scales. Factor 4, which might be called "Compulsively Defended/Delusional-Paranoid," accounted for 8% of the variance. Dominant themes included pervasive suspicions defended by rigid emotional controls with periodic explosive outbursts. High positive loadings were found on the Compulsive, Paranoid, and Delusional Disorder scales. Relatively high positive loadings were found on the Aggressive/Sadistic and Schizoid scales. Negative loadings were found on the Histrionic, Bipolar, Manic, and Negativistic scales.

Factor 5, which might be called "Submissive/Aggressive-Sadistic," accounted for 7% of the variance. This is a bipolar factor with one end represented by low self-esteem, self-abnegation, and submissiveness and the opposite extreme reflecting interpersonal hostility, exploitation, and intimidation with associated high self-confidence. Positive loadings were found on the Dependent and Self-Defeating scales and negative loadings were found on the Aggressive-Sadistic, Antisocial, and Narcissistic scales. Factor 6, which might be called "Addictive Disorders," accounted for 5% of the variance. Dominant themes included both alcohol and other drug addiction as well as antisocial personality features. Positive loadings were found on the Alcohol, Drug, and Antisocial scales. Factor 7, which might be called "Psychoticism," accounted for 4% of the variance. Dominant themes included the psychotic realm of frankly thought-disordered and delusional experiences, and chimerical or confused thinking. Positive loadings were found on the Delusional Disorder, Thought Disorder, and Paranoid Personality scales. Factor 8, which might be called "Self and Other Conflictual/Erratic Emotionality," accounted for 3% of the variance. Dominant themes included internal conflict, interpersonal ambivalence, and erratic and unstable emotionality. High positive loadings were found on the Borderline, Negativistic, and Self-Defeating scales.

A second factor analysis of the new MCMI-II, this one item based, showed 8 personality and 9 symptom factors for a patient sample as well as 7 personality and 7 symptom factors for a college student population (Retzlaff et al., 1989). Because the sample consisted of only 207 male VA patients and 278 college students, these results have to be interpreted with caution. Nevertheless, Retzlaff et al. felt that their data generally supported the scale keyings on the new MCMI-II.

Of the 13 personality scales of the MCMI-II, for instance, 9 are represented by factors in one or both of their samples. Only the Paranoid, Schizotypal, Negativistic, and Avoidant scales lack clear identification. Of the 9 clinical symptom scales on the MCMI-II, 5 are represented by the following factors in the samples: Somatoform, Mania, Dysthymia, Alcohol Abuse, and Drug Abuse. However, only nonsignificant aspects of the three psychotic scales were seen, and no factor for the Anxiety scale was found. The psychometric convergence of so many of the MCMI-II scales at the item level is noteworthy. This is particularly noteworthy, as Retzlaff et al. (1989) observed, because factor-analytic methods were not used in the construction of the MCMI-II, a test developed with techniques of domain theory, with items deliberately composed for a priori psychopathology constructs.

Strack, Lorr, Campbell, and Lamnin (in press) conducted separate factor analyses on the 13 personality scales and on the 9 clinical syndrome scales of the MCMI-II. They also examined both the BR scores and the "residual scores." Analyses using BR scores yielded four factors for the personality scales. Analyses using "residual scores" yielded what these researchers regarded as a more meaningful set of three bipolar factors for both the personality scales and for the clinical syndrome scales. Those authors also stated that their findings are generally supportive of Millon's (1969) contention that personality disorders are reliably associated with clinical syndromes. For example, the Strack et al. study showed that social introversion was strongly associated with disordered thinking and that traits of emotionality were strongly associated with substance abuse, depression, and anxiety.

McMahon, Kouzekanani, and Bustillo (1991) investigated the factor structure of the MCMI-II in a population of 278 male inpatient cocaine abusers selected from four treatment facilities in Florida. The McMahon et al. results indicate that the MCMI-II factor structure was highly similar to that found by McMahon and Davidson (1988) with the original MCMI and a sample of alcohol abusers. In addition, three of the four factors found in that analysis revealed clear similarities to Millon's (1987) factor analysis of the MCMI-II based on a psychiatric population. McMahon et al. described the first factor as reflecting a pattern of aggressive acting-out. The second factor was characterized as involving a detached interpersonal style accompanied by anxious–depressed emotionality. A dependent interpersonal style with anxiety and somatic complaints was reflected on the third factor, whereas the last factor revolved around compulsive personality features.

To sum up, scale-based factor analyses of the MCMI have generally produced solutions within a range of three to five factors. Such solutions have been interpreted with some consistency. Millon (1982) described his own findings as reflecting the classical tripartite distinctions for affective, paranoid, and schizophrenic disorders: moving toward, moving against, and moving away. Certain solutions have recalled Eysenck's (1976) triad of neuroticism, extraversion, and psychoticism. Evidence is available for factors that correspond closely to Millon's detached, dependent, and independent typology (McMahon, Gersh, & Davidson, 1989a). Among the factors that have emerged most consistently from scale-based studies, despite differences in naming or labeling as well as differences in order of emergence or percent of variance accounted for, paranoia, emotional lability, schizoid detachment, passive-aggressive, psychoticism, and general maladjustment appear to have been the most prominent across a variety of population samples.

Regrettably, a number of researchers continue to use questionably small samples for factor analysis or to neglect the role of important patient variables (e.g., sex, race, age, socioeconomic status, and diagnostic assignment). The former practice ignores Comrey's (1978) comments on the most common methodological problems in factor-analytic studies. Beyond being sufficiently representative to allow generalization of results, the sample should be large enough to give stable correlation coefficients.

All of the MCMI-II factor-analytic studies already discussed used the scale scores and had the problem that the high interscale correlations might have been dictating the stability of the test structure. Lorr, Strack, Campbell, and Lamnin (1990), however, have conducted an item factor analysis with the MCMI-II that overcomes this problem. Lorr et al. found seven factors using the personality scale items that they labeled Schizotypal, Social Introversion, Conformity, Submissiveness, Antisocial, Narcissism, and Hostile Aggression. The clinical syndrome scales led to five factors: Depressed-Anxious, Alcohol Dependence, Suicidal Ideation, Hypomania, and Drug Dependence. The keying of the items contributing to all of the factors seemed to support well Millon's (1987) keying of the same items. Unfortunately, the Lorr et al. sample contained only 248 male patients and no hierarchical analysis was done, so that the factors offered are not compatible with the more general factors obtained from an analysis of the scale scores.

Validity of the NCS Automated Report for the MCMI-I

The diagnostic accuracy of the computer-generated MCMI-I diagnoses was examined by DeWolfe, Larson, and Ryan (1985) using a sample of 48 patients suffering from a bipolar affective disorder. Only 13 of the 48 reports accurately classified the patients, a finding that the authors interpreted as showing that the computer-generated diagnoses left much to be desired. Such findings were further supported by Piersma (1986d) with 151 consecutively admitted psychiatric inpatients at a large private hospital. Piersma compared the computer-generated diagnoses with the diagnoses generated by the admitting psychiatrists. His results indicated that the computer-generated diagnoses underestimated the presence of the depressive disorders and overdiagnosed anxiety disorders. Finally, Bonato, Cyr, Kalprin, Prendergast, and Sanhueza (1988) compared diagnoses derived from the MCMI-I with those independently generated by both structured and unstructured interviews for 31 consecutive referrals to an outpatient clinic. Bonato et al. reported extremely low (15%) agreement between the MCMI-I and the criterion diagnoses.

The validity of the NCS report as a whole has been the subject of two additional studies. C. J. Green (1982) reported that 23 clinicians rated the information provided by these interpretative reports for 100 of their patients as adequate or better 89% of the time. The clinicians compared MCMI-I and MMPI-I interpretative programs on the basis of adequacy of report information, descriptive accuracy, and utility of the report format. They rated MCMI-I reports as valid, useful, and more accurate than MMPI-I programs in assessing interpersonal relations, personality traits, and coping styles. Green's accuracy figures were dismissed by Lanyon (1984) on the basis that there had been no standard against which to compare the reports. Lanyon also expressed a concern about the "Barnum effect," namely, that a report may be rated as highly accurate because it is filled with generalizations that apply to almost anyone rather than because it is a pointed description of the individual patient.

One way to deal with the Barnum effect is to have experienced clinicians rate the accuracy of two reports for each patient, with one report having been prepared in the usual manner and the other chosen at random (Webb, Miller, & Fowler, 1970). One can then take the difference between the two types of reports as a measure of the incremental validity of the reports prepared in the usual fashion over base rate. Moreland and Onstad (1987) implemented this strategy and had eight doctoral-level clinical psychologists in six different settings rate a total of 99 pairs of reports on their own patients. Seven report sections were rated separately. The researchers formed a composite rating of overall report accuracy by giving each report 1 point for each of the seven report sections rated as "accurate." Case reports obtained a median accuracy rating of 5 ($M = 4.16$, $SD = 2.20$, Mode = 6), whereas the control reports chosen at random obtained a median accuracy rating of 2 ($M = 2.66$, $SD = 2.23$, Mode = 1). The difference between the case and control ratings was highly significant ($p < .0001$). The researchers regarded this as a conservative estimate of the accuracy of the MCMI-I interpretative reports because, for purposes of analysis, report sections that were rated as "unclear" or "don't know" were considered inaccurate. Evaluated singly, five of the report's seven sections exceeded chance accuracy. The researchers noted that those sections of the report that demonstrated the greatest incremental validity, namely, those dealing with Axis I and Axis II diagnoses and narratives, are also those for which the best empirical support exists (Millon, 1983). Moreland and Onstad (1987) concluded that the NCS system "for the MCMI can be much more accurate than the ascription of symptoms, traits, and so on, at random" (p. 114). This work, however, was criticized as possibly having methodological problems, such as using a sample of clinicians that might not have represented the field at large (Cash, Milkulka, & Brown, 1989). Although Moreland and Onstad recognized some limitations of their data, they were able to defend their "cautious" conclusions in a follow-up article (Moreland & Onstad, 1989).

Effect of Subject Variables

4

It may be possible to show that particular subject attributes such as the person's sex, race, age, socioeconomic status, or education influence the results obtained on the MCMI. Traditionally, this effect has been called "test bias" and is an unwanted error of the measurement, a factor that lowers the validity of the instrument.

With regard to the effect of the subject's race, the outcome of recent litigation has demanded that evaluations not lead to a disproportionate number of individuals being chosen from one race as opposed to another, even if the difference in test performance could be explained in terms of the characteristics of the minority groups involved (e.g., *Larry P. v. Wilson Riles* [Lambert, 1981]; "golden rule" settlement [Anrig, 1987]; *Watson v. Fort Worth Bank & Trust* [Bersoff, 1988]). This particular interpretation continues to be controversial (Denton, 1988) because it is just as logical to argue that the test is measuring what it is supposed to measure and that different groups in American society simply have different qualities or attributes.

Regardless of our viewpoint on the cause of group differences, it seems imperative for the clinician to be aware of the effect that particular subject variables may have on the test results. If women were much more prone than men to score higher on the Self-Defeating scale of the MCMI-II, for instance, then an elevation on this scale in the case of a woman would be seen as less pathological than would that of a man.[1] Such knowledge could

---

[1] This example was chosen because part of the controversy surrounding the discussion of the masochistic personality disorder during the development of the *DSM–III–R* involved the concern that this diagnosis would be used much more frequently with women. The controversy eventually led the *DSM–III–R* Task Force to relegate the diagnosis to an appendix of "proposed diagnostic categories needing further study" (American Psychiatric Association, 1985, p. 367). Because the prototype, however, was used for the MCMI-II, the concern regarding possible bias should obviously be extended to the test.

57

then be used to modulate our interpretations. A marginally elevated score may be disregarded in some cases as unimportant, whereas more significant elevations may be seen as partly constituting a socioculturally determined defense. In the review that follows, we examine the available literature from that perspective, not necessarily seeing any differences found between groups as a flaw of the test but as data with which clinicians must be familiar.

Gender

The standardizing data for both of the versions of the MCMI have shown that men and women respond differently to this test. As a result, Millon (1982, 1987) has judged it necessary to use different tables for the conversion of raw scores to BR score for men and women. It is important to examine how effectively the use of different conversion tables equalizes the test results if one is going to offer the same interpretation to the similar elevations regardless of the person's gender.

Although still inadequate, the information available on sexual differences on the MCMI-I suggests that the test may pathologize stereotypically feminine traits. Piersma (1986c), for instance, discovered that women scored significantly higher than men on 5 of the MCMI-I scales at the time of admission and 5 scales at the time of discharge. However, the 5 scales at the time of admission were not the same ones at the time of discharge. The three scales on which women scored significantly higher than men at both times were Dependent, Psychotic Depression, and Psychotic Delusion.

Similarly, Cantrell and Dana (1987) reported significant sex differences using the MCMI-I in their sample of psychiatric outpatients. Women obtained significantly higher scores on six scales—Dependent, Borderline, Anxiety, Somatoform, Dysthymia, and Psychotic Depression—and tended to have a greater number of scales elevated above a BR score of 74. Although men also scored higher than women on some scales in both of these studies, the incidence of such occurrences was less frequent and the mean differences were less pronounced.

The fact that scores on the same scales were not consistently found to be more elevated when one gender was compared with the other spoke for using the findings with caution. Nevertheless, both studies showed women to score higher on the Dependent and Psychotic Depression scales. Table 2 shows the means and standard deviations of these scales taken from Cantrell and Dana (1987). The difference found with the Psychotic Depression scale seemed less critical but, as can be seen, the average female score on the Dependent scale was above the usual clinical cutoff of 74. The obvious concern would be that, using the MCMI, women would be erroneously diagnosed as suffering from a dependent personality disorder. As a result, readers are strongly encouraged to interpret elevations of the Dependent

Table 2

Means and Standard Deviations for Men and Women on Millon Clinical Multiaxial Inventory Scales Showing Gender Differences

Scale	Women		Men	
	M	SD	M	SD
Dependent	82	23	58	24
Psychotic Depression	65	12	57	14

Note. Data are taken from Cantrell and Dana (1987). Used by permission.

scale with caution in the case of women, making sure that the patient clearly meets *DSM–III–R* criteria before this diagnosis is given.

Race

Public and scientific debate over the adequacy of psychological instruments in evaluating members of a minority group have been around for more than six decades (Cronbach, 1975). Although the original conversion tables for the MCMI did not distinguish between individuals of different races, a 1984 manual supplement included separate conversion tables for Black, White, and Hispanic subjects.

In spite of Millon's efforts, racial differences have been noted with the MCMI-I. Pochyly, Greenblatt, and Davis (1989; Davis, Greenblatt, & Pochyly, 1990) examined the effect of race and level of education on the Asocial, Avoidant, Schizotypal, Psychotic Thinking, and Psychotic Delusions scales. Their sample consisted of patients diagnosed as schizophrenic and those having nonpsychotic diagnoses. The particular scales were chosen because they are purported to show maximal differences between the two diagnostic groups in question. A multivariate analysis of variance showed race to be the only main effect that reached significance. Subsequent univariate tests showed that White patients scored significantly lower on the Asocial, Avoidant, and Psychotic Thinking scales.

Using a similar sample from another VA hospital, we have also examined the issue of racial differences with the MCMI-I (Choca, Peterson, & Shanley, 1986b; Choca, Peterson, & Shanley, 1986c; Choca et al., 1990). We used the *DSM–III* discharge diagnoses to examine the predictive power of the test for Black compared with White patients. Data analysis showed that there were differences in the way that the MCMI-I predicted the *DSM–III* diagnoses for anxiety disorders, affective disorders, substance abuse disorders, and psychotic disorders but not for personality disorders.

We then matched subjects according to diagnostic groups in order to

Table 3

Means and Standard Deviations for Men on the Millon Clinical Multiaxial Inventory Scales Showing Racial Differences

Scale	Whites		Blacks	
	M	SD	M	SD
Histrionic	53	23	59	19
Narcissistic	56	23	66	21
Antisocial	59	23	68	23
Paranoid	66	19	77	17
Hypomania	50	33	64	28
Dysthymia	85	16	81	16
Alcohol Abuse	73	19	77	18
Drug Abuse	64	24	75	21
Psychotic Delusion	63	18	70	16

Note. Data are taken from Choca, Shanley, Peterson, and Van Denburg (1990).

conduct an item analysis. Differences between Black and White subjects were found in 45 of the 175 items of the MCMI-I. At the scale level, an analysis of variance indicated a significant overall effect for race. Scores obtained by the Black and White groups were significantly different on 9 of the 20 scales. White patients scored higher on the Dysthymia scale, whereas Black patients scored higher on the Histrionic, Narcissistic, Antisocial, Paranoid, Hypomania, Alcohol Abuse, Drug Abuse, and Psychotic Delusion scales. Table 3 shows the means and standard deviations for the two races on these scales. We also conducted two factor analyses, done separately, with each of the racial groups. This work, however, led to identical solutions.

In other words, our data indicated that there are MCMI-I items that tend to be answered differently by White and Black patients; similarly, some of the scales tend to lead to a higher score with one racial group as opposed to the other. However, the fact that the structure of the instrument remains the same suggested that the instrument measures the same global attributes regardless of race.

One possible explanation for the differences we obtained at both the item and the scale levels is that the two racial groups were not similar psychopathologically. It could be argued, for instance, that the symptoms of one of the groups were more severe than the other. It could also be argued that the categories used to match the two groups were too general and therefore did not adequately equalize the groups as far as the characteristics measured by the MCMI-I. For example, matching subjects with regard to the presence or absence of a personality disorder does not mean that the resulting groups are going to be similar in their histrionic tendencies. Ideally, the two groups should have been matched for every one of the disorders that are covered by the test, a goal that could not be accomplished with the limitations of our sample. Finally, both of the studies cited used VA populations that may not be representative of the rest of the community. Nevertheless, the findings suggest using caution when interpreting the elevations obtained by Black subjects on certain scales, especially if the scores seem higher than would have been expected from the clinical picture.

When the MCMI-I items were being evaluated for the construction of the MCMI-II, item-endorsement frequencies for Black, White, and Hispanic subjects were studied in an effort to reduce potential minority biases. Millon (1987) randomly selected 200 patients from each of these three groups and performed a full replication study. When the endorsement frequencies were calculated on all 171 clinical items for the first 100 patients in each ethnic–racial group, significant differences among the groups were found for 36 items. When the endorsement frequencies were calculated on all clinical items for the second 100 patients in each ethnic–racial group, significant differences among the groups were again found for 13 of those 36 items. Those 13 items were then set for replacement in the MCMI-II.

Unfortunately, 39 of the 45 items that we found to be problematic in our study went on to be included in the MCMI-II. We would expect, as a result, that the newer test would also contain differences in the way items are endorsed by White and Black subjects. Although the MCMI-II manual includes "preliminary norms" for Black and Hispanic patients, these conversion tables are not being used at this time because the sample size was considered inadequate (Millon, 1987). As a result, it is possible that the scale differences that have been found with the MCMI-I would be even more pronounced with the newer version because no allowance is currently made for cultural differences. Indeed, the preliminary data that are available with the MCMI-II suggest a general trend for the nonpsychotic Black psychiatric patient to score higher on the MCMI-II Schizophrenia and Paranoid scales (Davis, Greenblatt, & Choca, 1991).

So as not to mislead readers, we note that the kind of racial differences found with the MCMI are typical of psychological tests in general. As the reviews by Reynolds (1982, 1983) and Jensen (1980) indicated, this problem plagues most of the measures of intellectual ability. The MMPI has been defended by those who feel that documented racial differences were attributable to methodological problems (Dahlstrom, Lachar, & Dahlstrom, 1986; Pritchard & Rosenblatt, 1980). Nevertheless, the fact remains that most MMPI studies on the topic have shown differences between minority cultures and White Americans (Butcher, Braswell, & Raney, 1983; Costello, Fine, & Blau, 1973; Costello, Tiffany, & Gier, 1972; Davis, Beck, & Ryan, 1973; Genther & Graham, 1976; S. B. Green & Kelley, 1988; Gynther, 1972, 1981; Gynther & Green, 1980; Hibbs, Kobos, & Gonzalez, 1979;

Holcomb & Adams, 1982; Marsella, Sanaborn, Kameoka, Shizuru, & Brennan, 1975; McCreary & Padilla, 1977; McGill, 1980; C. Miller, Knapp, & Daniels, 1968; C. Miller, Wertz, & Counts, 1961; Page & Bozlee, 1982; Plemons, 1977; Pollack & Shore, 1980).

Gynther (1989) reviewed six summaries of Black–White MMPI studies that were published from 1960 to 1987. Some of his comments made with regard to racial bias issues in the MMPI appear to be relevant to racial bias issues in the MCMI-I and II. He noted a surprising lack of response to the joint recommendations of Pritchard and Rosenblatt (1980) and Gynther and Green (1980) that studies be done to generate data to which the accuracy test can be applied in order to assess test fairness. He concluded by favoring a strategy of "underinterpretation" that involves a very conservative approach in evaluating the MMPI profiles of Black people. In this approach, moderate elevations on Scales F, 8, and 9 in particular, for blue-collar job applicants especially, would not be viewed as indicating the same degree of deviant behavior as they would for White people.

Age

A number of theorists have talked about adult developmental trends. Contemporary theorists have expanded on Jung's (1933) notions of male mid-life as a time for the development of contrasexual characteristics (for a review, see Neugarten, 1975). Most notably, Gutmann (1980, 1987) contended that men typically move from deriving pleasure through active mastery of the social and physical environment to discovering the varied pleasures of the senses and of warm human relationships (Gutmann, 1987). Similar themes are echoed in Levinson's (1978, 1980) theory of adult development.

In other words, the theory posits that men become less assertive or competitive and more dependent and affectively involved as they age. Following these ideas, we had a chance to study the scores generated by 277 Black and 761 White male psychiatric inpatients (Hoffman, Choca, Gutmann, Shanley, & Van Denburg, 1989). We expected that the Dependent scale scores would show increases with age and that the Histrionic, Narcissistic, and Antisocial scale scores would show decreases. Although women are theoretically supposed to experience the opposite trend, our population came from a VA facility and the sample did not include enough women to study female trends.

Our results using the MCMI-I showed that the two races behave differently as they age. For White subjects, age was positively correlated with Dependent scale scores and negatively correlated with Histrionic and Narcissistic scale scores, as expected, but no changes were seen on Antisocial scale scores. In the case of Black subjects, Antisocial scale scores were negatively correlated with age.

Table 4

Frequencies for Which a Personality Scale Constituted the Highest Elevation Among the Millon Clinical Multiaxial Inventory (MCMI) Personality Scales

MCMI scale	Percentiles		Aging change
	20–44	45–99	
No scale elevated	1.9	5.4	−3.5
Schizoid	7.4	6.7	.7
Avoidant	18.0	14.5	3.5
Dependent	18.8	29.1	−10.3
Histrionic	7.1	4.2	2.9
Narcissistic	13.4	6.4	7.0
Aggressive	8.0	6.2	1.8
Compulsive	5.2	10.8	−5.6
Negativistic	20.2	16.7	3.5

Note. Data are taken from Hoffman, Choca, Gutmann, Shanley, and Van Denburg (1989). We used the usual BR cutoff score of 75 for determining the records in which no scale score was elevated. The aging change was computed by subtracting the percentile of the older group from that of the younger group.

We also examined the relative frequencies with which the different personality scales constituted the highest elevation for the older and younger groups. As can be seen in Table 4, the biggest change between the younger and the older subjects was the frequency with which the Dependent scale received the highest elevation: This scale constituted the highest elevation in only 18.8% of the younger group but was the highest scale on 29.1% of the older group. Next was the difference in the frequency with which the Narcissistic scale was the highest elevation. The trend with this scale was in the opposite direction, with the scale constituting the highest elevation for the younger group in 13.4% of the cases, whereas it was the highest elevation in only 6.4% of the cases for the older group.

Our results supported the current theories of adult development. The findings also address the issue of interpreting elevated scores on the MCMI. Of the 922 male patients in the normative sample of the MCMI-I, 15% were aged 18–25, 27% were aged 26–35, 27% were aged 36–45, 23% were aged 46–55, and 8% were 56+ (Millon, 1982); the age distribution for the MCMI-II was even more skewed toward the younger subjects (Millon, 1987). Because the great majority of the standardizing populations was under 55, the norms are going to be much more reflective of the way younger people fill out the inventory and clinicians may not have to be concerned with the aging trends at that end of the continuum. Our data would suggest, however, that clinicians have to be more careful with older men who have elevated scores on the Dependent scale. We contend that such an elevation has to be interpreted in light of the aging trends and that caution has to be exercised before making statements that make an older man appear pathologically dependent.

Another study also done with veterans by Davis and Greenblatt (1990) similarly reported main effects for age and race. Those authors found an overall trend for older patients to obtain lower scale scores. Several design differences, however, prevent their data from addressing the controversy of whether there are personality changes in adulthood.

Whether personality changes as the result of aging is clearly controversial. In a recent review of their studies on adult personality changes, McCrae and Costa (1990) offered convincing support for their contention that no major changes actually take place as people age. They summarized many studies with cross-sectional as well as longitudinal designs, so their evidence cannot be easily disregarded. Perhaps the best way of integrating the available information is to note that all of their studies were done using their own inventory, designed to reflect the five-factor model of personality (Costa & McCrae, 1985), and it may be that this inventory is not a sensitive measure of the traits that do change with age.

Invalidity and Defensiveness

5

In order to assess the validity of the answers obtained, and the response set or answering tendencies of the subject, the MCMI-I enjoyed only the most rudimentary of measures. The original measures consisted of four items that were blatantly implausible and an index involving the aggregate raw score of the eight personality scales (Millon, 1977). The assessment of validity and defensiveness was considerably improved for the MCMI-II with the addition of two new scales (Millon, 1987). The measures are then used to adjust certain scale scores. Readers should be aware that the adjustments are not strong enough to correct for many cases (McNiel & Meyer, 1990) and obscure the issue of where the subject's scores actually fall in comparison to the standardizing population on any of the adjusted scales (Choca et al., in press). Because of the complexities involved, it is important for MCMI users to be particularly knowledgeable of the data available for these scales. In this chapter, we discuss what is known about all of these measures and review the kind of score profiles that may be expected with subjects who are attempting, consciously or unconsciously, to portray a particular image on the test.

Interpreting the Validity Scale

The first score one looks at when interpreting the MCMI is the score obtained on the Validity scale. Validity scores above 1 most probably mean that all other results are uninterpretable. Such a score indicates that the subject was not reading and understanding the inventory for some reason so that the answers are likely to be random choices. Because the items are keyed such that they only elevate the scale score if they are answered "true," the scale is very sensitive to random responding as long as the response set was not that of answering all of the items "false" (Retzlaff, Sheehan, & Fiel, 1991).

Although Millon accepts protocols containing a Validity score of 1 as valid, much caution should be used with those protocols. After all, a score of 1 on the Validity scale means that the subject claimed that one blatantly absurd item was true about himself or herself. (For instance, the subject may claim never to have had any hair on any part of his or her body.) The reason a Validity score of 1 is acceptable is that, unfortunately, many subjects used in the standardization studies scored some points on this scale; as a result, a score of 1 was not statistically out of the acceptable range. Even if statistically acceptable, clinicians have to consider whether the same person who would make some outlandish claim on the MCMI can evaluate accurately, for example, the connotations of believing that the world would be a better place if people's morals were improved.

Thus, users should look very carefully at protocols that have a Validity score of 1. If it is possible to explain such a score in a way that still allows the thinking that the rest of the items were answered accurately, the rest of the scores may be examined. If no such explanation is obvious, the user is encouraged to disregard all of the other findings. In our own practice, we typically tell the subject that the test was invalid and suggest that he or she may not have been paying close attention to all of the items. In the great majority of cases, one can have the subject fill out the inventory again, this time making certain to read the items carefully.

In cases in which the bad Validity scale item is explainable in some way, we are then inclined to examine the rest of the scores to see whether they make clinical sense. If the rest of the scores are in any way surprising for the particular patient, we are again inclined to see the protocol as invalid and disregard the findings. For our research work, we have used only those protocols with a Validity score of zero.

Interpreting the Disclosure Index

The Disclosure Index is a composite score derived from the raw scores obtained on the personality scales. For the MCMI-I, this index is a simple addition of the applicable raw scores. The MCMI-II uses an equation in order to weigh the raw scores of the different personality scales in a way that makes theoretical sense. In either case, Millon (1982, 1987) gave the acceptable and the average range for each of the two versions of the inventory.

If the index score obtained is outside of the acceptable range, the validity of the scores obtained is again in question. An unacceptably low index score is obtained by individuals who mark the great majority of the items "false." One possibility is that the individual did not read or understand the inventory. It should be noted that if all items are answered "false," the Validity scale score would be zero because the items were written in a way that they indicate an invalid protocol only if they are answered "true." If this possibility seems to have been the case, refer to the comments in the previous section on invalid protocols.

Another possibility that may lead to an unacceptably low Disclosure Index score would be that the subject is very defensive. In that case, the individual might have read and understood all of the items but claimed that very few of the traits or psychological attributes included in the inventory applied to him or her. Unfortunately, this index tended to remain in the acceptable range when subjects were asked to "fake good" in the inventory (Retzlaff, Sheehan, & Fiel, 1991; Van Gorp & Meyer, 1986). In cases in which the unacceptably low Disclosure Index is attributable to defensiveness, the thinking would be that the defensiveness is so profound that little can be learned from looking at any other score and that the protocol should be seen as invalid. It may be possible in such cases to coach the individual into completing the inventory again, this time in a less defensive manner.

When accompanied by a Validity scale score of 1 or above, an unacceptably high Disclosure Index score is usually associated with an invalid protocol. For these cases, refer to the discussion in the first part of this chapter. Otherwise, an unacceptably elevated Disclosure Index score is an indication of "faking bad" on the subject's part. Such an individual is usually claiming to have so many symptoms and psychological traits that it does not seem possible, even when the person is compared with the most disabled of psychiatric patients. The validity of the Disclosure Index in the case of fake bad conditions was supported by both of the studies available (Retzlaff, Sheehan, & Fiel, 1991; Van Gorp & Meyer, 1986).

Disclosure Index scores within the acceptable range may be outside of the average range. In such cases, the protocol is seen as valid but the index betrays a particular response set that the individual is using. In that case, Millon would use the score to adjust the weighted scores of the clinical scales so that they may better represent the actual clinical picture. In addition, however, the fact that the Disclosure Index is outside of the normal range is interpretable. When the index score is elevated, the indication would be that the individual has a tendency to think that he or she has more traits or symptoms than the average patient in the standardizing population. In the case of a low (but acceptable) Disclosure Index score, the implication would be one of defensiveness. (See the next section for further discussion of defensive personality styles.)

Interpreting the Desirability and Debasement Scales

The Desirability and Debasement scales are new to the MCMI-II. Desirability measures the tendency to portray oneself in a "good" light. Items included make the subject look confident, gregarious, cooperative, efficient, well organized, and allege a regard for authority and a respect for the rules of society.

The Debasement scale, on the other hand, was designed to tap an attempt to "look bad" in the inventory. Prominent items deal with feeling physically and emotionally empty, having low self-esteem, becoming angry or tearful at the slightest provocation, feeling unwanted or disliked, feeling tense, being uncomfortable in the presence of others, or feeling guilty and depressed. Erratic moods, a desire to hurt people, a suspicious attitude, and mental confusion may also be present.

Millon (1987) used the difference between the scores obtained on these two scales to modify some of the clinical scales so that they better reflect the picture that others may see looking at the individual. Elevations of these two scales, however, are obviously interpretable, using the descriptions provided previously.

Reztlaff, Sheehan, and Fiel (1991) found these two scales to have only modest effectiveness in their ability to detect malingering. In their study, only 52% of their fake good groups were screened by the scales; the scales detected 48% of the subjects in one of their fake bad groups and 92% on the other.

Wetzler and Marlowe (1990), on the other hand, reported that 17% of their psychiatric inpatients scored higher than a BR of 84 on the Debasement scale. Their finding suggested that this index may reflect a "cry for help" and be an expression of distress rather than intentional dissimulation in the case of severely disturbed subjects.

Defensive Personality Styles and Fake Good Response Sets

We have argued that elevations among the eight basic personality scales are only associated with a particular personality *style* and are not necessarily suggestive of psychopathology. Nevertheless, an MCMI protocol containing no elevations is theoretically indicative of a healthy personality. It is possible to obtain such a personality profile, referred to as *Profile 000,* in a nondefensive manner, a manner that leads to acceptable Disclosure Index levels and average scores on the other modifier indices. Subjects fitting such a profile typically admit having some dependent traits, some narcissistic traits, some competitive traits, and so on, but would not have enough of an inclination in any one of these areas to cause an elevation on the particular personality scale score.

Such people may be described as not having a characteristic style, a ready-made routine, or typical way in which he or she reacts to environmental events. Being this way may have the advantage of allowing the individual to readily vary his or her response in accordance with the situation. It may have the disadvantage of preventing the individual from having an automatic response, a pattern of behavior that comes out naturally and predictably regardless of the situation at hand.

It must be remembered, however, that the great majority of individuals taking the MCMI will have at least one elevation in one of the personality scale scores. In Repko and Cooper's (1985) sample of nonpsychiatric worker's compensation cases, for instance, only 4% did not have any elevated scores. Thus, when no elevations are obtained, one possibility to be considered is that of defensiveness on the subject's part. In our own work we have come to recognize two defensive "no-elevation" profiles.

In the first such profile, the Compulsive scale is the highest elevation of the protocol and is significantly more elevated than the rest of the personality scales. We refer to this style as *Profile 070* and describe it as indicative of a person who has an air of perfectionism and a tendency to deny faults or limitations. Typically, this profile refers to an individual who is guarded, private, and uncommunicative. Interpersonally, they seem distant and unavailable and have difficulty expressing emotions. In spite of appearing somewhat uncomfortable, they may speak of themselves in an overly superficial manner and try to project the image of a person who is doing well after having solved most of his or her problems. Behind this facade one may find an individual who is feeling very vulnerable and insecure, at least with regard to the outcome of the psychological testing.

The other profile we have come to recognize is very similar to the first but, instead of having only the Compulsive scale score elevated above the rest, the Compulsive and the Narcissistic scale scores are prominent. We refer to this profile as *Profile 075* and describe it as follows: The compulsive aspects shown by the MCMI suggest that this individual places an emphasis on perfectionism and maintaining good control of his or her environment. Similar individuals are somewhat defensive and unlikely to admit failures or mistakes. At times, they may be seen as being too inflexible, formal, or proper and may relate to others in a somewhat distant manner. Together with these compulsive elements, this individual may have a tendency to feel that he or she is a special kind of human being and is also inclined to deny the presence of faults. Similar individuals believe that they are more capable or worth more than most of the other members of society. These individuals attempt to tell others what to do and are most comfortable when placed in a position of leadership, but they usually share little of their own private affairs with those around them.

In support of these contentions, Retzlaff, Sheehan, and Fiel (1991) noted that the fake good groups tended to yield a narcissistic-compulsive profile. Both their work and the work of Van Gorp and Meyer (1986) served to point out that it is difficult to distinguish between fake good malingering and a valid profile. This would be especially true in the case of a person with mild emotional problems because, in those cases, the lack of significant elevations among the symptom scales cannot be used as further evidence that the inventory was not completed in a meaningful manner.

Additionally, Bagby, Gillis, Toner, and Goldberg (1991) showed that the fake good condition tended to elevate the Desirability Index scores and that it may depress both the Debasement and Disclosure scores of the MCMI-II.

Fake Bad Response Sets

By contrast, the fake bad profiles are much more discernible on the MCMI-I. Typically, such profiles have many scales above a BR score of 85, the Disclosure and Debasement scale scores are moderately high, and the Desirability scale score is moderately low. The clinical scales that tend to be elevated include the Schizoid, Avoidant, and Negativistic personality scales, as well as the Anxiety and the Dysthymia scales (McNiel & Meyer, 1990; Retzlaff, Sheehan, & Fiel, 1991; Van Gorp & Meyer, 1986).

In terms of the modifier or validity indices of the MCMI-II, the fake bad condition may lower the Desirability scale score while causing elevated scores on the Disbasement and Disclosure scales (Bagby et al., 1991).

PART II

Interpreting the MCMI

6 Interpreting Personality Styles

Our own approach is to view the original eight personality scales as measures of personality *styles* rather than as personality *disorders* (Choca et al., in press). In other words, we view these scales as measuring basic assumptions, predominant attitudes, and typical ways of interacting, and we do not consider an elevation in these scales scores as necessarily pathological. We feel that our approach makes the results of the MCMI more valid because, if these scales are interpreted as measuring personality disorders, the MCMI-I tends to overpathologize subjects (Cantrell & Dana, 1987; Holliman & Guthrie, 1989; Piersma, 1987; Repko & Cooper, 1985; Wetzler, Kahn, Cahn, van Praag, & Asnis, 1990). Because this is the area in which we differ the most from the automated interpretations generated by the NCS program for the MCMI, we would like to share the methodology and narratives that we use for our own discussions of test profile patterns.

The least sophisticated way of interpreting psychological inventories such as the MCMI would be to take one elevated scale score at a time and describe what that particular elevation indicates about the subject taking the test. Although adequate, that particular method is simplistic and forfeits a certain amount of information that could be derived from an integrative view of the elevated scales. Consider, for instance, 2 subjects for whom the Negativistic scale (Scale 8A) constitutes the highest elevation. One such person may have as a second elevation the Dependent scale (Scale 3); in that case, one may talk about an individual who feels inadequate but does not typically behave in a cooperative manner because he or she does not feel that other people are going to meet his or her dependency needs adequately. In contrast, if the second elevation is found on the Antisocial scale (Scale 6A), the negativistic tendencies may be more accurately discussed in terms of the juxtaposition of feelings of inadequacy and the view of life as a tournamentlike situation in which every person has to fend for himself or herself. Therefore, the ideal would be a system that allows any one finding to be adjusted and expanded by any other finding.

Although the ideal is a good goal to strive for, those who are working with the MCMI typically operate in a way that represents a compromise between the simplistic interpretations based on "1-point" elevations and the ideal report that takes into account every scale elevation at the same time. For one thing, at times one may not have a clear idea of how the cluster of traits that are described by one elevation are altered by the presence of another elevation. Moreover, those who administer this test on a routine basis have ready-made interpretations, and the number of narratives needed would be prohibitive if every scale must be considered. The compromise we recommend involves first separating the personality style scales from the rest.

The theoretical underpinning of the personality style scales allows one to visualize what kind of personality would come from a mixture of different styles and makes it more feasible to produce an interpretation of the personality profile rather than interpreting the scales one at a time. Even here, however, there is a limit to the number of scales that one can interpret; we therefore recommend taking into account the three highest elevations among the eight personality scales. Because the number of permutations of eight different things taken three at a time is still a very sizable number (336), we still do not have enough narratives to cover every one of those permutations.

Our system involves giving an individual a narrative that approximates their particular profile, even if it does not exactly fit the elevations that the subject obtained.

In theory, all 336 of these permutations would constitute different and distinguishable personality profiles. Whether this is true empirically remains to be seen. Lorr and Strack (1990) conducted a cluster analysis of the personality scales of the MCMI-II using 166 male psychiatric patients. Four clusters were found with two different types of analyses: the antisocial-sadistic-negativistic cluster, the avoidant-schizoid cluster, the schizoid-dependent-compulsive cluster, and a cluster with a relatively flat profile. In a similar study, Donat (1991) found five clusters. In either case, the clusters found appeared to be fairly large groupings into which many of the different personality profiles could be subsumed, but it would not seem reasonable to limit our interpretative statements to such broad categories.

In the display that follows, a mapping of all possible profiles among the personality styles onto the narratives that are available. The coding of the profiles is performed in the following manner: The first number represents the highest elevation above the cutoff BR score of 75, the second number represents the second such elevation, and the third number represents the third such elevation. Profile 832, therefore, describes an individual who is negativistic, dependent, and avoidant. A zero is used to denote that no scale is elevated above the cutoff so that 120 means that the Schizoid and Avoidant scales were the only two scales having significant elevations. When less than three numbers are given, implied is that it does not matter which other scale is elevated; in other words, 51 means that the Narcissistic scale is the most elevated, followed by an elevation on the Schizoid scale, which may be followed by an elevation of any other scale or no other elevations. Having decided which narrative may constitute the best fit using the display, the reader can then go on to find the narrative later in the chapter.

The display that follows shows profile clusters (first number) and the narrative prototype that may be appropriate (after the arrow). A zero among the profile clusters means that no other scale is elevated above the BR score of 75. When only two numbers are given, the third elevation is unimportant (e.g., 14 means that the Schizoid scale [Scale 1] is the highest elevation, the Histrionic scale [Scale 4] is the second elevation, and it does not matter what else is elevated). Because in our system the Sadistic and the Self-Defeating scales (Scales 6B and 8B) are handled separately, "6" always means "6A" and "8" always means "8A."

0 → 000	20 → 200	30 → 300	40 → 400	50 → 500	60 → 600	70 → 700	80 → 800
070 → 070	210 → 120	310 → 320	41 → 400	51 → 500	610 → 612	71 → 720	810 → 812
075 → 075	213 → 321	312 → 321	42 → 400	52 → 520	612 → 612	72 → 720	812 → 812
10 → 100	214 → 200	314 → 320	430 → 340	53 → 530	613 → 612	730 → 370	813 → 800
120 → 120	215 → 200	315 → 320	431 → 340	540 → 540	614 → 600	731 → 370	814 → 800
123 → 231	216 → 200	316 → 320	432 → 340	541 → 540	615 → 600	732 → 370	815 → 800
124 → 120	217 → 200	317 → 320	435 → 340	542 → 540	617 → 612	734 → 370	816 → 800
125 → 120	218 → 182	318 → 320	436 → 340	543 → 540	618 → 612	735 → 370	817 → 800
126 → 120	230 → 230	320 → 320	437 → 340	546 → 546	62 → 260	736 → 736	820 → 820
127 → 120	231 → 231	321 → 321	438 → 438	547 → 540	63 → 600	738 → 738	821 → 820
128 → 128	237 → 327	324 → 320	450 → 450	548 → 548	640 → 468	74 → 740	825 → 820
130 → 132	234 → 238	325 → 340	451 → 450	56 → 564	641 → 468	75 → 750	826 → 826
132 → 132	235 → 238	326 → 340	452 → 450	57 → 750	642 → 468	76 → 670	827 → 820
134 → 138	236 → 238	327 → 327	453 → 450	58 → 580	643 → 468	78 → 837	823 → 823
135 → 138	238 → 238	328 → 328	456 → 456		645 → 456		824 → 823
136 → 138	24 → 238	340 → 340	457 → 450		647 → 468		830 → 380
137 → 137	25 → 250	341 → 340	458 → 458		648 → 468		831 → 380
138 → 138	26 → 260	342 → 340	46 → 468		650 → 650		832 → 382
14 → 100	27 → 720	345 → 354	470 → 470		651 → 650		834 → 380
15 → 100	280 → 280	346 → 340	471 → 470		652 → 650		835 → 380
16 → 100	281 → 280	347 → 340	472 → 470		653 → 653		836 → 380
17 → 170	283 → 238	348 → 348	473 → 470		654 → 650		837 → 837
180 → 182	284 → 280	350 → 530	475 → 468		657 → 650		84 → 840
182 → 182	285 → 280	351 → 530	476 → 470		658 → 658		850 → 800
183 → 138	286 → 826	352 → 530	478 → 468		67 → 670		851 → 800
184 → 138	287 → 280	354 → 354	480 → 480		680 → 680		852 → 800
185 → 138		356 → 356	481 → 480		681 → 680		853 → 800
186 → 138		357 → 357	482 → 480		682 → 680		854 → 800
187 → 138		358 → 356	483 → 480		683 → 680		856 → 856
		36 → 360	485 → 458		684 → 680		857 → 857
		370 → 370	486 → 468		685 → 658		860 → 860
		371 → 370	487 → 480		687 → 680		861 → 860
		372 → 327					862 → 826
		374 → 370					863 → 860
		375 → 370					864 → 864
		376 → 370					865 → 856
		378 → 387					867 → 860
		380 → 380					870 → 800
		381 → 380					871 → 800
		382 → 382					872 → 800
		384 → 380					873 → 837
		385 → 380					874 → 800
		386 → 380					875 → 857
		387 → 387					876 → 800

The narratives just provided were generated as part of our clinical work so that each of them was originally written for one particular patient. Repeated use of the narratives led to further refining of the descriptions, often involving the omission of statements that did not apply to the subsequent patients obtaining the same test profile. Nevertheless, the narratives have not been validated in a systematic and experimentally valid manner; they are offered only as an aid to the diagnostician who would still be expected to decide what part of the narrative if any applies to his or her particular patient.

In spite of our attempt to make the narratives as benign as possible, we still use a fair number of negative terms in describing our patients. There are two reasons for this. First, negative terms unfortunately tend to be more meaningfully descriptive: Most people would claim to be cooperative but only a few would admit being submissive or compliant. Second, the MCMI is designed to be used with a psychiatric population so that we are often in the position of having to emphasize the problem areas rather than the areas of psychological strength.

If read in sequence these narratives are very repetitive because they often describe traits that were already described in a previous narrative. We intend for the reader to use them in a cookbook fashion, examining only the one that applies for the particular subject in question.

Profile 100: Schizoid

The Schizoid scale of the MCMI contains items that deal with a lack of close relationships with others and a lack of interest or ability in expressing feelings or emotions. Patients who obtain elevated scores on this scale are probably private and prefer to be alone than to be with others. The detachment that they show does not appear to be a defense mechanism because the MCMI suggested that they may be quite comfortable when they are involved in a social situation. Rather, the findings indicated that they may be loners by nature or by choice.

Similarly scoring people tend to be uninsightful and are not interested in exploring their personal feelings. Their detachment may result from enjoying inanimate objects and not caring about interpersonal rewards. They lead unemotional lives and are not inclined to get too disturbed when things do not go their way, but they also do not experience much excitement when good things happen. This tendency to remain on an even keel can be a real asset because emotions will seldom interfere with the decision-making process. These people may be seen, however, as being emotionally bland and lacking an effective rapport with the people around them.

Given this personality style, these patients may have some difficulty in becoming involved in a therapeutic situation. Establishing a therapeutic alliance is likely to be problematic because such patients are not likely to value the explorations and insights that are often seen as being an important part of therapy. Modes of treatment that place less value on the emotional rapport or the understanding of psychodynamics may be more in tune with patients' approaches to life. In addition, the therapist must be comfortable with having distant relationships with these patients and must accept that, although cooperative, such clients may never be aggressive collaborators in the therapeutic process.

Profile 120: Schizoid-Avoidant

High scores on these scales of the MCMI characterize people who keep a significant emotional distance from others. Such individuals are most comfortable when they are doing something alone. They tend to like jobs or hobbies that involve objects and that have minimal human contact. In extreme cases, these individuals may be single and their history may show signs of an inability or unwillingness to establish a meaningful relationship outside of the nuclear family. Otherwise, these individuals restrict the number of relationships that they form and tend to have superficial friendships when those exist, alliances that are more similar to acquaintanceships than strong friendships.

For these patients, the inclination to be loners seems to be the result of two different dynamics. First, they appear to be uninterested in interpersonal relations. They are not too adept at understanding and enjoying the subtleties and nuances of interpersonal emotions and communications, a situation that might then have led to their being apathetic about the relationship itself. They typically do not have very strong emotions and live fairly bland affective lives.

A second dynamic that seems to be operating in these patients' cases is that they seem to be sensitive and afraid of being rejected by others. As a result, social situations are a source of significant tension, leaving them feeling nervous and not looking forward to this type of activity. They would like to be accepted and appreciated and realize that they have to take part in social events in order to obtain that kind of satisfaction. Relating to others, however, is so uncomfortable that they avoid the situation in spite of the positive effects that it could have.

On the positive side, avoidant-schizoid individuals are self-sufficient people who do not depend on others for the fulfillment of their own needs. Often they lead lives that are fairly free of overemotionality and in which psychological issues tend not to interfere with their behavior. On the other hand, they may be perceived by others as loners who are isolated and who have somewhat empty and unproductive lives.

Given this personality style, such patients may have difficulty establishing therapeutic alliances. The discomfort that they experience in interpersonal relationships will probably make the sessions unenjoyable. In addition, a therapist would also have to be concerned about patients feeling rejected any time that an uncomplimentary interpretation is made. Inasmuch as treatment plans involve giving patients negative feedback or guiding them to confront objectionable aspects of their personalities or behavior, the therapeutic situation will be experienced as threatening or stressful. In order to maintain the alliance but contribute to patients' growth, a very careful balance has to be struck between the uncritical support and the threatening therapeutic work. The therapist must also be ready to allow the emotional distance that patients may need and to tolerate patients' inability to talk about their lives and feelings in a nondefensive manner. These patients will feel most enhanced with a therapist who treats them with admiration and respect.

Profile 128:   Schizoid-Avoidant-Negativistic

The scores that patients obtain on these scales of the MCMI characterize people with introversive, avoidant, and negativistic elements in their personality styles. They have little interest in experiencing the subtle aspects of interpersonal relationships. Because of their lack of interest in interpersonal matters, these patients might have turned their attention toward areas that do not involve people, such as reading or art. At worst, such individuals may be perceived as being emotionally insensitive in a distant and apathetic way. Such people probably have very few friends and little real interpersonal involvement.

High scores on these three scales also suggest that these patient are generally unresponsive to stimuli. This is true regardless of whether the stimulus comes from their own processes or from the outside. Similar individuals are not particularly energetic or enthusiastic and their thinking is usually vague, unclear, and somewhat impoverished. They are not prone to understanding or interpreting past events or to planning for their own future. At times, they may appear evasive and overly defended, but most typically they just seem somewhat apathetic, dull, and uninteresting.

In these patients' cases, the detachment from others is accompanied by conflicts that they experience in social situations. These MCMI scale scores indicate that they feel somewhat inadequate and often wish that someone would provide nurturance, shelter, and guidance. They fear, however, that when others get to know them, they will reject them. As a result, they often seem nervous and tend to be somewhat moody and resentful. At times, they may be friendly and cooperative, but anger and dissatisfaction soon color most of their relationships.

Given their personality styles, these patients may have some difficulty establishing therapeutic alliances. The discomfort experienced in interpersonal relationships will probably make the sessions unenjoyable. In addition, a therapist would also have to be concerned about patients feeling rejected any time that an uncomplimentary interpretation is made. Finally, patients' dependency conflict will mean that they are likely to respond to the therapist's leadership in a negativistic manner so that it may be difficult to get them to be motivated collaborators in the treatment. The therapist must be ready to allow the emotional distance that patients may need and to tolerate their inability to talk about their own lives and feelings nondefensively. If care is taken not to issue many directives or advice, the resentments that patients usually develop when they feel dependent on a relationship may be minimized.

Profile 132: Schizoid-Dependent-Avoidant

The MCMi personality style cluster for patients scoring highly on these scales emphasizes introversive aspects of the personality, which are also observed with cooperative and avoidant traits. Similarly scoring individuals are characterized by a lack of interest in the emotional area of human functioning. They do not seem happy when things come out well but are also not too upset by unfortunate events. These individuals are not very interested in interpersonal situations. They are quiet and often stay by themselves and take the role of passive observers. They remain uninvolved, very seldom taking sides or verbalizing a strong position. Rarely the center of attention, these individuals typically fade into the social background. They have a small number of friends and the relationships that do exist tend to be superficial. They are socially indifferent and have little apparent need to communicate or to obtain support from others.

Together with the emotional indifference, such patients have a predominant dependent trait and tend to feel less important or capable than most other people. Similar individuals are easily led by others and relate in a submissive and dependent manner. They are uncomfortable with highly competitive situations and are humble and try to be as congenial as possible to the people around them. Often they are afraid of being rejected by others and, as a result, feel some discomfort when relating to others.

These patients are probably detached and uninvolved. Cooperative and agreeable people, they may be perceived as easygoing and emotionally stable. However, they may be criticized as being somewhat dull, quiet, indifferent, dependent, or apathetic.

In light of this personality style, the difficulty for a therapist attempting to work with these patients may be in establishing the therapeutic alliance. The therapist will have to be tolerant of patients' somewhat distant way of relating. A somewhat unexciting course of treatment can also be expected. A supportive relationship will be one in which the therapist takes a protective and parentallike attitude, reassuring clients that their problems can be worked out and that help will be available.

Profile 137: Schizoid-Dependent-Compulsive

The MCMI personality style cluster for patients scoring highly on these scales emphasizes introversive aspects of the personality, which are seen together with cooperative and disciplined traits.

Accordingly, these patients are probably characterized by a lack of interest and awareness of emotional feelings and interpersonal situations. They usually have relatively unemotional existences and do not seem particularly happy when things turn out well, but they are not too saddened by unfortunate events either. These individuals tend to be quiet loners who often stay by themselves and are passive observers. They remain uninvolved, very seldom taking sides or any strong position. Rarely the center of attention, they often fade into the social background. They have a very small number of friends and, when relationships do exist, they tend to be superficial. It is not that such people fear or actively avoid others but that they are somewhat indifferent and apparently have little need to communicate or to obtain support from others.

Together with the emotional indifference, these patients tend to feel less important or capable than most other people. Individuals with the same pattern of scores tend to be led by others and to relate in a submissive and dependent manner. They also tend to shy away from highly competitive situations. They are humble and try to be as congenial as possible to the people around them.

These patients probably assume that if they do not make mistakes, they can depend on other people to provide for their needs. The compulsive trait is compatible not only with the dependency needs but also with their tendency to be distant from others because it emphasizes a control of emotions and the benefits of keeping things to oneself. The emphasis on avoiding mistakes often makes these individuals seem somewhat rigid, inexpressive, and excessively formal. The compulsive trait, however, probably makes them orderly, dependable, well organized, and responsible.

Individuals with similar profiles tend to be detached, uninvolved, and objective. However, they may also be perceived as being somewhat dull, quiet and colorless, indifferent, dependent, and apathetic.

Profile 138: Schizoid-Dependent-Negativistic

Patients scoring highly on these scales have a personality style that can be characterized by the prevalence of introversive and cooperative traits, although they seem to be uncomfortable with their dependency. Such individuals tend to be unemotional. When things turn out well for them, they do not seem particularly happy, but they are not too saddened by unfortunate events either. They tend to be quiet, private people who prefer to stay by themselves and be passive observers. Often they remain uninvolved, seldom taking sides or a strong position. Rarely the center of attention, these individuals tend to fade into the social background. They have a small number of friends and their relationships are usually superficial. It is not that they fear or actively avoid people but that they are somewhat indifferent and apparently have little need to communicate or to obtain support from others.

Perhaps partly as the result of the lack of interpersonal interest and know-how, these patients tend to have low self-esteem and to be submissive to others. They probably avoid competitive situations and try to be congenial and conciliatory. In order to do this, they may cover up their feelings, especially if such feelings are aggressive or objectionable.

Some submissive individuals feel comfortable when they are able to establish a dependent relationship with another person who seems to be competent and trustworthy. The lack of emotional interest and awareness that these patients show makes it hard to establish a strong relationship of this type. As a result, they probably have some chronic discomfort that may be observed in a generally moody emotional makeup. Other individuals of this type may demonstrate this discomfort by relating in a somewhat negativistic way.

Profile 170: Schizoid-Compulsive

High scores obtained on these scales of the MCMI characterize individuals who are fairly distant and controlled. Similar individuals have little interest in or ability to experience the subtle aspects of interpersonal relationships. Because of this, they usually concentrate on matters that do not involve people, such as reading or art. They may be perceived to be emotionally insensitive to others in a distant and apathetic way. The end result is that they probably have very few friends and little real interpersonal involvement. Similar individuals also tend to be unresponsive to nonsocial stimuli, regardless of whether the stimulation is coming from inner processes or the outside.

Additionally, such patients tend to be overly controlled, disciplined, and proper. It is as if the emotions that they feel are so confusing or threatening that the feelings have to be hidden. Individuals with similar personality profiles feel that people should try very hard to avoid making a mistake. They are orderly, conscientious, well prepared, and controlled. They try to be efficient, dependable, industrious, and persistent. To those in authority, these individuals relate in an overly respectful and ingratiating manner. This style of relating often changes when the relationship is with a subordinate. In that case, patients may become somewhat perfectionistic and may treat the other person with some disdain. Often these individuals believe in discipline and practice self-restraint. This overcontrol of emotions often gives these individuals a characteristic flavor: They may be too formal and proper and may be perceived to be rigid or indecisive when they have not had a chance to study all possible alternatives. However, they tend to be well organized and do a good job in situations in which it is important to be accurate and meticulous.

Profile 200:   Avoidant

Patients scoring highly on this scale have a personality style marked by avoidant traits. Typically, such individuals are somewhat hypersensitive to the possibility of rejection. They assume that people will not value their friendship and are often concerned with the risk of an interpersonal humiliation. This fear has the effect of making them ill at ease in social situations because they feel that they have to put their best foot forward and constantly be on guard. Even though they are often sensitive people who can show understanding and compassion for others, they tend to be nervous and uncomfortable. In order to avoid the discomfort that is most commonly attached to interpersonal contact, similar individuals tend to shy away from social situations. This probably presents a problem for them because they would like to have friends and to be well accepted. However, the discomfort associated with the social risk often makes it easier to forfeit the support that they could have derived from others than to do otherwise. Similar individuals, as a result, tend to be somewhat isolated and to function best in situations in which they do not have to interact with many other people.

Profile 230:   Avoidant-Dependent

High scores on these scales characterize individuals with predominant avoidant and dependent traits. Individuals with similar scores usually do not have any close friends and tend to remain detached and isolated. They often view themselves as weak, inadequate, unresourceful, and unattractive. Strongly wishing to be liked and accepted by others, they nevertheless have a great fear of rejection. This concern tends to put them on guard and makes them uncomfortable so that social situations are experienced negatively. They seem apprehensive when relating to others and are shy or nervous in social situations. Relating to others is a difficult and threatening experience that these patients try to avoid. In so doing, however, they give up the support and affection that the avoided relationship could have brought. Thus, life is experienced as a conflict between taking a risk and accepting the discomfort of forming a relationship or retreating to the unfulfilling safety of their isolation. These individuals are usually sensitive, compassionate, and emotionally responsive. However, they are often nervous, awkward, mistrustful, and isolated.

Profile 231:   Avoidant-Dependent-Schizoid

High scores on these scales characterize patients with interpersonal apprehensiveness, feelings of inadequacy, and introversiveness. An overriding concern for individuals with similar scores is that of being liked and appreciated by those around them, but they are always afraid that others will reject them. These attitudes place them in a bind: If they avoid interacting with others, they feel comfortable and at ease but worry about the lack of social support. If, on the other hand, they decide to take the risks of attempting to form relationships, the fear of rejection makes them tense, nervous, and uncomfortable as long as they are involved in the interaction.

Two other traits are also evident, which may help explain the feelings just described. First, there is some evidence that these patients feel inadequate and insecure compared with others. They tend to feel devalued and to think that other people are more capable or more worthy than they are. As a result of these feelings, such patients probably try to be cooperative to the point of submissiveness. This dependency fits well with the discomfort in interpersonal relationships because it supports the assumption that if others were to really get to know them, they would see how worthless they really are and would lose interest in their friendship.

The other trait is that of a lack of interest in personal feelings or interpersonal communications. Individuals obtaining similar score profiles are often unaware of their own emotions and tend to remain aloof and detached. They are distantly complacent, appear somewhat apathetic, and do not experience strong emotional ties with others. They are private individuals, often loners, who may have some acquaintances, but typically do not have an intimate friendship.

Profile 238: Avoidant-Dependent-Negativistic

High scores on these MCMI scales indicate that the central traits in these patients' personality makeup are a fear of rejection, feelings of inadequacy, and a tendency toward mood changes. They want very much to be liked by others but feel that it is much too likely that their social approaches will be rejected.

They are probably dependent and cooperative. People with similar personality profiles usually underestimate themselves: When they compare themselves to others, they feel that they are less capable, less attractive, or worth less as human beings. They tend to be unassertive people who seldom demand anything from others, although they can be controlling in a dependent and submissive manner. Similar individuals seem more comfortable when they can rely on others to make the important decisions and obtain enough guidance and protection. The feelings of inadequacy are consistent with the fear of rejection because they assume that people will eventually develop uncomplimentary opinions about them and will reject them.

As a result of this basic personality structure, such patients tend to be apprehensive when relating to others. Probably seen as shy and nervous, they are likely to feel uncomfortable in social situations. They are often caught in a bind: On one hand, they would like very much to interact with others and to be liked and appreciated. On the other hand, they tend to avoid social situations in order to avoid the anxiety that the situations evoke.

The psychic conflict may be seen behaviorally in a vacillation or ambivalence that the patients may have. At times, they may be more open and friendly and at other times will seem aloof, distant, abrasive, moody, or disinterested in others. Occasionally, similar individuals project the feelings created by the frustration of their basic conflict. In such instances, they may be even more distrusting or become hostile and prone to blame others for their failures. This pattern will be short-lived and eventually these individuals come back to feeling inadequate and blaming themselves for everything that happens to them.

In light of this personality style, these patients can be expected to have some difficulties in establishing a therapeutic alliance. A certain amount of discomfort in the relationship and an inability to develop enough trust so that they can truly confide in the therapist will have to be overcome. Even after the relationship has been established, the therapist will need to be careful not to offer interpretations that can be experienced as rejections. A tolerance for moodiness and overt or covert expressions of resentment will also be needed. If successful, however, these patients may derive much benefit from experiencing the closeness of the therapeutic relationship because they may not have many other opportunities for emotional closeness.

Profile 250: Avoidant-Narcissistic

Patients scoring highly on these MCMI scales have a personality style that is characterized by avoidant and confident traits. Typically, these individuals are hypersensitive to the possibility of rejection. They assume that people will not value their friendship and are often concerned with the risk of humiliation. This fear causes them to feel ill at ease in social situations because they feel that they have to put their best foot forward and constantly be on guard. Even though they are often sensitive people who can show understanding and compassion for others, they tend to be nervous and uncomfortable. In order to avoid the discomfort that is most commonly associated with interpersonal contact, these individuals tend to shy away from social situations. They probably would like to have friends and to be well accepted. However, the discomfort associated with the social risk often makes it easier to forfeit the support that they could have derived from others rather than take the risk of being mistreated. As a result, they tend to be isolated and may function best in situations in which they do not have to interact with many other people.

Part of the fear of rejection comes from the tendency that they have to overestimate their own value. Individuals obtaining similar scores on these MCMI scales feel that they are "special" and that they are superior to most other people. A tendency to exaggerate their abilities and positive attributes and construct rationalizations to inflate their own worth is typically present. Individuals characterized by this profile usually view themselves as intelligent, outgoing, charming, and sophisticated. They have a need to evoke affection and attention from others. Whenever they feel slighted, rejected, or mistreated by others, they are likely to use projection as a defense and depreciate those who refuse to accept or enhance their self-images. Thus, these patients may be a bit grandiose, egocentric, and unappreciative of others.

In light of this personality style, these patients can be expected to have some difficulties in establishing therapeutic alliances. A certain amount of discomfort in the relationship and an inability to develop enough trust so that they can truly confide in the therapists will have to be overcome. Even after the relationships have been established, the therapist will need to be careful not to offer interpretations that can be experienced as rejections. A tolerance for expressions of resentment will also be needed. These patients will feel most enhanced with a therapist who treats them with admiration and respect. Allowing them to be as much in control as possible during the therapy sessions will make them feel comfortable. A relationship in which the therapist is treated more like a colleague than a superior will also be experienced as ego syntonic and supportive. Inasmuch as the treatment plan involves giving patients negative feedback or confronting objectionable aspects of the personality or behavior, the therapeutic situation will be experienced as threatening or stressful. In order to maintain the therapeutic alliance but contribute the patients' growth, a very careful balance has to be struck between the uncritical support and the threatening therapeutic work.

Profile 260: Avoidant-Antisocial

According to the elevated scores that patients obtain on these MCMI scales, they have a personality style characterized by avoidant and competitive traits. Typically, these individuals are hypersensitive to the possibility of rejection. They look at their environment as a competitive place and feel that in order to function in it, they have to fend for themselves. As a result, most individuals with this view are somewhat distrusting and suspicious. They see themselves as assertive, energetic, self-reliant, strong, and realistic. They imagine that they have to be tough in order to make it in the "rat race." Justifying their assertiveness by pointing to the hostile and exploiting behaviors of others, they may be contemptuous of the weak and not care whether they are liked, claiming that "good guys come in last."

Individuals with this type of personality are concerned that other people will take advantage of their friendship if they are not careful. This fear causes them to be uncomfortable in social situations because they feel that they have to be constantly on guard. As a result, they tend to be nervous and uncomfortable.

In order to avoid the discomfort that is commonly attached to interpersonal contact, they shy away from social situations. These patients probably would like to have friends, but the discomfort associated with the social risk often makes it easier to forfeit the support that could have been derived from others rather than take the chance of being mistreated. Such individuals are typically isolated and may function best in situations in which they do not have to interact with many other people.

People obtaining similar MCMI scores on these scales are usually impulsive. They are typically perceived as being somewhat aggressive and intimidating, perhaps somewhat cold, callous, or insensitive to the feelings of others. They may be argumentative and contentious, even abusive, cruel, or malicious. When matters go their way, they may act in a gracious, cheerful, and friendly manner. More characteristically, however, their behavior is guarded, reserved, and resentful.

In light of this personality style, these patients can be expected to have some difficulties in establishing a therapeutic alliance. A certain amount of discomfort in the relationship and an inability to develop enough trust so that they can truly confide in the therapist will have to be overcome. Even after the relationship has been established, the therapist will need to be careful not to offer interpretations that can be experienced as rejections. Inasmuch as the treatment plan involves giving patients negative feedback or confronting objectionable aspects of their personalities or behaviors, the therapeutic situation will be experienced as threatening or conflictual. In order to maintain the therapeutic alliance while contributing to patients' growth, a very careful balance has to be struck between the uncritical support and the threatening therapeutic work.

Profile 280:   Avoidant-Negativistic

Elevated scores on these MCMI scales indicate the presence of avoidant and negativistic traits in the personality style.

The avoidant trait may be observed in a hypersensitivity to rejection. Interpersonal situations are probably perceived as risky, often leading to humiliation or rejection. The conflict that similar individuals face is that they would like to be appreciated, but the fear of rejection makes them apprehensive; they would like to meet people and establish strong emotional ties, but they are so uncomfortable in social situations that they tend to avoid interpersonal contacts altogether. Typically, these people are loners to some degree. They retreat into their own worlds and are interpersonally nervous and uncomfortable. They tend to be sensitive, however, aware of their own feelings and the emotional reactions that they evoke in others.

Individuals with similar MCMI profiles tend to question their own abilities and to see themselves as not being very interesting or worthwhile. However, they do not see others as being much better and, in fact, tend to perceive humanity as cold and rejecting. So, in spite of their poor self-images, they do not idolize others and are generally very aware of the limitations that other people may have.

When these patients are able to establish significant relationships, the interactions tend to be conflictual. There is a tendency for them to be moody and resentful: They may be friendly and cooperative at times, but they may become negativistic or hostile, only to feel guilty later on and behave contritely. In some cases, these mood fluctuations are less noticeable, with patients handling the conflict through a more stable form of covert obstructionism.

In light of this personality style, these patients can be expected to have some difficulties in establishing a therapeutic alliance. A certain amount of discomfort in the relationship and an inability to develop enough trust so that they can truly confide in the therapist will have to be overcome. Even after the relationship has been established, the therapist will need to be careful not to offer interpretations that can be experienced as rejections. A tolerance for moodiness and overt or covert expressions of resentment will also be needed. It may be possible to minimize some of the hostility that may eventually be projected onto the therapist by trying not to give advice to the clients and allowing them to control any aspect of the therapy sessions that do not need to be controlled by the therapist. Interpretations dealing with both the fear of rejection and the tendency to blame others can also be helpful. If successful, the clients may derive much benefit from experiencing the closeness of the therapeutic relationship because they may not have many other opportunities for emotional closeness.

Profile 300: Dependent

Patients scoring highly on this MCMI scale have a cooperative personality style. These individuals feel that they are not very able to take care of themselves and must find someone dependable who will protect them and support them, at least emotionally. They tend to feel inadequate or insecure and to see themselves as being less effective or capable than everyone else. They also tend to form strong attachments to people who will be the decision makers, but they shy away from competitive situations. They are followers rather than leaders and are often submissive in social interactions.

Concerned with the possibility of losing friends, similar individuals may cover up their true emotions when the feelings are aggressive or objectionable. These are humble people who try to be as congenial as possible to those around them. They are probably well liked but may occasionally be considered wishy-washy because they never take a strong position on controversial issues. Similar individuals could be criticized for their inclination toward submissive dependency, their lack of self-esteem, and always looking outside of themselves for help.

In light of this personality style, these patients can be expected to form a quick alliance with any therapist willing to play a benevolent parental role. An approach in which they are given guidance in an affectionate and understanding manner would be experienced as supportive. It may be difficult if part of the treatment plan is to move the patients toward more independence or increase their ability to compete in an assertive or effective manner. In that case, these patients may feel vulnerable and threatened and may respond with unadaptive behaviors.

Profile 320: Dependent-Avoidant

High scores on these scales indicate a personality style with high cooperative and avoidant components. These individuals tend to have low self-esteem and see others as being more capable or more worthwhile. They tend to be followers rather than leaders, often taking passive roles. They would like to seek emotional support and the protection of others but, together with these wishes, they experience a certain amount of discomfort.

The discomfort comes from the assumption that if others get to know them as well as they know themselves, people would develop the same uncomplimentary views that they have of themselves. As a result, these patients probably tend to be guarded and apprehensive when relating to others. Similar people try to "put their best foot forward" and tend to hide their true feelings, especially when the feelings are aggressive or otherwise objectionable. These individuals may seem tense, nervous, and distant. Because they feel ill at ease in social situations, they often avoid them, resulting in loneliness and isolation.

Given the personality style just described, these clients will experience as supportive a relationship in which the therapist has a benevolent and protective attitude toward them. Feeling that the therapist is a powerful expert and will give good advice and guidance will be reassuring for them. Their fear of rejection may require frequent reaffirmation and the promise of support.

Profile 321: Dependent-Avoidant-Schizoid

High scores on these MCMI scales are characteristic of a personality style with high cooperative, avoidant, and introversive components. These individuals tend to have low self-esteem
and to perceive others as being more capable and worthy. They tend to be followers rather
than leaders, often taking passive roles. They would like to seek emotional support and the
protection of others but, together with these wishes, they are uncomfortable in social relationships. Additionally, they often have trouble understanding the feelings and motivations of
others and appear somewhat bland and apathetic.

Individuals with similar scores tend to assume that if others get to know them as well as
they know themselves, people would develop the same uncomplimentary views that they have
of themselves. As a result, they tend to be guarded and apprehensive when relating to others.
They try to put their best foot forward and tend to hide their true feelings, especially when the
feelings are aggressive or otherwise objectionable. They may seem tense, nervous, and distant.
Because they feel ill at ease in social situations and because they lack interest and understanding in the interpersonal area, they often do not have any strong relationships. Thus, they are
frequently lonely and isolated from others. However, these patients may be fairly cooperative
and gentle, seldom experiencing intense feelings and feeling fairly pleasant and controlled.

Given the personality style just described, these clients will experience a supportive therapeutic relationship if the therapist has a benevolent and protective attitude toward them.
Feeling that the therapist is a powerful expert who will offer helpful advice and guidance will
be reassuring for them. Their fear of rejection may require frequent reaffirmation and the
promise of support as well as tolerance for the clients who may be somewhat uncomfortable
during the sessions.

Profile 327: Dependent-Avoidant-Compulsive

Patients scoring highly on these scales have a personality style with high cooperative, avoidant,
and disciplined elements.

Individuals with similar scores tend to have low self-esteem and to see others as being
more capable and worthy. They are followers rather than leaders, often assuming passive
roles. They would like to seek the emotional support and protection of others but, together
with that wish, they experience a certain amount of discomfort.

The discomfort comes from the assumption that if others get to know them as well as they
know themselves, these people would develop the same uncomplimentary views that they have
of themselves. As a result, these patients are probably guarded and apprehensive when relating to others. Similar people try to put their best foot forward and have a tendency to hide
their true feelings, especially when these feelings are aggressive or objectionable. They may
seem tense, nervous, and distant. Because they feel uncomfortable in social situations, they
often avoid such affairs and are frequently lonely and isolated.

Thus, one way in which these clients defend against the insecurity that their low self-
esteem may bring is by counting on the guidance and protection of others. Another defense
mechanism that they use is thinking that if they manage to avoid making mistakes, they can
always expect the outcome to be a positive one. Individuals with a similar "compulsive" bent
are orderly and plan for the future. They prepare in a conscientious manner and do the work
on schedule. Other characteristics of these people include efficiency, dependability, in-
dustriousness, persistence, extreme respectfulness and ingratiating behavior, perfectionism,
and self-discipline. They tend to be indecisive and have significant problems making decisions
by themselves. The compulsive inclination may also serve to strengthen the feelings of inadequacy that are beneath it in that, whenever bad things happen, they will be inclined to look for
what mistakes they made that might have led to the undesirable outcome.

Given the personality style just described, these patients will experience as supportive a
therapeutic relationship in which the therapist has a benevolent and protective attitude. Feel-

ing that the therapist is a powerful expert who will advise and guide will be reassuring for them. Their fear of rejection may require frequent reaffirmation and the promise of support.

Profile 328:   Dependent-Avoidant-Negativistic

High scores on these scales of the MCMI characterize patients who have cooperative, avoidant, and negativistic personality traits. Individuals with similar scores tend to have low self-esteem. Furthermore, they are likely to assume that if others get to know them, those people would develop the same uncomplimentary views that they have of themselves. They would like to seek the emotional support and protection of others but, at the same time, they fear rejection. As a result, they may experience much interpersonal discomfort and tend to be guarded and apprehensive. They may seem tense, nervous, and distant when they are with others. Because they feel ill at ease in social situations, they often avoid them and become loners.

According to their scores, such patients are somewhat resentful of others and are inclined to blame negative events on external factors. The anger may be expressed overtly or covertly. In either case, they may occasionally become uncooperative and hard to handle. The projective defense mechanism fits in well with the social avoidance because the hostility tends to alienate other people. Projections also give them a rationale for rejecting others before they have a chance to be rejected. At the same time that they resent the control of others, however, they are probably uncomfortable in competitive situations in which they have to act independently and make their own decisions. This discomfort creates a vicious cycle of needing to depend on others but feeling resentful of that need.

The presence of a dependent, avoidant, and resentful personality style suggests that these clients will have difficulty establishing a good therapeutic alliance. They may be most at ease in a situation in which they feel protected, supported, and safe: not likely to be rejected or humiliated. This same relationship, however, is likely to activate a conflict over dependency, a fear of rejection, and discomfort with intimacy. As the conflicts are activated, such clients may become critical of the therapist and it may be more difficult than ever to keep them in treatment. It may be necessary to make appropriate interpretations and help them understand how the defensive resentment is generated. Through this understanding, clients may be able to become less dependent, defensive, or conflicted.

Profile 340:   Dependent-Histrionic

The indications from scores on these MCMI scales are that these patients have a cooperative personality style with dramatic overtones.

Probably the most prominent personality trait for these patients will be low self-esteem. Individuals with similar scores tend to feel less gifted or worthy when they compare themselves with others. The poor self-image usually leads to feelings of insecurity and anxiety, especially when they are in competitive situations.

There are indications that these patients also have fairly high needs to get attention from others. They may always be seeking to be conspicuous and to have constant affirmation of approval and affection. Individuals with similar profiles take an active role in obtaining the needed attention. They often develop a sensitivity to the moods of others and use this knowledge to evoke the reactions that they desire. They may seem charming and outgoing, dramatic or seductive.

These types of people are usually cooperative and congenial, colorful, and in touch with their emotions. However, they may have a difficult time in situations in which they feel alone or have to depend on themselves. The loss of meaningful others is often strongly felt.

With regard to psychotherapy, these patients would feel the most comfortable when the therapist re-creates a parental role and offers a good deal of attention, support, nurturance, and protection. In spite of the dependency, similar patients tend to be occasionally contrary and conflictual in the therapeutic relationship as a result of the histrionic overtones. The therapist should be tolerant on these occasions. Therapeutic change may come from processing the perceived lack of support, from encouraging patients to be more independent, and from enhancing their understanding of their primitive needs for attention and support.

Profile 348: Dependent-Histrionic-Negativistic

With regard to this personality style, such patients seem to have a combination of cooperative, dramatic, and negativistic elements. Their MCMI scores on these scales suggest that they are caught in the bind of having low self-esteem but feeling that they have to conceal their true appraisal of their own worth and appear confident and self-assured.

Individuals with similar MCMI scale scores tend to feel less gifted or valuable when they compare themselves with others. The poor self-image probably leads to feelings of insecurity and results in anxiety when they are in a competitive situations. Similar people are followers rather than leaders, usually trying to be cooperative and to get along well with others. They are "people who need people": They tend to relate to others in an easy and meaningful manner but often depend on those relationships in order to function. Because they trust others to protect and guide them, the patients may not be well prepared to take independent responsibility for attaining goals or life accomplishments.

The elevation on the Histrionic scale score indicates that these patients need a certain amount of attention from others. They may seek to be conspicuous and to have frequent reaffirmation of approval and affection. Individuals with similar profiles take an active role in involving others. They often develop a sensitivity to the feelings of the people around them and use this knowledge to evoke the reactions they desire. They can be charming and outgoing, colorful, dramatic, or seductive. Depending on how functional they are, they may use this ability to cope effectively with the environment or they may come across manipulative and ungenuine.

These patients may be friendly and cooperative when they are feeling more inadequate. Soon, however, they probably begin to feel that they should be projecting a different image and change to a more arrogant and demanding posture. They may become bored with stable relationships and displace some of their inner conflicts into interpersonal resentments. Thus, they may seem moody and easily irritated, unpredictable, or negativistic.

Given their personality style, these patients will benefit from a therapeutic relationship in which the therapist takes a dominant role and offers parentallike guidance and protection. An emphasis on formalities such as being on time for the session or keeping an interpersonal distance during the session is likely to feel unfriendly and dissatisfying. The type of relationship that would feel ego syntonic to the patients would be one in which they are very much the center of attention and demonstrations of affection and support flow readily, especially from the therapist to the patient. The limits to the support that the therapist can offer, however, may eventually become an issue if patients become clingy, demanding, and dissatisfied. If not handled properly, such developments may threaten the therapeutic alliance. One way to handle such issues is to make them aware of their inappropriate expectations and help them work through their dependency conflict.

Profile 354: Dependent-Narcissistic-Histrionic

Elevated scores on these MCMI scales characterize patients who have cooperative, confident, and dramatic overtones. Probably the most prominent personality trait for these patients is low self-esteem. Individuals with similar scores tend to feel less gifted or worthy when they compare themselves with others. This poor self-image usually leads to feelings of insecurity and some anxiety when they are in competitive situations.

Such individuals also tend to publicly overrate their own self-worth. This tendency may come from disparate assumptions that they hold about themselves so that—even though they do not value themselves in some areas—they seem to be very confident in others. Often, however, this ego inflation is a defensive reaction to the low self-esteem. In either case, there is an obvious conflict between the two images that they try to project. This conflict may surface in vacillations between relating in a congenial way and seeming somewhat arrogant and obstructionistic.

There are indications that these patients also have fairly high needs for attention from others. They may be always seeking to be conspicuous and to have constant affirmation of approval and affection. Individuals with similar profiles actively pursue the needed attention. They often become sensitive to other people's moods and use this knowledge to evoke the reactions they want. They may seem charming and outgoing, dramatic or seductive in their relationships with others.

These individuals are usually cooperative and congenial, colorful, and in touch with their emotions. However, they may have a difficult time in situations in which they feel alone or have to depend on themselves. The loss of meaningful others is often strongly felt.

Profile 356: Dependent-Narcissistic-Antisocial

According to the MCMI scores on these scales, these patients generally feel inadequate. As a result, they are often cooperative and ingratiating. Similar people want to be liked by others and often try to be generous and congenial. However, they also feel that they are very special. In spite of assessing themselves as being less capable than others, they feel that they have some quality or innate worth that indeed makes them superior to others.

The way that these patients have adapted to their often conflictual life assumptions is by developing a somewhat defensive posture that allows both of the assumptions to remain in place. Individuals obtaining similar scores can be characterized as having a bit of a "tough" image. They emphasize the competitive aspects of the world and see themselves as having to be tough in order to come out ahead. Seeing the world in a "realistic" manner that pictures everyone in competition for the same limited assets, they focus on the advantages of having personal strength. They often try to hide their own inadequacies because they assume that if others learn about them, the knowledge will become a liability that will work against them. Although they do feel emotionally dependent on others, they try to appear as if they do not need other people and can make it on their own. They try to control others and may be somewhat mistrusting.

The maladaptive defensive element of this power-oriented stance can be observed when their positions are somehow undermined. When confronted by people who will question their control, they may have an abrasive or hostile reaction that represents their attempt to bolster their own self-confidence.

Profile 357: Dependent-Narcissistic-Compulsive

Elevated scores on these MCMI scales characterize patients who have cooperative, confident, and disciplined traits. Probably the most prominent personality trait is low self-esteem. Individuals with similar scores tend to feel less gifted or worthy when they compare themselves with others. They try to be cooperative and feel most comfortable when they are under the guidance and protection of a powerful mentor. Their poor self-image usually leads to feelings of insecurity and anxiety when they are in competitive situations.

Individuals with similar MCMI profiles also tend to be proud and occasionally publicly overrate their own self-worth. This tendency may come from disparate assumptions that they hold about themselves so that, even though they do not value themselves in some areas, they seem to be very confident in others. This ego inflation—their proneness to rationalize away their failures and paint themselves in a good light—may be seen as a defensive reaction to the low self-esteem, a way of quieting their insecurities and comforting themselves.

These patients may also use compulsive ways of enhancing their self-images. Similar individuals are likely to be proper and respectful in their relationships with others and to adopt a somewhat perfectionistic and moralistic outlook. They are usually hard-working people who see the world in right–wrong terms (black–white) and who may be somewhat meticulous and picayunish. This proper and disciplined facade is frequently used to emphasize their intrinsic value and combat the fear that they may not be very worthwhile.

Profile 360: Dependent-Antisocial

Patients scoring highly on these MCMI scales have a cooperative personality style with competitive overtones. The life assumption of similar individuals is that they are not capable of taking care of themselves and must find someone dependable who will support and protect them. They tend to feel inadequate or insecure and see themselves as less effective or able than everyone else. They tend to form strong attachments to people who will be the decision makers and take responsibility for their welfare. Concerned with the possibility of losing friends, similar individuals may hide their true emotions when the feelings are aggressive or objectionable. These are humble, congenial people.

Such individuals perceive the environment as a competitive place. As a result, they are somewhat mistrustful and suspicious of others. Typically, their behavior is guarded and reserved, but they hope that, with the help of the people they have risked depending on, they can be strong, realistic, and determined in the rat race of life. Although they do not feel tough or secure by themselves, they look to others to provide protection from a cruel and insensitive world in which people are interested only in personal gain.

In light of the personality style just described, these patients can be expected to form an alliance with any therapist willing to play a benevolent parental role, even if they are guarded and distant at first. An approach in which guidance is given in an affectionate and understanding manner will be experienced as supportive. If part of the treatment plan is to move patients toward more independence or increase their ability to compete in an effective or aggressive manner, there may some difficulty. In that case, patients may feel vulnerable and threatened and may respond with unadaptive behaviors.

Profile 370: Dependent-Compulsive

According to these MCMI scale scores, patients tend to have low self-esteem and an orderly and disciplined nature. Similar individuals believe that other people are more capable, interesting, or valuable than they are. They are humble and personable and are often capable of forming strong interpersonal relationships. They aim to be as congenial as possible in order to obtain the support they need. As a result, similar people tend to be fairly submissive, or at least compliant. They shy away from competitive situations because such situations make them feel unsupported and vulnerable. When they feel protected, however, they tend to be quite at ease and conflict-free.

Thus, one way in which these patients defend against the insecurity that their low self-esteem may bring is by counting on the guidance and protection of others. The second defense mechanism used is thinking that if one avoids "making a mistake," one can always expect the outcome to be a positive one. Individuals with a similar "compulsive" bent are orderly and plan for the future. They prepare in a conscientious manner and do the work on schedule. They try to be efficient, dependable, industrious, and persistent. Often, these individuals relate in an overly respectful and ingratiating manner, but they may be somewhat perfectionistic and demanding. Similar individuals believe in discipline. They may be indecisive and have significant problems making decisions by themselves. The compulsive tendency may also serve to strengthen the feelings of inadequacy that are beneath it in that whenever bad events happen, they will blame themselves for the outcome.

Given the personality style just described, these patients will benefit from a therapeutic relationship in which the therapist has a benevolent and protective attitude toward them.

Feeling that the therapist is a powerful expert who will give appropriate advice and guidance will reassure them. These patients can be expected to establish a strong therapeutic alliance without much difficulty and to find such a relationship helpful.

Profile 380: Dependent-Negativistic

Patients scoring highly on these MCMI scales are both dependent and negativistic. Individuals with similar scores tend to feel insecure and to have low self-esteem. They are inclined to feel uncomfortable in competitive situations and are not the kind of natural leaders who assert themselves and take for granted that others will follow.

Many individuals with low self-esteem look to others for protection and support. However, they seem to have a conflict in this area. Although they feel unsure of their own abilities and feel that they need to depend on others, they also tend to be mistrustful of others. These individuals do not feel that other people are reliable or dependable and resent being in the vulnerable position of needing others but not being able to assure that their needs will be met.

Some people faced with this conflict externalize it by appearing to be cooperative and compliant but actually resist the leader in some way. Others tend to vacillate. Sometimes they are very friendly and cooperative but begin to feel resentful and may become mistrustful and angry, only to feel guilty and contrite and begin the cycle again.

Given their personality style, these patients need a therapeutic relationship in which the therapist assumes the dominant role and offers parentallike guidance and protection. The limits to the support that the therapist can offer, however, may eventually become an issue if patients become clingy, demanding, and dissatisfied. If not handled properly, such developments may threaten the therapeutic alliance. One way to handle such issues is to make patients aware of their inappropriate expectations and help them work through the dependency conflict.

Profile 382: Dependent-Negativistic-Avoidant

High scores on these MCMI scales characterize individuals with predominant dependent, negativistic, and avoidant personality traits. Such individuals tend to feel that they are not very capable or gifted and that if they are left to their own devices, they would not be able to make ends meet. They would like to have someone else take care of them and provide for their needs, but they tend to distrust and resent the capacity of others, a fact that closes the option of becoming dependent on some benefactor.

These patients tend to be moody and to change their overall feelings without an obvious reason. At times, they may be friendly and engaging; they then become angry and resentful. Later yet, they may feel guilty and behave contritely. The cycle is completed when they again become friendly and cooperative. In other words, they defend against their insecurities by projecting blame, sometimes onto themselves and sometimes onto others. A different defensive substyle of the same basic personality makeup involves the use of a negativistic defense. In that case, patients try to control resentment through obstructionistic maneuvers that allow the venting of anger in covert ways, without blatantly jeopardizing the dependent relationship.

Most individuals with similar MCMI scale scores have considerable feelings of insecurity. They tend to perceive others as being more gifted, more capable, or more worthy than they are. In addition, they fear that others may recognize their lack of value and reject them; they also tend to be nervous and uncomfortable in social situations because they fear that the other person does not really like them and that they are imposing. They avoid some of the discomfort by avoiding social relationships altogether. As a result, similar individuals tend to isolate and may establish fairly distant relationships, which they see as untrustworthy and judgmental.

Similarly scoring individuals are sensitive people who would like to be appreciated by others and to be able to relate better than they do. They are caught, however, between wanting to depend on others but being concerned that if they trust others, they will be hurt in the end.

In view of the personality style that these patients demonstrate, they will probably demand much attention and reassurance in the therapeutic situation. They may be somewhat distant and mistrustful, but they may also react negatively to either the unavailability of the therapist or the therapist's attempts to control their behaviors. It may be useful to set clear limits in the therapeutic relationship and to give them as much independence as possible, getting them to make their own decisions rather than offering suggestions or recommendations because any advice given is likely to become involved in their dependence–independence conflict.

Profile 400:   Histrionic

Patients scoring highly on this scale show a predominance of dramatic traits in the basic personality structure. Histrionic individuals are colorful and emotional, and seek stimulation, excitement, and attention. They tend to react very readily to situations around them, often becoming very invested, but typically the involvement does not last. This pattern of getting involved and ending up bored is repeated time after time.

Histrionic patients are very good at making positive first impressions. Their ability to react to unexpected situations, their alertness, and their search for attention make them colorful and charming socialites at parties or other social gatherings. Often, however, they can be too loud, exhibitionistic, and dramatic. They can be demanding and uncontrollable, especially when they are highly involved. Histrionic people may have intense emotional moments in friendships, but these friendships may be short-lived and replaced when boredom sets in. Their dependency has a very different flavor from the dependency of inadequate individuals in that they need the attention of others rather than protection and guidance. As a result, they may be much less submissive than other types of dependent individuals.

Given the histrionic personality style, an emphasis on formalities, such as being on time for the session or keeping an interpersonal distance during the session, is likely to feel unfriendly and dissatisfying. The therapist may need to be tolerant of patients' emotionality and even a certain amount of conflict. The type of relationship that would feel ego syntonic to these patients is one in which they are very much the center of attention and demonstrations of affection and support flow readily, especially from the therapist to the patient.

Profile 438:   Histrionic-Dependent-Negativistic

Elevated scores on these scales show a combination of dramatic, dependent, and negativistic traits in the basic personality structure. Similar individuals are colorful and emotional, and seek stimulation, excitement, and attention. They react very readily to situations around them, often becoming very emotionally involved, but typically this involvement does not last. The pattern of getting involved and ending up bored is repeated over and over.

The scores suggest that these patients are caught in the bind of having low self-esteem but having to conceal this self-appraisal and appear confident and self-assured. Individuals with similar scores tend to feel less gifted or valuable when they compare themselves with others. Nevertheless, these patients are aware that dependency on others projects an undesirable image and are uncomfortable with that particular coping strategy. Faced with this conflict, some individuals externalize it by appearing to be cooperative and compliant but actually resist their leader in some covert way; others may vacillate. At times, they may be friendly and cooperative, but they start to feel resentful and may become angry and aggressive, only to feel guilty and contrite and begin the cycle again. Such a solution allows them to reconcile the wish to be protected and the wish to appear independent and self-sufficient at the expense of being in frequent conflicts with others.

These patients may be criticized for being somewhat loud, exhibitionistic, or overly dramatic. Such individuals are often seen as needing much support from others. They may also be seen as moody or temperamental. However, they are often colorful and expressive people who are able to engage others effectively in a reasonably short period of time.

Given this type of personality style, an emphasis on formalities, such as being on time for the session or keeping an interpersonal distance during the session, is likely to feel unfriendly and dissatisfying. The therapist may need to be tolerant of patients' emotionality and conflict. The type of relationship that would feel ego syntonic to such patients is one in which they are the center of attention and demonstrations of affection and support flow readily, especially from the therapist to the patient. The lack of exciting issues during the sessions, or the limits to the support that the therapist can offer, may eventually become an issue, with patients becoming clingy, demanding, or dissatisfied. If not handled properly, such developments may threaten the therapeutic alliance. One way to handle such issues is to make patients aware of their inappropriate expectations and help them work through the attentional needs and dependency conflict.

Profile 450:   Histrionic-Narcissistic

Individuals with elevated scores on these the MCMI scales have a need for attention and conspicuousness. They tend to feel that they are special and may view themselves as being intelligent, outgoing, charming, or sophisticated. Often, they discuss their own abilities in an exaggerated manner, constructing rationalizations to inflate their own worth and belittling others who refuse to enhance the image they try to project. They make good first impressions because they are able to express their feelings, have a flair for the dramatic, and a natural ability to draw attention to themselves. In addition, they are colorful and may have a good sense of humor.

These patients are probably perceived as being friendly and helpful; they may actively seek praise and may be entertaining and somewhat seductive. However, they are probably easily bored and lack self-definition when they are alone.

Given this personality style, such patients may find it easier to establish a relationship with a therapist who is attentive and inclined to appreciate their charm and successes. Allowing patients to take a leading role in the therapeutic situation and to control as much as possible what goes on in the sessions would also contribute to making the treatment palatable. Once the therapeutic relationship is well established, the therapist will undoubtedly need to offer occasional interpretations that will sound negative if psychological growth is to occur. Care should be taken, however, to choose both the timing and manner of such interpretations in order not to injure patients' narcissism beyond the point they can tolerate.

Profile 456:   Histrionic-Narcissistic-Antisocial

A dramatic personality style with confident and competitive overtones is found in people scoring highly on these scales. Individuals obtaining similar scores have a great need for attention and affection. They constantly seek stimulation and conspicuousness with a dramatic flair. Typically, they are adept at manipulating social situations so that others give them the attention they need. They do this partly by becoming sensitive to others so that they can decide what reactions will evoke the reactions they want.

These individuals often express their feelings easily and have fairly intense, short-lived emotions. They may appear outgoing, charming, and sophisticated. However, their other-directedness makes them vulnerable to the lack of acceptance from others. They may be somewhat capricious and intolerant of frustration. At times, their dramatic presentations may appear shallow, phony, or overly seductive rather than as expressions of real feelings. They may also have some difficulties in developing a self-identity.

For these patients, the histrionic style has narcissistic and antisocial components. This finding suggests that in striving for attention, they may feel that they are very special and that they will be quite successful in most enterprises, especially in getting attention from others. These individuals tend to feel that they are better than everyone else, a feeling that comes through in their interactions with others. They also view the world as being competitive: Everyone is competing for attention and only those who are better in obtaining attention will actually have their needs fulfilled. As a result of these attitudes, they may be somewhat abrasive or conflictual at times.

Given this personality style, patients may find it easier to establish a relationship with a therapist who is attentive and inclined to appreciate their charm and successes. Allowing patients to take a leading role in the therapeutic situation and control as much as possible what goes on in the sessions would also help to make the treatment palatable. Accepting patients' matter-of-fact, tough, and antisocial views of the world may also help to establish rapport.

Once the therapeutic relationship is well established, the therapist will undoubtedly need to offer occasional interpretations that will sound negative but have to be made if patients are to grow psychologically. Care should be taken, however, in choosing the timing and manner of such interpretations in order not to injure patients' narcissism beyond the point they can tolerate.

Profile 458: Histrionic-Narcissistic-Negativistic

Elevated scores on these MCMI scales indicate a personality composed of dramatic, confident, and negativistic traits. These scores characterize people with prominent needs for attention who live fast-paced lives, enjoying stimulation and excitement; they may be thrill-seekers who are easily interested in the prospects of some new adventure. Coming through as charming socialites, these patients are probably colorful, dramatic, and emotional; they can be flippant, capricious, and demanding but also skilled at attracting others and appearing in a good light. These individuals are easily infatuated, but their enthusiasm is often short-lived. They tend to be immature, unable to delay gratification, undependable, and often lack discipline. However, they are lively extraverts who present themselves with a certain color and flair.

The MCMI scores also show that these patients have a fairly high self-regard: They tend to feel that they are better or more capable than most people. As a result, they are prone to behaving in a confident and self-assured manner and to be comfortable taking a strong position on important issues, even when other people disagree. This trait, however, may also present a problem in that they may treat others in a disdainful and insensitive manner or be threatened when someone questions their superiority.

When these patients encounter some sort of opposition, the negativistic elements are likely to emerge. The picture then may be that of angry and provocative individuals who can show their feelings in aggressive or even hostile ways. This highly emotional state is probably short-lived, at which time the other aspects of their personalities will again become more prominent.

Given the personality style just described, these patients may find it easier to establish a relationship with a therapist who is attentive and inclined to appreciate their charm and successes. Allowing patients to take a leading role in the therapeutic situation and control as much as possible what goes on in the sessions would also help the treatment. Another strategy that should be kept in mind is that of refraining from giving patients directives or setting up unnecessary rules because they are prone to eventually resent any controls. Part of the therapist's task is to maintain patients' perceptions that the therapist is on their side; otherwise, the relationship becomes competitive and conflictual and the patients' goals are no longer solving their problems but winning the fight with the therapist.

Once the therapeutic relationship is well established, the therapist will undoubtedly need to offer occasional interpretations that will sound negative but must be said. The timing and manner of such interpretations should be chosen carefully so as not to injure their narcissism beyond the point they can tolerate.

Profile 468: Histrionic-Antisocial-Negativistic

Elevated scores on these MCMI scales characterize dramatic, competitive, and negativistic patients. Individuals with similar scores enjoy being the center of attention. In addition to being somewhat emotional and dramatic and enjoying social situations, they are also colorful and lively but can be seen as somewhat superficial and not serious enough in their approach to the world. Because they have a tendency to get bored easily, they may not always finish a project before moving onto another.

Another important aspect of the personality pattern characterizing these patients is a competitive worldview: They feel that there is a limited supply of the things for which everyone is striving. As a result, life is a little bit of a rat race and the world is a somewhat cruel and unfriendly place in which no one can really be trusted and in which people have to fend for themselves. Most of these individuals see themselves as tough realists and are always trying to prevent getting into situations in which they may be taken advantage of.

These two tendencies usually cause conflict for these people. The attention-getting tendency is people-loving and tends to make the patients somewhat dependent on others. The antisocial outlook, on the other hand, makes them unwilling to trust others. Therefore, they are probably caught in this conflict and may have resolved it in one of two ways. Some individuals handle the conflict through mood fluctuations: They start by being friendly and cooperative, then become afraid that they will be taken advantage of and suddenly seem resistant, distant, and mistrustful or even angry and aggressive. In more pronounced cases, they may even become explosive and hard to handle. Other people may handle the conflict in a passive-aggressive manner by superficially complying but actually being negativistic and obstructionistic and thus acting out their aggressive impulses.

Given this personality style, patients may find it easier to establish a relationship with a therapist who is attentive and inclined to appreciate their charm and successes. Allowing patients to be dominant and control as much as possible what goes on in the sessions would also help the therapy. Another strategy is avoiding giving the patients directives or setting up unnecessary rules because they are prone to eventually resent any controls. Part of the therapist's task is to maintain patients' perceptions that the therapist is on their side; otherwise, the relationship becomes competitive and conflictual and the patients' goals are no longer solving problems but winning the fight with the therapist. On the other hand, it is just as important to stand firm when a rule has been established, making sure that infractions carry an appropriate consequence. Clarity, firmness, and certainty about what areas are controlled by whom can eventually lessen some of the conflicts that would otherwise occur.

Once the therapeutic relationship is well established, the therapist will undoubtedly need to offer occasional interpretations that will sound negative but must nevertheless be said. The therapist should carefully choose the timing and manner of such interpretations in order to avoid getting involved in an antisocial struggle and evoking a defensive and unproductive reaction.

Profile 470: Histrionic-Compulsive

High scores on the Histrionic and Compulsive scales characterize colorful and emotional people who usually seek stimulation, excitement, and attention. They tend to be conspicuous and actively search for affirmation of approval and affection. They often become sensitive to other people's moods and use this knowledge to evoke the reactions they want. They respond readily to situations around them, often becoming very emotionally involved, but typically the involvement does not last. These individuals are very good at making positive first impressions. Their ability to react to unexpected situations, their alertness and interest, and their search for attention make them colorful socialites at parties and similar gatherings.

These patients probably value a compulsive type of image hinging on propriety and dependability. They also want to appear conscientious, efficient, dependable, industrious, and persistent, and may place a high value, for instance, on "dressing right," having a clean and orderly house, and so on.

In some ways the histrionic and the compulsive tendencies are in conflict with one another. Histrionic patients, for instance, tend to be very emotional, intense in their relationships, and impulsive. Compulsive patients, on the other hand, overcontrol their emotions, are somewhat distant when relating to others, and plan their behaviors carefully. Individuals who have these two tendencies together are often unable to integrate them well and are conflicted as a result. They may then seem moody or emotionally labile. At times, they may be more emotional and intense, then develop some fears as to where this behavior would lead and become more rigid and controlled.

Profile 480:   Histrionic-Negativistic

High scores on these MCMI scales characterize individuals with dramatic and competitive traits. Elevations on the Histrionic scale suggest that such patients often seek to be the center of attention. They are dramatic, emotional, sensitive, and perceptive about other people's moods, using that knowledge to fulfill their needs for attention and support. They are often colorful socialites who can charm and entertain others and who thrive in the superficial relationships of parties and social gatherings. However, they usually need a certain amount of stimulation and become easily bored. In that case, they are prone to move on to something different without much forethought.

These patients are probably very aware of the images that people project. For them, the building of this image is partly based on a negative attitude toward others. These individuals are prone to putting others down or showing a certain amount of disdain. This aspect adds a particular flavor to their basic personality makeup by introducing an aggressive or hostile element. Some such people handle this aggressiveness by being consistently obstructionistic and negativistic, allowing them to vent the aggressive element without jeopardizing their ability to gain emotional support and be the center of attention. Otherwise, they may try to control or repress their angry feelings. In this case, the aggressive element will eventually surface through some kind of hostile explosion. After such an incident, however, the individuals are prone to feel guilty and apologize, an action that they hope will appease the offended party and place them back in their original position. Such a mode of operation may make these patients seem moody, overemotional, and unpredictable.

Given this basic personality style, these patients need a therapeutic relationship in which they are the center of attention. Tolerating displays of emotion and accepting a certain amount of conflict will be needed by the therapist. Care must be taken not to unduly foster the patients' enthusiasm and positive responses to the treatment when it occurs and to prepare them for the times ahead when the treatment will become more mundane and they are ready to terminate it. It may also be important to keep some distance and not to intrude in decisions that the patients can make on their own in order to avoid their future resentment.

Profile 500:   Narcissistic

High scores on the Narcissism scale of the MCMI characterize patients whose basic assumption in life is that they are special. They probably feel superior to others and have a tendency to exaggerate their abilities and positive attributes, construct rationalizations to inflate their own worth, and depreciate others who refuse to accept or enhance their own self-images.

Such patients typically view themselves as being intelligent, outgoing, charming, and sophisticated, and have a need to be conspicuous and to evoke affection and attention from others. They often make good first impressions because they are likely to have their own opinions and have a natural ability to draw attention to themselves. They are proud people, carry themselves with dignity, and may have a good sense of humor. However, they have trouble if they do not feel properly recognized or are forced to accept the opinions of others or to compromise.

Given these factors, these patients can be expected to be most comfortable in situations in which they feel admired or at least respected. If confrontation is used in therapy, much tact has to be exercised so as not to injure their narcissism more than they can tolerate. On the other hand, there is also a danger that a therapist would be so supportive of patients' narcissism that no negative feedback is given and growth is not facilitated. Thus, it is important to find ways of helping patients accept their fallibilities and work on their problems without feeling unrecognized or humiliated.

Profile 520:   Narcissistic-Avoidant

People obtaining high scores on these scales assume that they are special and feel superior to most other people. They tend to exaggerate their abilities and positive attributes, construct rationalizations to inflate their own worth, and depreciate others who refuse to accept or enhance their own self-images. Viewing themselves only in positive terms, they tend to think of themselves as intelligent, outgoing, charming, and sophisticated. Any negative attributes that they do accept are usually minimized.

For these patients, however, there is also a certain amount of apprehension regarding relationships with others. They tend to feel that other people are not going to appreciate how capable and outstanding they really are. These individuals are very sensitive to any sign of rejection because a rejection is interpreted as a negation of the kind of image that they feel they must have in order to be comfortable. As a result, when they interact with others, they always feel they have to put their best foot forward. They tend to be tense, nervous, and self-conscious with most of the people with whom they interact. Therefore, their social outlook is very conflicted: In some ways they would like to relate to people well so that they would be appreciated, but they are so socially uncomfortable that they find themselves avoiding people altogether much of the time. This tends to be a life conflict with them, one with which they struggle for years before some resolution is reached.

Profile 530:   Narcissistic-Dependent

According to these MCMI scale scores, these patients have predominant confident and cooperative traits in the personality makeup. The juxtaposition of these two styles is a bit unusual and possibly problematic. An elevation on the Narcissistic scale usually indicates that they value themselves highly. Such individuals are prone to assuming that they are more capable than others; they often think of themselves as being special in some way. As a result, they tend to exaggerate their own positive attributes and to minimize their liabilities. They like to be conspicuous and relate to others with an air of self-assurance. They wish to be leaders, to hold positions of status and power, and are not particularly interested in following somebody else's directions.

The problem with this personality profile is that the second elevation occurrs on a scale that is almost the direct opposite of the first. The Dependent scale characterizes individuals who are followers rather than leaders. Patients' scores indicate that they are very unsure about their own abilities. Given those two divergent assumptions about one's role in life, the test scores suggest that the patients normally experience much conflict. Sometimes they relate in a submissive and overly congenial manner and at other times they may be very assertive and try to play a dominant role.

The task in establishing a therapeutic relationship with these patients may involve catering to both of the basic emotional needs. The therapist may need to provide the parentallike guidance and support that patients seem to need while, at the same time, allowing them to control enough of the situation that they do not feel humiliated. In some ways they will need to be treated in a parent-to-child manner but will still have to be afforded the respect of a parental figure. The conflict between the two opposing tendencies may lead to a certain amount of anger and interpersonal discomfort that the therapist will have to handle well for the treatment to be successful.

Profile 540: Narcissistic-Histrionic

The main assumption that individuals scoring highly on these scales have about themselves is that they are special and probably superior to most other people. A tendency to exaggerate their abilities and positive attributes, emphasize their past achievements, and depreciate those who refuse to accept their inflated self-images may be present. This narcissism is probably manifested in an air of conviction and self-assurance. When extreme, these individuals are perceived as conceited and arrogant.

Something that these individuals pay attention to when feeling superior to others is their personal images. They seem to value appearances: A good person is one who looks intelligent, outgoing, competent, sophisticated, and so on. Beneath this surface, however, there is a need for approval and a striving to be conspicuous, to evoke affection, and to attract attention from others. These types of individuals may be very impressive at first glance because they may be able to express their thoughts easily, have a flair for the dramatic, and enjoy a natural capacity to draw attention to themselves. However, they may be capricious and intolerant of frustration. They are often emotional, but the emotions may be short-lived. There is also an inclination to be easily bored, at which times they may go do something else.

Given these factors, such patients can be expected to be most comfortable in situations in which they feel admired or at least respected, as well as the center of attention. If confrontation is used in therapy, much tact has to be exercised so as not to injure their narcissism more than they can tolerate. On the other hand, there is also a danger that a therapist would be so supportive of patients' narcissism that no negative feedback is given and growth is not facilitated. Thus, it is important to find ways of helping patients accept their fallibilities and work on their problems without feeling unrecognized or humiliated.

Profile 546: Narcissistic-Histrionic-Antisocial

High scores on these scales suggest a personality style characterized by confident, dramatic, and competitive elements. The main assumption these individuals have about themselves is that they are very special and that they are superior to most other people. A tendency to exaggerate their abilities and positive attributes, emphasize their past achievements, and depreciate those who refuse to accept their inflated self-images may be present. This narcissism is probably manifested in an air of conviction and self-assurance. When extreme, some individuals are perceived as being conceited and arrogant.

There is evidence that these patients pay strict attention to their personal images when they are feeling superior to other people. They seem to value appearances: A good person is someone who "appears" intelligent, outgoing, competent, sophisticated, and so on. Beneath this surface, however, there is a need for approval and a striving to be conspicuous, to evoke affection, and to attract attention from others. These individuals may be very impressive at first because they express their thoughts easily, have a flair for the dramatic, and enjoy a natural capacity to draw attention to themselves. They may be capricious, however, and intolerant of frustration. They are often emotional, but the emotions may be short-lived; they become bored easily and may move from one enterprise to another.

Another factor in their superiority complex may be related to their tendency to view the environment as a competitive place. They feel that they have to fend for themselves in order to function. As a result, they are somewhat mistrustful and suspicious. Assertive, energetic, self-reliant, strong, and realistic are adjectives they use to describe themselves. They feel that they have to be tough to survive in a tough world. For them, compassion and warmth are "weak" emotions that will place them in an inferior position. The competitive outlook fits in well with the feelings of superiority as long as these patients are in situations in which they have a good chance of "winning."

Given these factors, such patients require a therapeutic situation in which they feel admired or at least respected. They also need to be the center of attention. If confrontation is used in therapy, tact must be used to avoid injuring their narcissism more than they can tolerate. A problem could arise if patients interpret the confrontation as being part of a competitive relationship and fight it rather than accept it as useful feedback. On the other hand, there is also a danger that a therapist would be so supportive of patients' narcissism that no negative feedback is given and growth is not facilitated. Therefore, it is important to find ways to help patients accept their fallibilities and work on their problems without feeling unrecognized or humiliated.

Profile 548: Narcissistic-Histrionic-Negativistic

Patients who obtain high scores on these MCMI scales assume that they are special and superior to other people. They tend to exaggerate their abilities and positive attributes, construct rationalizations to inflate their own worth, and depreciate others who refuse to accept or enhance their own self-images.

In addition, they want to appear intelligent, outgoing, charming, and sophisticated, and have a need to be conspicuous and evoke affection and attention from others. They typically make good first impressions because they are able to express their feelings, have a flair for the dramatic, and have a natural ability to draw attention to themselves. They are colorful, usually have a good sense of humor, and can be perceived as being very friendly and helpful in interpersonal relationships. Actively solicitous of praise, they may be entertaining and somewhat seductive. Their preoccupation with external rewards and approvals may leave them with a somewhat undefined identity when they are alone.

In theory, this type of personality style may result from a home situation in which the parents tended to overestimate their child's charms and abilities. The parents might have also reinforced the area of personal image that the patient stresses as important. Many of these individuals were somewhat pampered and indulged as youngsters and received much attention and prominence in the home.

These patients also tend to be conflicted. On one hand, they see themselves as colorful, more capable, and generally superior to others. On the other hand, however, they are dependent on a flow of attention and approval from others. With some individuals, this conflict surfaces in a hypersensitive or negativistic way of reacting: They may be compliant but in a resentful and negativistic manner. Others handle this conflict by showing some mood changes: They may be submissive and compliant at times, become resentful and angry in other instances, and on still other occasions, become contrite, apologetic, and overly cooperative.

Profile 564: Narcissistic-Antisocial-Histrionic

Elevated scores on these scales characterize individuals who are confident, competitive, and dramatic. A major assumption they have is that they are very special; they probably feel superior to most other people. A tendency to exaggerate their abilities and positive attributes, construct arguments to emphasize their own worth, and depreciate those who refuse to accept their self-images may be present. This tendency is probably externalized through an air of conviction, security, and self-assurance. When extreme, these people can be perceived as conceited and arrogant.

Some of their feelings of superiority come from their tendency to view the world in competitive terms. They feel that they have to fend for themselves in order to function. As a result, they are somewhat mistrustful and suspicious. They see themselves as being assertive, energetic, self-reliant, strong, and realistic, and feel that they have to be tough to make it in a tough world. These individuals usually justify their aggressiveness by pointing to the hostile and exploitive behavior of others. In their views, compassionate or warm people are weak and will be taken advantage of. This antisocial outlook fits in especially well with their feelings of superiority if they are in situations in which they can assume a chance of winning.

There are indications that these patients pay particular attention to their images when they are feeling superior to others. They seem to value appearances: A good person is someone who appears intelligent, outgoing, charming, sophisticated, and so on. Beneath this surface, there is typically a need for approval and a striving to be conspicuous, to evoke affection and attract attention from others. These individuals usually make good first impressions because they express their thoughts and feelings easily, have a flair for the dramatic, and naturally draw attention to themselves. However, they may be capricious and intolerant of frustration.

Given these factors, therapy will be more effective if the patients feel admired or at least respected by the therapist. They also need to be the center of attention frequently. If confrontation is used in therapy, tact must be used so as not to injure their narcissism more than they can tolerate. If confrontation is used, patients could interpret it as part of a competitive relationship and fight it rather than accept it as useful feedback. On the other hand, it is also possible that a therapist could be so supportive of patients' narcissism that no negative feedback is given and growth is not facilitated. Therefore, it is important to find ways to help patients accept their fallibilities and work on their problems without feeling unrecognized or humiliated.

Profile 580:   Narcissistic-Negativistic

Individuals scoring highly on these MCMI scales have confident and explosive personality traits. They assume that they are special and superior to most people. They tend to exaggerate their abilities and positive attributes, construct rationalizations to inflate their own worth, and depreciate others who refuse to accept or enhance their own self-images.

These patients want to appear intelligent, outgoing, charming, and sophisticated, and have a need to be conspicuous, evoking affection and attention from others. They typically make good first impressions because they can be friendly and helpful in interpersonal relationships. However, they are often unable to accept criticism and project whatever feelings of inadequacy they have, attempting to dismiss their failures as resulting from the irresponsibility or incompetence of others.

Indications that some patients wanted to have some supremacy over others were seen concomitantly with indications that they had low self-esteem. Individuals with similar MCMI scores tend to be conflicted. On one hand, they want to see themselves as superior to others. On the other hand, they are insecure and painfully aware of their own limitations. With some individuals, this conflict surfaces in a hypersensitive or negativistic way: They may be compliant but resentful and negative. For others, this conflict is manifested in mood changes: They may be submissive and compliant at times, become resentful and angry in other instances, and be contrite, apologetic, and overly cooperative on still other occasions.

Given this personality style, these patients will benefit most from a therapeutic relationship in which they feel admired or at least respected. If therapists confront patients, they should use tact to avoid injuring their narcissism more than they can handle. On the other hand, therapists should not be so supportive of patients' narcissism that no negative feedback is given so that patients do not grow psychologically. Thus, it is important to find ways of helping them accept their fallibilities and work on their problems without feeling unrecognized or humiliated.

In addition, it may be important not to try to control patients in ways that are not necessary for the therapy to function. Because these patients are bound to resent any control that is placed on them, this tactic can prevent the therapeutic relationship from becoming overly conflictual. They may also benefit from learning how they normally operate and project negative feelings onto others.

Profile 600:   Antisocial

Competitiveness is the major trait found in individuals scoring highly on this MCMI scale. These individuals look at their environments as a competitive place and feel that they have to fend for themselves to function. As a result, most individuals with this view are somewhat mistrustful and suspicious of others. They see themselves as being assertive, energetic, self-reliant, strong, and realistic. In order to make it in the rat race, they have to be tough. These individuals usually justify their assertiveness by pointing to the hostile and exploitive behavior of others. They may be contemptuous of the weak and do not care whether they are liked because "good guys come in last."

Individuals with this type of personality are typically impulsive. They are often perceived by others as being somewhat aggressive and intimidating. At times, they may appear cold, callous, and insensitive to the feelings of others. They may be argumentative and contentious. Some such people may even be abusive, cruel, or malicious. When matters go their way, they may act in a gracious, cheerful, and friendly manner. More characteristically, however, their behavior is guarded, reserved, and competitive. When crossed, pushed on personal matters, or faced with embarrassment, they may respond impulsively and become angry, vengeful, and vindictive.

Profile 612:   Antisocial-Schizoid-Avoidant

Competitive, introversive, and avoidant traits characterize individuals obtaining high scores on these three scales. Such patients see their environments as if they were tournaments or contests, with one person pitted against the other. To be able to function in such a situation, they feel that they have to fend for themselves. These are self-sufficient people who do not depend on others to fulfill their needs. They may be somewhat mistrustful and suspicious of others. They see themselves as being assertive, energetic, self-reliant, strong, and realistic. In order to make it in the rat race, they believe they must adopt a tough stance. Their assertiveness is justified by pointing to the hostile and exploitative behavior of others. They may be contemptuous of the weak and not care whether they are liked, claiming that good guys come in last.

People with this type of personality may be seen as somewhat cold, callous, or insensitive to the feelings of others and may tend to be argumentative and contentious. When matters go their way, they may act in a gracious, cheerful, and friendly manner. More characteristically, however, their behavior is guarded, reserved, and aggressive. When crossed, pushed, or embarrassed, they may respond impulsively and may become angry, vengeful, and vindictive.

In addition, these patients seem to keep an emotional distance from others and to some degree, they are uninterested in interpersonal relations and may not be too adept at understanding and enjoying the subtleties and nuances of emotions, which could result in apathy about the relationship itself. Moreover, they may be afraid of being rejected by others who are also looking out for themselves in the competitive world. As a result, social situations are avoided because they are uncomfortable and tension provoking. They restrict the number of relationships that they form and tend to have superficial friendships when those exist, alliances that are more similar to acquaintanceships than strong friendships.

In light of the personality style that these patients appear to have, establishing therapeutic alliances may be somewhat difficult. Such patients are not inclined to see psychotherapy as valuable unless it offers a very tangible material benefit, such as a way out of a jam of some sort. One approach to establishing an alliance in spite of this difficulty may be to accept, at least temporarily, the same competitive outlook that the patients favor. The therapist may then be in the position to help them explore the behaviors and attitudes that get in the way of their being a "winner."

Profile 650: Antisocial-Narcissistic

Elevated scores on these scales suggest a personality style characterized by competitive and confident traits.

Because their environments are perceived to be competitive by nature, they feel that they have to fend for themselves in order to function. Most individuals with this view are, as a result, somewhat distant, mistrustful, and suspicious of others. They see themselves as being assertive, energetic, self-reliant, strong, and realistic. For them, one must be tough to make it in this "dog-eat-dog" world. These individuals usually justify their assertiveness by pointing to the hostile and exploitive behavior of others. They may not object if they are not liked; after all, good guys come in last.

Another aspect of the personality style pattern portrayed by such patients is an inflated self-image. They probably think that they are more capable, more interesting, and more worthwhile than other people. This tendency is often externalized through an air of conviction, independent security, and self-assurance. When extreme, this tendency may make them appear to be somewhat conceited and arrogant.

Other people may perceive these patients to be somewhat aggressive and intimidating. Often their assertiveness is sensed as a cold insensitivity to the feelings of others. These individuals tend to be argumentative and contentious and may even be abusive, cruel, or malicious at times. When things go their way, they may act in a gracious, cheerful, and friendly manner. More characteristically, however, their behavior is guarded, reserved, and resentful. When crossed, pushed on personal matters, or faced with embarrassment, they may respond quickly and become angry, vengeful, and vindictive.

In light of this personality style, establishing a therapeutic alliance may be somewhat difficult. These patients will likely not see the benefit of psychotherapy unless it offers a tangible material benefit, such as a way out of trouble. They also resent the kind of superior-like position that the therapist has in the therapeutic situation, perhaps because the therapist is the "expert" whose opinions are solicited during the therapy session.

One approach to establishing an alliance in spite of the difficulties may be to accept, at least temporarily, the same competitive outlook that they favor. The therapist may then be in the position to help them explore the behaviors and attitudes that prevent them from being winners. Treating them with as much respect and deference as possible may also contribute to the formation of the therapeutic alliance.

Profile 653: Antisocial-Narcissistic-Dependent

High scorers on these scales have predominant competitive, confident, and cooperative traits in their personality makeup. The juxtaposition of these three styles is a bit unusual and possibly problematic. An elevation on the Antisocial scale is typically associated with viewing the environment as a contest in which people are pitted against each other. In order to be able to function, these individuals feel that they have to fend for themselves. As a result, they are somewhat distant, mistrustful, and suspicious of others. They see themselves as assertive, energetic, self-reliant, strong, and realistic, and feel that they have to be tough in order to make it in a tough world. These individuals may not care whether they are liked because good people finish last.

Another aspect of the personality style portrayed by these patients is an inflated self-image and a tendency to think they are more capable, more interesting, and more worthwhile than other people. They like to be conspicuous and admired. Their wish to be leaders who hold positions of status and power and their lack of interest in following somebody else's directions may become externalized through an air of conviction, independent security, and self-assurance. When extreme, this tendency may make them look somewhat conceited and arrogant.

These people may be perceived as aggressive or intimidating; often their assertiveness is sensed as a cold insensitivity to the other people's feelings. When things go their way, they may act gracious, cheerful, and friendly. At other times, however, their behavior is guarded, reserved, and resentful. When crossed, pushed on personal matters, or faced with humiliation, they may become angry and vindictive.

The inflated self-image fits in well with the competitive outlook in that it provides the security that these patients need to engage in the rivalry they may feel when they are with others. The problem with this personality profile is that the third elevation can occur on a scale that is almost the direct opposite of the first two. The Dependent scale usually characterizes people who are followers rather than leaders. High scores on this scale indicate patients who are very unsure about their abilities and would feel more comfortable if they had someone whom they trusted enough to take care of them. One way of integrating all of the findings would be to think of the patients as actually feeling fairly inadequate but compensating against these feelings by putting up an overconfident facade.

In light of this personality style, establishing a therapeutic alliance may be difficult because they probably will not see psychotherapy as valuable unless they will benefit from it in a tangible way. They are likely to resent the kind of superiorlike position of the therapist: The therapist is the expert whose opinions are solicited during the therapy session. One approach to establishing an alliance may be to temporarily accept the same competitive outlook that the patients favor. The therapist may then be able to help them examine the behaviors and attitudes that keep them from being successful. It will also help to treat them with respect and deference.

Profile 658: Antisocial-Narcissistic-Negativistic

Individuals scoring highly on these scales will likely have a competitive personality style with confident and negativistic elements.

People with this personality style view their environments as being primarily competitive and to be able to function, they must fend for themselves. As a result, most individuals with this view are somewhat distant, mistrustful, and suspicious of others, but they see themselves as being assertive, energetic, self-reliant, strong, and realistic. They feel that they have to be tough to survive in such a competitive environment and usually justify their assertiveness by pointing to the hostile and exploitive behavior of others. They probably will not care whether other people like them because one does what one must do to get ahead.

An unfortunate effect of adversarial relationships is that the loser suffers as a result of the other person winning. Although this may not be the goal of behaving in a particular way, the patients probably try not to be bothered by humanistic sentiments or guilt. In fact, they may feel that worrying about those issues implies some weakness or liability instead of something admirable. These patients want others to see them as tough, thick-skinned, streetwise, and capable of taking care of themselves.

Another aspect of the personality style pattern portrayed by these patients is inflated self-images. They probably think they are more able, more interesting, and more worthwhile than others. There is an air of conviction, independent security, and self-assurance. When extreme, they may appear to be conceited and arrogant.

These individuals can be perceived as aggressive, intimidating, cold, and insensitive. They tend to be argumentative and contentious and may even be abusive, cruel, or malicious at times. When everything is fine, they may be gracious, cheerful, and friendly. More characteristically, however, they are guarded, reserved, and resentful. When crossed, pushed on personal matters, or embarrassed, they may respond quickly and become angry, vengeful, and vindictive.

In fact, high scores on these scales suggest some conflicts in the way these patients relate to others. At times, they want to have closer and warmer relationships and may regret having mistreated others in the antisocial struggle. The unresolved conflict is apparently projected in the form of a negativistic resentment or anger. Instead of venting the resentment overtly, some individuals are more inclined to be obstructionistic or negativistic.

The predominance of the antisocial personality style probably makes these patients function particularly well in situations that are inherently competitive such as business, sales, or aggressive sports (e.g., boxing, football). The superficiality in interpersonal relationships and the aggressive attitude, on the other hand, may have a negative effect in situations in which loyalty and team coordination are needed.

In light of the personality style that these patients appear to have, establishing a therapeutic alliance may be hard. They probably will not see psychotherapy's value unless they will tangibly benefit from it. The therapist's superior position will be resented because the therapist is the expert whose opinions are solicited during the therapy session. The therapist should accept, at least temporarily, the same competitive outlook that the patients favor. The therapist may then be better able to help them figure out what behaviors and attitudes hinder them being winners. The therapist may also have to remain unintrusive, being careful not to take a stance if it is not necessary. Not taking a position will encourage patients to make their own decisions and will decrease the amount of conflict present in the therapeutic relationship. Interpretations at times when patients are using dysfunctional projective mechanisms may be necessary. However, any confrontation has to be carried out with care because they will be inclined to approach such feedback in a antisocial manner and to fight the insights that are offered. The therapist must try to protect the therapeutic alliance, doing whatever is necessary to keep the patients feeling that the therapist is on their side.

Profile 670:   Antisocial-Compulsive

Elevated scores on these MCMI scales suggest a personality style characterized by competitive and disciplined traits. High scorers view life as a sort of tournament. Everyone, in their view, is competing for the same things, and they believe that these valuables are in limited supply. To be able to function well in this situation, they feel they have to fend for themselves. As a result, most such individuals are somewhat mistrustful or even suspicious of others. They see themselves as assertive, energetic, self-reliant, strong, and realistic, and feel that they have to be tough in order to make it in the world. These individuals may be somewhat contemptuous of the weak and not care whether they are liked, claiming that "good guys come in last." Characteristically, their behavior is guarded and reserved.

Additionally, these patients assume that the most important thing in life is to avoid making a mistake. They are usually orderly, plan for the future, conscientious, prepare well, and do the work on schedule. They tend to be efficient, dependable, industrious, and persistent. Often, these individuals believe in discipline and practice self-restraint, especially when it concerns their own emotions, which are usually kept under control. The overcontrol of the emotions gives them their typical flavor: They are formal and proper and somewhat unlikely to open up and act spontaneously in front of others. They are sometimes perceived as perfectionistic, somewhat distant, occasionally inflexible, and perhaps indecisive before they have a chance to study all possible alternatives. In other words, their strategy to win the rat race is to be careful, deliberate, dependable, and hard-working.

Profile 680:   Antisocial-Negativistic

This MCMI personality profile indicates a predominance of competitive traits with negativistic elements. Patients tend to experience life as if it were a tournament. Assuming that everyone is struggling for things that exist in limited supply, they are probably somewhat mistrustful and superficial in the way they relate to others. They need to be strong and self-sufficient. They feel that asking others for help is counterproductive because it lessens their own chances of ending up ahead of those on whom they depend. These individuals are proud of their "realistic" views, which stress tangible achievements and material gains.

A perhaps unfortunate effect of adversarial relationships is that the loser suffers as a result of the other person winning. Although this may not be the goal of behaving in a particular way, such patients probably try not to be bothered by humanistic sentiments or guilt. In fact, they may feel that worrying about those issues implies some weakness or liability instead of something to be admired. They want other people to perceive them as tough, thick-skinned, streetwise, and capable of protecting their own interests.

However, these patients may have some conflicts in the way that they relate to others. At times they may want closer and warmer relationships and may regret having mistreated others in the competitive struggle. The unresolved conflict is typically projected in the form of a negativistic resentment or anger. Instead of venting the resentment overtly, some individuals may use an obstructionistic or passive-aggressive strategy.

The predominance of the antisocial personality style probably makes such patients function particularly well in situations that are inherently difficult, such as business, sales, or competitive sports. The superficiality in interpersonal relationships and the aggressive attitude, on the other hand, may have a negative effect in situations where loyalty and team coordination are needed.

In light of the personality style that these patients appear to have, establishing a therapeutic alliance may be difficult. Patients are not likely to see psychotherapy as valuable unless it offers a very tangible material benefit. They also resent the therapist's superior position in the therapeutic situation, perhaps because the therapist is the "expert" whose opinions are solicited during the therapy session. One approach to establishing an alliance is to accept, at least temporarily, the same competitive outlook that the patients favor. The therapist may then be able to help patients identify the behaviors and attitudes that hinder their being winners.

The therapist may also have to remain unintrusive, careful not to take a stance. Not taking a stance will encourage patients to make their own decisions and will decrease the amount of conflict present in the therapeutic relationship. Giving interpretations when the patients are using unadaptive projective mechanisms may be necessary. However, any confrontation has to be done carefully because they will be inclined to react to such feedback in an antisocial manner and to fight the insights that are offered. The therapeutic alliance must be protected, and the therapist has to do whatever is necessary to keep the patients feeling that the therapist is on their side.

Profile 700: Compulsive

Elevated scores on this MCMI scale suggest that disciplined traits tend to be prominent in this personality structure. Individuals with this type of personality profile assume that people should work hard to avoid making a mistake. These patients are usually orderly and plan for the future. They are conscientious, typically prepare well, and do work on schedule. They tend to be efficient, dependable, industrious, and persistent. To people in authority, these individuals act overly respectful and ingratiating. This style of relating often changes when the relationship is with a subordinate. In that case, patients may become somewhat perfectionistic and demanding.

These individuals often believe in discipline and practice self-restraint, especially when it concerns their own emotions, which are usually kept under control. The overcontrol of emotions tends to give them a characteristic flavor: They are formal and proper and unlikely to open up and act spontaneously in front of others. They are sometimes seen as perfectionistic, distant, occasionally inflexible, and perhaps indecisive before they have a chance to study all possible alternatives. However, they are often careful, deliberate, righteous, honest, dependable, and hard-working people.

This type of personality style may make it hard for patients to work with some aspects of the environment. For instance, situations that can change abruptly from one moment to the next in an unpredictable manner or situations in which following the rules does not lead to the desired outcome can be particularly stressful. However, disciplined individuals are very well suited for situations in which it is important to be accurate and meticulous.

Unfortunately, an elevation on the Compulsive scale can also be obtained with people who are not all that proper or orderly but who are interested in "looking good" in the testing or are defensive psychologically. This is because such patients do not accept any personality "flaw" and answer the testing in a perfectionistic manner. If this is thought to be the case with these patients, the description just given has to be changed to emphasize the defensive outlook rather than the meticulousness, orderliness, or the interest in careful future planning.

If patients do have a compulsive personality style, however, they would find it easier to establish a therapeutic alliance with a professional who is formal, proper, punctual, and predictable. Keeping some distance and allowing them to control significant parts of the session would also make them feel at ease. Explanations of the diagnosis, the nature of the "illness," and the expected course of treatment will probably be very appreciated. It may, however, be difficult to move them from a superficial therapeutic alliance to a more meaningful dependency on the relationship. Helping them explore the defenses that they use or enhancing their tolerance for allowing others to hold the controls can also be hard to accomplish.

Profile 720: Compulsive-Avoidant

People with high scores on these MCMI scales have disciplined and avoidant tendencies in their personality structure. An important motivational force behind this basic personality structure is avoiding making a mistake. This trait might have originated as a reaction formation, a mechanism by which people espouse perfectionistic and righteous ways of thinking in order to convince themselves that they are not imperfect, incapable, or worthless. It might also have emerged as a response to being punished whenever they made a mistake and given no incentive to take risks.

Whatever the origin, such individuals tend to be orderly and plan for the future. To those in authority, they are inclined to be overly respectful, ingratiating, and dependent. This probably changes when they relate to a subordinate. In that case, they may become somewhat arrogant, perfectionistic, or disdainful. Often, they believe in discipline and practice self-restraint, especially when it concerns their own emotions, which are always kept under control.

The indications are that these patients would like to relate to others and have their affection and appreciation. People in general, however, present a problem to such patients because people can be emotional and unpredictable. This unpredictability and emphasis on emotional aspects of relationships can make these patients somewhat uncomfortable. Thus, relating to others represents a risk that makes them feel particularly vulnerable. They may be inclined to avoid relationships or to relate in a cold and distant manner in order to minimize the risk taken.

These individuals also tend to be somewhat proper and formal. They are usually conscientious, well prepared, efficient, dependable, industrious, and persistent. However, they may also be perceived as perfectionistic, rigid, picayune, and indecisive.

Given this type of personality style, these patients may find it easier to establish a therapeutic alliance with a professional who is formal, proper, punctual, and predictable. Keeping some distance and allowing them to control significant parts of the session will also make them feel at ease. Explanations of the diagnosis, the nature of the illness, and the expected course of treatment can be very important to them. It may be difficult to move them from a superficial therapeutic alliance to a more meaningful dependency on the relationship. Helping them to explore the defenses that they use or enhancing their tolerance for allowing others to be in control can also be hard to accomplish.

Profile 736: Compulsive-Dependent-Antisocial

The scores that patients obtain on these MCMI scales indicate that their personality style has predominant disciplined, cooperative, and competitive elements. These individuals tend to feel inadequate and have low self-esteem. Superficially, they may appear to be very cooperative and congenial and to be searching for support from others. However, they tend to have their own ideas about things and, although at times they may comply with the wishes of others, they are not likely to enthusiastically support someone else's ideas.

These patients see the world as a competitive place. Because they feel that people are out to satisfy their own needs, they are somewhat mistrustful in their relations with others; they probably will not share all of their feelings and will be suspicious that other people are trying to use them. Combined with their feelings of inadequacy, the competitive view of the world reinforces the compulsive traits because they feel that they have to avoid making mistakes, which can be used to gain advantage over them.

These patients may seem somewhat rigid, unsure, distant, and mistrustful. On the other hand, well-adjusted individuals with this personality cluster may be able to use some of these traits to their benefit. Their disciplined nature may contribute to their being conscientious hard workers with an ability to pay attention to detail and follow the rules. The dependent inclinations may then translate into a certain congeniality and motivation, moved by the desire to be liked and appreciated. Finally, their competitiveness may make them realistic people who are mature enough to appreciate that people do not usually get something for nothing and that one has to look at the risks and alternatives before making a decision.

Profile 738: Compulsive-Dependent-Negativistic

Disciplined, negativistic, and dependent traits tend to be emphasized in this basic personality structure. People with high scores on these scales assume that people should work hard to avoid making mistakes. Such people are usually orderly and plan for the future. They are also conscientious, typically prepare well, work on schedule, efficient, dependable, industrious, and persistent.

In spite of their perfectionistic inclinations, they fear not being very capable or gifted so that, if left completely to their own devices, they would not be able to make ends meet. They would like to have someone else take care of them and provide for their needs, but they tend to resent any control that others may exert as the price for the emotional support. This resentment closes the option of becoming dependent on some benefactor.

The conflict of wanting support but fighting control and dependency also makes these patients likely to change their overall feelings without an obvious reason. At times, they may be very friendly and engaging; they may then become angry and resentful. Later yet, they may feel guilty and contrite. The cycle is completed when they again become friendly and cooperative. In other words, they defend against their insecurities by projecting blame, sometimes against themselves and sometimes at others. A different style brought about by the same basic conflict involves the use of a passive-aggressive defense. In that case, they try to control their resentment through obstructionistic maneuvers that allow them to vent their anger in covert ways, without blatantly jeopardizing the dependent relationship.

The compulsive element in this personality style may make it hard for patients to deal with some aspects of the environment. For instance, situations that can change abruptly from one moment to the next unpredictably or situations in which following rules does not lead to the desired outcome can be stressful for disciplined individuals. However, they are very well suited for situations in which it is important to be accurate and meticulous.

Given the type of personality style described, these patients may find it easier to establish a therapeutic alliance with a professional who is formal, proper, punctual, and predictable. Keeping some distance and allowing them to control significant parts of the session would also make them feel better. Explanations of the diagnosis, the nature of the illness, and the expected course of treatment can also help. Moving them from a superficial therapeutic alliance to a more meaningful dependency on the relationship may be difficult. Helping them explore the defenses that they use or enhancing their tolerance for not being in control of things can also be hard to accomplish. These patients will probably demand some support and reassurance in the therapeutic situation. It may be useful to set clear limits and to give them as much independence as possible, getting them to make their own decisions rather than offering suggestions or recommendations.

Profile 740:   Compulsive-Histrionic

Individuals obtaining high scores on these MCMI scales have a personality style with predominant disciplined and dramatic traits. In some ways, the dramatic and the disciplined tendencies conflict with one another. Dramatic people, for instance, tend to be very emotional, intense in their relationships, and impulsive. Disciplined individuals, on the other hand, overcontrol their emotions, are somewhat distant when relating to others, and plan their behaviors carefully. Individuals who have these two tendencies together are often unable to integrate them well and tend to be conflicted. As a result, patients may seem moody or emotionally labile. At times, they may be more invested and intense and then develop some fears as to where this behavior would lead and become more rigid and controlled.

The indications would be that these patients tend to emphasize appearances, placing a premium on propriety and dependability and living their lives trying to avoid the appearance of making a mistake. A high value may be placed, for instance, on dressing right, having a clean and orderly house, and so on. They probably try to be conscientious, efficient, dependable, industrious, and persistent.

Nevertheless, there is a side to these patients that is not all that conscientious or dependable and that often breaks through the controls that they try to exert. That other side is one that seeks stimulation, excitement, and attention and is colorful and emotional. Thus, at times, these patients are going to be conspicuous and actively search for affirmation of approval and affection. They often become sensitive to other people's moods and use this knowledge to evoke the reactions they desire. They are very reactive to their environments and often become deeply involved, but typically this involvement does not last.

They are probably good at making positive first impressions. The ability to react to unexpected situations, the alertness and interest, and the search for attention help make them colorful at parties and similar gatherings. However, they may have some difficulty with the balance between the disciplined control of their emotions and their needs to get attention, stimulation, and affection.

Given this personality style, forming a therapeutic alliance may be easier if the therapist conducts the sessions in a formal and orderly fashion. Even more important, however, will be making sure that they are the center of attention and receive a great deal of reassurance, affection, and support.

Profile 750:   Compulsive-Narcissistic

The pattern of scores obtained on these scales indicate the prominence of disciplined and confident personality traits. The disciplined aspects suggest that there is an emphasis on perfectionism and maintaining good control of the environment. People scoring highly on these scales are somewhat defensive and unlikely to admit to failures or mistakes. At times, they may be seen as too inflexible, formal, or proper and may relate to others in a somewhat distant manner.

Together with these disciplined elements, these patients have a tendency to feel that they are more special, capable, and worthy than most other people. They are field-independent people who rely more on their own feelings or judgments than they do on the opinions of others. A confident air of self-assurance may be present. They may have trouble accepting somebody else's ideas and doing what they are told. Such situations may cause conflict between them and the other people involved.

Given the type of personality style described, patients may find it easier to establish a therapeutic alliance with a professional who is formal, proper, punctual, predictable, and able to admire them in some manner. Keeping some distance and allowing them to control significant parts of the session would also make the patients feel at ease. Other helpful things include explaining the diagnosis, the nature of the illness, and the expected course of treatment. It could be difficult to move them from a superficial therapeutic alliance to a more meaningful dependency on the relationship. Helping them to find out what their defenses are and enhancing their tolerance for not being in control could also be hard.

Profile 800:   Negativistic

A conflictual personality style characterizes people who obtain high scores on this MCMI scale. This style results from holding two assumptions about the world that are difficult to integrate. These individuals first assume that they need to rely on others because they are not able to do well without their support; they are "people who need people." The second premise that conflictual individuals hold is that they cannot afford to depend on others. They may feel that others are not interested enough to be dependable, that the dependence on others is not socially acceptable and will make them look bad, and that others would take advantage of them if they are not constantly on guard.

These two assumptions about life typically bring about one of two different behavior patterns. In the *negativistic style,* the conflict is handled by being compliant on the surface but not fully supporting the efforts of others along the way. In the *explosive style,* individuals typically vacillate between feeling that they are lucky and get more out of life than they have a right to expect and feeling cheated or mistreated. Their behavior changes accordingly. At times, these people treat others in an agreeable and friendly manner and on other occasions they may be irritable, aggressive, or hostile; at still other times, they may experience guilt and appear eagerly cooperative and remorseful. Frequently, they may be optimistic and see the future as bright, but this changes, seemingly without reason, into the opposite view. An energetic and productive mood together with high goals may characterize them on some occasions but in other instances, they are inclined to lower their goals and become less productive.

Such people can be very flexible and changeable, sensitive, and responsive to their environments, but they may also seem moody and unpredictable. Projection is an important defense, but whom it is directed at (self or others) tends to change. Mostly, they tend to be angry, conflicted, and resentful people who are often difficult to handle and present problems wherever they go.

Given this personality style, it may be useful to try not to control these patients in ways that are not necessary for both the therapist and patients to be able to function. Because these patients are bound to resent any control that is placed on them, this tactic can prevent the therapeutic relationship from becoming overly conflictual. They may also benefit from learning how they normally operate and tend to project negative feelings onto others.

Profile 812:   Negativistic-Schizoid-Avoidant

Patients who score highly on these scales have a negativistic personality style that also has introversive and avoidant elements. This style results from holding two assumptions about the world that are difficult to integrate. Individuals first assume that they need to rely on others because they are not able to do well without their support; they are "people who need people." The second premise that conflictual individuals hold is that they cannot afford to depend on others. They may feel that others are not interested enough to be dependable, that the dependence on others is not socially acceptable and will make them look bad, and that others will take advantage of them if they are not careful.

These two assumptions about life typically cause one of two different behavior patterns. In the negativistic style, the conflict is dealt with by being compliant on the surface but not fully supporting the efforts of others along the way. In the other behavior pattern, the individuals are explosive and typically vacillate between feeling that they are lucky and get more out of life than they have a right to expect and feeling cheated or mistreated. Their behavior changes accordingly. At times they are agreeable and friendly; at other times they may be irritable, aggressive, or hostile; at still other times, they may experience guilt and appear overly cooperative and remorseful. Frequently, they may be optimistic and see the future as bright, but this changes, seemingly without reason, into the opposite view. An energetic and productive mood, together with high goals, may characterize them on some occasions, but in other instances, they are inclined to lower their goals and become less productive.

These people can be very flexible and changeable, sensitive, and responsive to their environment, but they can also seem moody and unpredictable. Projection is an important defense that can be aimed at themselves or others. Mostly, they tend to be angry, conflicted, and resentful people who are often difficult to handle and are inclined to present some problems wherever they go.

In addition, these patients seem to keep an emotional distance from others. To some degree, they are uninterested in interpersonal relations and may not be too adept at understanding and enjoying the subtleties and nuances of emotions, something that may lead to being apathetic about the relationship itself. Moreover, they may be afraid of being rejected by others. As a result, social situations are uncomfortable and tense and are avoided. They restrict the number of relationships that they form and tend to have superficial friendships when those do exist, alliances that are more similar to acquaintanceships than friendships.

In trying to establish a therapeutic relationship, it might be useful for the therapist to avoid trying to control the patients in ways that are not necessary for the therapist and patients to be able to function. Because patients are bound to resent any control that is placed on them, not trying to control them can prevent the therapeutic relationship from becoming overly conflictual. Patients may also benefit from learning how they normally operate and about their tendency to project negative feelings onto others.

Profile 820:   Negativistic-Avoidant

Elevations on these scales suggest a personality style characterized by conflictual and avoidant traits. Individuals with high scores usually have low self-esteem and see themselves as inadequate, not very interesting, or unworthy. Projection is an important part of their psychological defenses because the tendency to search for someone to blame is quite prevalent. They not only see themselves as responsible for anything that goes wrong, but they are inclined to feel that others are also to blame. In their somewhat pessimistic view of the world, other people are usually portrayed as cold and rejecting. So, in spite of their poor self-images, they do not put others up on a pedestal, and they tend to be very aware of the limitations that other people may have.

These patients probably have some conflicts in their interpersonal relationships. They are afraid that they may not be seen in a good light. Interpersonal situations are associated with having to take considerable emotional risks. The conflict that they face is that, on one hand, they would like to be appreciated by others. On the other hand, the fear of rejection fills them with apprehension. They would like to meet people and relate to them, but they are so uncomfortable in social situations that they tend to avoid them. Most of these individuals are loners who retreat into their own world of fantasy and are nervous and uncomfortable when they are with others. They tend to be, however, sensitive people who are aware of their own feelings and the emotional reactions that they evoke in others.

Together with the conflict over whether they should relate to others, these individuals tend to be moody and resentful. Thus, they may be friendly and cooperative at times, but they then may become obstructionistic, negativistic, or hostile, only to feel guilty later and behave contritely. In some cases, these mood fluctuations are less noticeable and the conflict is handled through covert obstructionism. This dualism works well because it allows the patients to cope with their conflict over their dependency needs and whether they should relate to others. Thus, the negativistic response allows cooperation without submission and contributes to the formation of relationships that keep others at a distance. It should be noted that even the dualism may have a positive side because some individuals are able to excel while taking the rebel's role in society.

Patients such as these are likely to be ambivalent about the prospect of therapy and will probably be quite uncomfortable during the session. The therapist may be able to make establishing the therapeutic alliance easier by finding ways of minimizing the controls and demands that are made on them in order to make the relationship more conflict-free. Although reassurance of acceptance may be necessary, the therapist should not be too warm and engulfing because it would be too threatening to individuals who have been able to keep some interpersonal distance. In spite of these strategies, the therapist may have to be tolerant of patients who may be irritable or even somewhat hostile in their defensive projection of blame toward others.

Once the therapeutic alliance has been established, the therapist might want to use the relationship to help the patients explore their emotional reactions and develop more productive ways of dealing with their feelings. The therapist has to be careful not to be perceived as being on the other side of the fence and joining the mass of individuals who are, in these patients' views, callous and rejecting.

Profile 823:   Negativistic-Avoidant-Dependent

Individuals with elevated scores on these MCMI scales have predominantly conflictual, avoidant, and dependent traits. They tend to be moody and to change their overall feelings without any obvious reason. At times, they may be very friendly and engaging; they may then become angry and resentful; and later yet, they may feel guilty and contrite. The cycle is completed when they again become friendly and cooperative. A different substyle of the same basic personality makeup is seen in individuals who vent their resentment through obstructionistic maneuvers that allow them to dissipate their anger without threatening their interpersonal support.

Most of these individuals have considerable feelings of insecurity. They tend to feel that others are more gifted, capable, and worthy than they are. However, they feel that if other people got to know them, the people would recognize their lack of value and reject them. They tend to be nervous and uncomfortable when relating to others and often feel that other people do not actually like them and that they are imposing. By avoiding social relationships altogether, they can avoid some of their discomfort. As a result, these people tend to lead lonely lives, fairly distant from other people, whom they see as untrustworthy and judgmental.

These individuals are sensitive: They would like to be appreciated by others and wish they could relate better than they do. However, they are conflicted about wanting to depend on others but feel that if they trust others, they will be hurt in the end. The emotional changes and other possible maladaptive developments are simply the surface behaviors that their basic conflict brings about.

These patients are likely to be highly ambivalent about the prospect of therapy and will probably be uncomfortable during the session. Establishing the therapeutic alliance may be made easier by finding ways to minimize the controls and demands that are made on such patients in order to reduce conflict. Reassurance of acceptance may need to be done frequently. Be careful, though, because a relationship that is too warm and engulfing may also be threatening to an individual who has to be able to keep some interpersonal distance. In spite of these strategies, the therapist may have to be tolerant of patients who may be irritable or even somewhat hostile in their defensive projection of blame toward others.

Once the therapeutic alliance has been established, it will be possible to use the relationship to help patients explore their emotional reactions and help them develop more productive ways of dealing with their feelings. This plan has to be executed very tactfully so that the therapist is not perceived as being the enemy and joining the mass of individuals who are, in the patients' views, callous and rejecting.

Profile 826: Negativistic-Avoidant-Antisocial

High scores on these MCMI scales characterize individuals who have conflictual, avoidant, and competitive traits. Probably the most predominant feature of these patients' personality style is their ambivalence when relating to others. They seem to have low self-esteem and to feel that they are not particularly able or gifted. They tend to generalize this assessment to also include other people. Thus, even though they do not feel good about themselves, they are inclined to put others down and to feel that they are just as unworthy.

Because these patients have low self-esteem, they usually feel that they need the help of others in order to make ends meet. However, they have difficulties accepting the help of others because they see the world as a competitive place where everyone is struggling to obtain the same limited benefits. To them, relying on others is likely to be useless because they assume that people will take advantage of their trust and use the relationship for their own purposes.

As a result of their low self-esteem, these patients also probably tend to be quite sensitive to negative feedback from others. They fear that others may form a poor opinion of them and would not value their friendship. The end result is that they are always looking out for signs of rejection when they are in social situations. They experience interpersonal relationships as anxiety producing and uncomfortable. Because they tend to be nervous when they are relating to others, they often choose to avoid this stress by keeping to themselves. When they do relate, they are distant, superficial, and apprehensive.

By adopting an ambivalent way of relating to others, such patients seem to have adjusted to their interpersonal conflicts. These individuals are often somewhat obstructionistic and negativistic in a distant sort of way. Thus, they may not work through the objections they may have about particular aspects of their lives; instead, they may resent others and vent the resentment by "dragging their feet." Otherwise, the adaptation involves fluctuations in mood such that the individual may go from being very cooperative to being unable to control their anger, which can be explosive. The hostile feelings eventually subside and leave them in a contrite mood so that they will try to be friendly and cooperative once more.

When treating patients with this personality style, the therapist should consider that such patients are likely to be quite ambivalent about therapy and will be uncomfortable during the sessions. The therapist may be able to facilitate establishing a therapeutic alliance by minimizing the controls and demands made on the patients in order to reduce conflict in the relationship. However, the therapist should not be too warm and engulfing because this may be threatening to individuals who have to be able to keep some interpersonal distance. In spite of these strategies, the therapist may have to be tolerant of patients who are irritable or even somewhat hostile in their defensive projection of blame toward others. Once the therapeutic alliance has been established, the relationship could be used to help patients explore their emotional reactions and develop more productive ways of dealing with their feelings. The therapist should be careful not to be perceived as being on the other side of the fence and joining the mass of people who are, in the patients' views, callous and rejecting.

Profile 837: Negativistic-Dependent-Compulsive

People who obtain high scores on these scales have negativistic, dependent, and disciplined traits. They do not have a very high regard for their abilities or accomplishments and feel that they need the help of others in order to make ends meet. However, they tend to be perfectionistic: They have set ideas about how things should be done and very seldom will others be able to meet their expectations. Their world is highly idealistic and void of heroes because neither they nor their cohorts can measure up. This kind of situation leaves them in a bind. On one hand, they feel inadequate to meet their own needs and would like to have another person on whom they could depend. However, they have reservations about the abilities of others and often object to the kind of help that they might receive.

In many individuals scoring highly on these scales, the psychological adaptation to these forces is evident in the clinical picture. At times, they may seem cooperative and wanting a lot of help, attention, and reassurance. However, they also come across as proper, formal, and controlling. Although occasionally they may seem obstructionistic and angry, this anger will be kept well under control and will tend to be vented in covert ways.

Profile 840:   Negativistic-Histrionic

Elevated scores on these scales indicate a personality profile that has predominant negativistic and dramatic traits. People obtaining similar profiles do not have a high opinion of themselves or others. Other people are not viewed as empathetic, caring, or understanding. Their relationships may be intense at first but eventually become somewhat threatening or unexciting so that the friendship "cools down."

Some individuals who are insecure about their own abilities can obtain peace of mind by finding someone on whom they can depend. The interpersonal attitude that these patients seem to have, however, tends to close this as an option. Similar individuals feel that the dependency on others is not acceptable, that the dependency would make them look bad, and that eventually people would criticize them for needing this type of relationship. As a result, these patients probably face an unsolvable approach–avoidance conflict: If they do not depend on others, they feel uncomfortable because they fear that they will not be able to provide for their needs. On the other hand, if they form dependent relationships, they do not have to worry about making ends meet, but they will become uncomfortable about the type of position in which they are placed.

Individuals with high scores on these scales usually fluctuate in their patterns of behavior. At times, they may be quite friendly and congenial. Soon, however, they resent others and may become inappropriately aggressive or even hostile; this may also change and turn into guilt and repentance. The friendly and congenial behavior that may follow completes the behavioral cycle. In contrast, other individuals with similar scores work out their conflict with a more stable pattern of behavior. This pattern involves appearing to be friendly and congenial on the surface while covertly playing a negativistic and obstructionistic role.

Given this personality style, it may be useful to avoid trying to control these patients in ways that are not functional for therapist or patients. Because patients are likely to resent any control that is placed on them, this tactic can prevent the therapeutic relationship from becoming overly conflictual. A supportive relationship would be one in which patients are the center of attention. The therapist should have tolerance for displays of emotion and be able to accept some conflict. Care must be taken to prepare them for the times ahead when they will be angry at the therapist, the treatment has become mundane, and they are ready to terminate. Patients may also benefit from learning how they normally operate and about their tendency to project negative feelings onto others.

Profile 856:   Negativistic-Narcissistic-Antisocial

High scores on these MCMI scales suggest a basically conflictual personality style with confident and competitive traits. This combination often leads to resentments and difficulties handling anger. Many people who have the same pattern of scores appear conflicted and moody and change their feelings and behaviors from one moment to the next. They may seem negativistic, unstable, and erratic, and are easily upset and have a low tolerance for frustration. They may vacillate between being enthusiastic and cheerful or sad and despondent. At times, such patients may feel guilty and try to be friendly and cooperative, but they may soon start resenting others and become critical, angry, or spiteful. Instead of being moody or explosive, other people with this pattern of scores vent their resentment in negativistic or oppositionistic ways. Their anger may be less obvious but, in their negativism, irresponsibility, and passivity, they "get even" by making others angry.

Part of the resentment comes from feelings that they are better than most of the people around them. They also see the world as a competitive place where every person has to fight for the same limited goods. However, they are unable to integrate those two assumptions about the world because, if they were truly superior, they should have their needs fulfilled without having to compete with "lesser" human beings. It is this conflict and lack of integration that often leads to whatever problems they present in terms of their psychological functioning.

On the positive side, individuals with this personality style are independent people who do not cling to others in a needy or dependent manner. They tend to be proud and avoid situations in which they may be humiliated, an issue that may be an important one for these patients.

In light of the personality style that these patients have, the therapist should pay much attention to their narcissistic needs for a strong therapeutic alliance. There will be a tendency, for instance, for patients to reject any interpretation that sounds critical. Feeling threatened, they may become angry and blame the therapist for real or imagined faults or mistakes. Keeping the relationship balanced so that the patients feel that the therapist is on their side and avoiding antisocial or conflictual dealings will require a certain amount of ability and care. A balance has to be struck between being unconditionally supportive and dealing with these patients' issues in an aggressive manner. Often, such a balance will require the therapist to allow them much control over the relationship and will require limiting the areas of exploration in which negative feedback may be given to them.

Profile 860:   Negativistic-Antisocial

Elevated scores on these scales suggest a basic personality style with negativistic and competitive traits, a combination that leads to conflicted and moody individuals who are inclined to change their feelings and behaviors from one moment to the next. At their worst, they may seem negativistic or obstructionistic, unstable or erratic in their feelings. Similarly scoring individuals are easily upset and have a low tolerance for frustration. At times, these patients may feel guilty and try to be friendly and cooperative, but they may soon start resenting others and become more critical, which may even have an angry or spiteful element.

This kind of vacillation theoretically results from conflictual views with regard to the self and the environment. On one hand, such patients tend to be aware of their own limitations and may feel that they need to depend on others to provide for some of their needs. On the other hand, they seem to view the world as a competitive place, a rat race in which one has to be strong, dominant, adequate, and willful in order to survive. These patients may be inclined to suppress the softer emotions of kindness, generosity, and gentility because these emotions will make them weak and vulnerable to the exploitation of others. Probably, in their minds, the way to survive is to be assertive, energetic, self-reliant, and on guard. They feel that they must be aware of the possible manipulations of others and try to gain the upper hand whenever possible.

In light of this personality style, the therapeutic approach that we advocate would be one of remaining unintrusive, being careful not to take a position among the options available unless necessary. This stance will encourage patients to make their own decisions and will decrease conflict in the therapeutic relationship. Interpretations may need to be made when patients use maladaptive projective mechanisms. However, any confrontation has to be done carefully because they will be inclined to perceive the feedback in an antisocial manner and fight the insights that are offered. The therapist must protect the therapeutic alliance and do whatever is necessary to keep these patients feeling that the therapist is on their side.

Profile 864:   Negativistic-Antisocial-Histrionic

Conflictual, competitive, and dramatic elements characterize people who obtain high scores on these MCMI scales. Such individuals tend to be angry and moody and are inclined to change their feelings and behaviors from one moment to the next. Typically, they are perceived as negativistic or obstructionistic, inclined to approach life by turning everything around and seldom accepting something in the manner in which it is presented.

Evidence suggests that there is a conflictual aspect to their oppositionism such that they are typically aggressive, if not hostile, in their interactions with others. Similarly scoring individuals tend to emphasize their ability to remain independent and are not inclined to do what others tell them to do. They are antisocial by nature and may be seen as behaving in a callous manner in the struggle to get ahead of everyone else. They are likely to be mistrustful, to question the motives of others, and to assume that they have to be vigilant and on guard if they are to protect themselves. These patients tend to blame others for anything that goes wrong. They are "touchy": excitable and irritable, easily upset and unstable in their feelings, easily frustrated, treat others in a rough or mean manner, and become angry whenever they are confronted or opposed.

The anger and emotional lability that such patients seem to have theoretically results from conflictual views regarding the self and the environment. On one hand, they tend to be aware of their own limitations and may feel that they need to depend on others to provide for some of their needs. On the other hand, they seem to view the world as a competitive place in which one has to be strong, dominant, adequate, and willful in order to survive. They may be inclined to suppress the softer emotions of kindness, generosity, and gentility, feeling that these emotions will make them weak and vulnerable to the exploitation of others. These patients probably feel that they must be aware of the possible manipulations of others and try to gain the upper hand whenever possible.

Patients' oppositionism may be partly fueled by their histrionic tendencies. They seem to need to be the center of attention and may become easily bored with any situation that becomes routine. Their contrariness probably serves to fulfill their need for attention—albeit in an abrasive and unproductive manner—because uncooperative behaviors are likely to be noticed. In fact, the oppositionism and the search for attention may create a vicious cycle that may be hard to break because their oppositionism tends to meet several of their psychological needs. Consistent with the histrionic tendencies, these patients may be superficial and guarded interpersonally and may not need interpersonal closeness.

7 Assessment of Psychopathology

In this chapter we focus on the use of the MCMI for the assessment of the different psychopathological patterns. We mostly use the *DSM–III–R* diagnostic entities, as well as the *DSM–III–R* distinction between clinical syndromes (Axis I) and personality disorders (Axis II). We discuss the personality disorders first because many of these disorders are related to the personality styles discussed in the previous chapter. Along with the *DSM–III–R* clinical syndromes, we also review the few articles that have dealt with pathologies that are not recognized *DSM–III–R* diagnoses by themselves, such as spouse abuse and thought disorders.

Personality Disorders

Table 5 shows our rendition of the data that Millon (1987) presented for the typical patient suffering from the different personality disorders. A knowledge of such typical profiles may be helpful in making decisions regarding patients' diagnoses. Remember, however, that there is much variance within any diagnostic group. When protocols are obtained that do not fit typical patients within a diagnostic category, the finding can often be used to further understand the patients and does not necessarily mean that they do not suffer from a particular clinical syndrome.

From our viewpoint, a person can have a personality disorder in one of two ways. Eight of the 11 *DSM–III–R* personality disorders constitute syndromes that we would see as exaggerations of basic personality styles. In other words, the clusters of personality traits that we have discussed repeatedly throughout this book are sometimes seen in a pathologically exaggerated or rigid fashion. Such a pattern can then be classified as a personality disorder.

115

Table 5

Expected Primary and Secondary Millon Clinical Multiaxial Inventory Elevations With the Different Personality Disorders

Disorder	Highest scale	Other elevations
Schizoid	Schizoid	Avoidant, Schizotypal
Avoidant	Avoidant	Schizoid, Negativistic, Self-Defeating, Dysthymia
Dependent	Dependent	Avoidant, Self-Defeating
Histrionic	Histrionic	Narcissistic
Narcissistic	Narcissistic	Histrionic, Aggressive/Sadistic
Antisocial	Antisocial	Narcissistic, Negativistic Aggressive/ Sadistic, Borderline, Paranoid, Drug Abuse
Compulsive	Compulsive	
Passive-Aggressive	Negativistic	Aggressive/Sadistic
Schizotypal	Avoidant	Schizoid, Negativistic, Self-Defeating, Schizotypal, Borderline, Anxiety, Dysthymia, Thought Disorder, Major Depression
Borderline	Borderline	Avoidant, Negativistic, Self-Defeating, Anxiety, Dysthymia, Major Depression
Paranoid	Aggressive/Sadistic	Narcissistic, Antisocial, Compulsive, Paranoid, Anxiety, Dysthymia

Note. Data were derived from the MCMI test manual (Millon, 1987).

In addition, there are three *DSM–III* personality disorders that are not represented among the personality styles: the borderline, the schizotypal, and the paranoid. The MCMI-II also has two scales representing personality disorders that the *DSM–III–R* considers to be in need of further study and that are not part of the current official nomenclature. All five of these life-long dysfunctional characterological tendencies, in our opinion, do not have a "normal" or nonpathological equivalent; in other words, the pattern is intrinsically pathological even in cases in which the disorder is not very severe.

Although a great deal of research using the MCMI personality scales is available, the studies have dealt mostly with the validity of the scales or the characterological issues related to particular clinical syndromes and have been covered elsewhere in this book. As odd as it may seem, the MCMI has almost never been used to examine personality styles or personality disorders in their own right.

One exception is the work that has been done with the dependent personality. Overholser, Kabakoff, and Norman (1989) compared individ-

Table 6

Expected Primary and Secondary Millon Clinical Multiaxial Inventory Elevations With Different Clinical Syndromes

Problem area	Highest scale	Other elevations
Anxiety	Anxiety	Avoidant, Negativistic, Self-Defeating
Somatoform	Somatoform	Anxiety, Histrionic, Compulsive
Mania	Hypomania	Dysthymia, Histrionic, Narcissistic, Negativistic, Self-Defeating
Dysthymia	Dysthymia	Avoidant, Negativistic
Alcohol abuse	Alcohol Abuse	Drug Abuse, Antisocial, Negativistic, Self-Defeating
Drug abuse	Drug Abuse	Alcohol Abuse, Histrionic, Antisocial
Thought disorder	Avoidant	Schizotypal, Schizoid, Negativistic, Self-Defeating
Major depression	Psychotic Depression	Dysthymia, Anxiety, Avoidant, Dependent, Self-Defeating
Delusion	Psychotic Delusion	Psychotic Thinking, Paranoid

Note. Data were derived from the MCMI test manual (Millon, 1987).

uals with a significant elevation on the Dependency scale with other psychiatric inpatients. They reported that this group was unlikely to be married and more likely to have been repeatedly hospitalized for psychiatric problems.

Another exception is the work conducted by Wetzler and Dubro (1990). In a validation study of 81 patients, results on the MCMI were compared with admitting diagnoses made by experienced psychiatrists. The MCMI was sensitive to identifying personality disorders (high rate of true-positives), but it showed poor specificity (too many false-positives). Wetzler and Dubro offered two possibilities for the poor predictive power of the test: Did the current acute Axis I pathology of the sample lead to a skewing of personality disorder scale test results? They speculated that "what the MCMI identifies as trait may in fact be state" (Wetzler & Dubro, 1990, pp. 262–263). To support this notion, they noted the high item overlap between clinical scales and personality disorder scales. They offered the second interpretation: Are psychiatrists using an unstructured interview format that underdiagnoses personality disorders and does the test more accurately reflect probable underlying personality pathology?

Clinical Syndromes

Table 6 shows our own rendition of the data that Millon presented for typical patients suffering from the different clinical syndromes. The sup-

porting data and Millon's own conclusions, which are occasionally somewhat different from the ones presented here, can be found in the test
manual (Millon, 1987). As before, remember that a knowledge of such
typical profiles may be helpful but that a great deal of variance exists within
any diagnostic group.

In the remainder of this chapter, we review the MCMI literature on the
different disorders. The issue of whether there is an underlying or predis-
posing personality has been present with almost every clinical syndrome,
and the MCMI has proved to be a good instrument for testing some of the
hypotheses. When such data are available, we present them first and then go
on to discuss any other information that we are aware of with regard to that
disorder.

Schizophrenic Disorders

Hogg, Jackson, Rudd, and Edwards (1990) investigated the frequency of
personality traits and disorders in a sample of 40 recent-onset schizophrenics. The instruments used were the MCMI-I and the Structured Interview for DSM-III Personality Disorders (SIDP). There was evidence that
57%–70% of the sample had a diagnosable personality disorder, although
there was poor agreement between the instruments in making specific personality disorder diagnoses. There was greater concordance between the
instruments when trait scores were used. Hogg et al. concluded that their
results support other research reporting it is common to find Axis II diagnoses in Axis I disorders.

Anxiety Disorders

Unfortunately, we could find little literature on anxiety disorders from the
viewpoint of the MCMI. Alnaes and Torgersen (1990) compared a group of
84 patients with anxiety disorders with other outpatients using the MCMI-I.
Those authors reported that the individuals with "pure" anxiety disorders
tended to be more schizotypal than depressed patients. They were also
more schizoid and avoidant and less histrionic than patients with other
mental disorders except depression. Some caution in accepting these results may be in order: A great number of chi-squares were performed between the different groups used in the study, so some of the findings might
have been obtained by chance.

Similarly, Wetzler et al. (1990) compared 20 patients with panic disorder with 23 depressed patients and 24 normal individuals. The findings
show that the patients with panic disorder scored higher than normal individuals on the Schizoid, Avoidant, Negativistic, Schizotypal, Borderline,

Anxiety, Somatic Preoccupation, Dysthymia, Psychotic Thinking, and Psychotic Depression scales of the MCMI-I. These patients scored significantly lower than the normal subjects on the Narcissistic and Compulsive scales (Wetzler et al., 1990).

Affective Disorders

The issue of whether there are personality traits that predispose the individual to having manic episodes or depressions has been raised frequently in the literature on affective disorders. As clinicians, we have all seen the overly serious, "all work and no play" type of individual who suffers from occasional depressions, or the energetic, flamboyant, and grandiose person who has manic episodes; in those cases, it is often very hard to say where the personality ends and the clinical syndrome begins.

Not surprisingly, the idea that affective disorders are associated with specific underlying personality patterns can be traced back to the pioneers of psychology (Chodoff, 1972). In the case of unipolar depressions, research has indicated that the disorder may occur in individuals who have predominant obsessive traits such as orderliness, rigidity, and guilt (Bech et al., 1980; Charney, Nelson, & Quinlan, 1981; Hirschfeld & Klerman, 1979; Julian, Metcalfe, & Coppen, 1969; Kendell & DiScipio, 1968; Nystrom & Lindegard, 1975; H. D. Palmer & Sherman, 1938; Rosenthal & Gudeman, 1967). Others have shown a connection between depression and increased need for dependence (Strandman, 1978) or a tendency toward social introversion (Donnelly, 1976; Hirschfeld & Klerman, 1979; Nystrom & Lindegard, 1975; Murray & Blackburn, 1974; Perris, 1966). In terms of *DSM–III* personality prototypes, depressed individuals without anxiety have been associated with schizoid and avoidant personality structures (Alnaes & Torgersen, 1990).

Bipolar affective disorders have been linked with hysterical character traits, such as the need for attention expressed in a dramatic, impulsive, and emotional manner (Charney et al., 1981; Cohen, Baker, Cohen, Fromm-Reichmann, & Weigert, 1954; Lazare & Klerman, 1968). The presence of premorbid personality characteristics observed in bipolar disorders, however, is more controversial than in the case of unipolar disorders: Several studies have shown relatively normal personality profiles when bipolar patients were tested during an asymptomatic period (Bech et al., 1980; Donnelly, 1976; Nystrom & Lindegard, 1975; Murray & Blackburn, 1974; Perris, 1966, 1971; Strandman, 1978; von Zerssen, 1982).

Complicating the issue of possible underlying personalities in patients with affective disorders is the problem that the mood state may influence personality traits. Hirschfeld et al. (1983) examined the personality patterns of patients with affective disorders during intake evaluations and again at a 1-year follow-up. The patients were divided into those who recovered after 1 year and those who did not. Personality traits were measured on 19 scales that assessed the characteristics of emotional strength, interpersonal dependency, and extraversion. The findings indicated that the state of depression strongly influenced scores on these three personality constellations and pointed to the need to measure personality patterns while patients are in a symptom-free or euthymic state.

We tried to clarify those issues by comparing a group of patients with affective disorders at a time when they were euthymic with nonpsychiatric controls. We did this to determine whether there would be personality traits that characterize patients with affective disorder that are not part of the acute symptomatology. We then compared patients in the different affective mood states in order to examine the difference that the mood state might make on the measures of patients' personalities when they are symptomatic.

According to our data (Alexander, Choca, Bresolin, et al., 1987), bipolar patients in remission were more narcissistic and histrionic than normal controls, as measured by the MCMI. Euthymic unipolar patients, on the other hand, scored significantly higher than normal controls on the Avoidant, Dependent, and Negativistic scales. We concluded, on the basis of our findings, that patients with affective disorders tend to have personality traits that are associated with their disorder and that remain with them even after the acute episode is in remission. Such a conclusion conflicts with the findings of J. Reich and Troughton (1988), who reported no MCMI differences between asymptomatic patients with a history of depressions and normal subjects.

When we examined the effect of mood state on patients' personalities, we found evidence that a depressed mood leads to elevations in scores on the Schizoid, Avoidant, and Negativistic scales in both unipolar and bipolar patients; these findings have been supported by Wetzler et al. (1990). On the other hand, the manic state did not seem to be associated with further elevations in any of the MCMI basic personality scales (Alexander, Choca, DeWolfe, et al., 1987).

In other words, people who suffer from depressions tend to be more avoidant, dependent, and negativistic even when they are not symptomatic; the depressive mood itself contributes to further increases in scores on the Schizoid, Avoidant, and Negativistic scales for both unipolar and bipolar patients. By contrast, manic-depressive patients tend to be more narcissistic and histrionic after the symptoms have abated, but the manic state by itself does not seem to affect MCMI scores very much. Our findings, and similar results obtained by Libb et al. (1990), suggested caution when interpreting elevated scores on the Schizoid, Avoidant, and Negativistic scales for depressed individuals because the scores obtained can be expected to moderate after the episode is over. Judging from our data, however, there should be less concern that the scores of individuals in a manic state might be inflated.

Another way of looking at the relationship between affective disorders and personality styles is to conceptualize the personality elements as defining different "depressive styles." Goldberg, Segal, Vella, and Shaw (1989), for instance, found two such styles after administering the MCMI to depressed patients. The first of these types was characterized by elevated scores on the Negativistic scale of the MCMI and was seen as being similar to Beck's (1983) "autonomous" depressive. Such individuals are described as typically feeling misunderstood and unappreciated; they tend to anticipate disappointment and to precipitate failures through obstructive behaviors. In contrast, the other type conceptualized by Goldberg et al. was marked by elevated scores on the Dependent and Avoidant scales of the MCMI and was seen as being similar to Beck's "sociotropic" subtype. These individuals were thought to be self-effacing, noncompetitive people who were constantly seeking relationships in which they could lean on someone for guidance and security.

Similarly, Overholser et al. (1989) examined the difference between dependent and nondependent depressed individuals. Their data indicated that dependent depressed subjects were more likely to be older and female than the nondepressed psychiatric controls and were more likely to demonstrate reduced activity and energy levels than the nondependent depressed subjects.

Finally, in terms of psychopathology as opposed to personality style, Wetzler et al. (1990) reported that the 23 depressed patients they studied had higher scores than the 24 normal subjects on the Schizotypal, Borderline, Anxiety, Somatic Preoccupation, Dysthymic, Psychotic Thinking, and Psychotic Depression scales of the MCMI-I.

Eating Disorders

Thanks to the work of Tisdale, Pendleton, and Marler (1990), information is available about eating disorders and the MCMI-I. These investigators compared a group of bulimic patients with a group of psychiatric patients who did not have an eating disorder and a group of normal controls. The data showed that bulimic patients obtained significantly higher scores on the Dependent, Avoidant, and Schizoid scales; their average score on the Narcissistic scale was significantly lower than the average score of the other two groups. The average BR score obtained by the bulimic patients on the Dependent scale was 75, indicating that most of those patients had a dependent personality style. Tisdale et al. considered their findings to be consistent with previous descriptions of bulimic women as dependent, unassertive, eager to please, and concerned with social approval.

Substance Abuse

The idea that substance abuse is fueled by characterological tendencies probably dates back to Freud. The Freudian contention that all alcoholic individuals represented an "oral" personality (the precursor of the modern dependent personality) has not been supported by the literature. Instead, the current thinking is that there are several alcoholic subtypes. In a comprehensive review of the literature, Nerviano and Gross (1983) identified seven such subtypes.

Several MCMI studies done by different investigators have revealed clusters among alcoholic patients, thus supporting the presence of at least four of the seven subtypes (Bartsch & Hoffman, 1985; Craig, Verinis, & Wexler, 1985; Gibertini & Retzlaff, 1988b; Mayer & Scott, 1988). In all of these studies there was a group of alcoholic patients with elevated scores on the Negativistic scale. It appeared that they often had additional elevations on the Borderline or Paranoid scales and were thought to be demonstrating moderate to severe personality dysfunctions. Specifically, the patients were characterized as having "substantial variations in mood, irritability, suspiciousness" and "an ambivalent and indecisive approach" to life (Bartsch & Hoffman, 1985, p. 711). Drinking often served a "self-medicating" function for them. This group tended to be anxious and demonstrated borderline and paranoid tendencies (Craig et al., 1985). In terms of its prevalence, this cluster accounted for 38% of Mayer and Scott's sample.

A second cluster of patients was defined by elevated scores on the Narcissistic and Histrionic scales. For those subjects, the drinking was conceptualized as "recreational in nature" and a "manifestation of a lifestyle of self-indulgence and thrill seeking" (Bartsch & Hoffman, 1985, p. 711). This cluster may account for 22% to 28% of the alcoholic population (Gibertini & Retzlaff, 1988b; Mayer & Scott, 1988).

Accounting for about 20% of the samples (Craig et al., 1985; Mayer & Scott, 1988) were the alcoholic patients with elevated scores on the Compulsive scale. Bartsch and Hoffman (1985) talked about this cluster as representing an "overly exuberant conscience" so that the function of the alcohol is to "permit escape from feelings of responsibility, or permit the expression of anger" (p. 711).

In all studies there was a cluster with schizoid, avoidant, and dependent elements that constituted as much as 28% (Craig et al., 1985) or as little as 5% (Gibertini & Retzlaff, 1988b) of the subjects. Besides the three MCMI personality scales that measure those three traits, some of the investigators found elevations on the Borderline and Schizotypal scale scores (Bartsch & Hoffman, 1985; Mayer & Scott, 1988) whereas Craig et al. (1985) described these subjects as being "anxious and depressed" (p. 159). Such individuals were thought to demonstrate "widespread and severe maladjustment" and to be typically "caught between feelings of loneliness and social apprehension"; drinking may serve to "mediate social anxiety to a level that produces self-assurance and permits social contact" (Bartsch & Hoffman, 1985, p. 712). Participation in self-help groups such as Alcoholics Anonymous was thought to be especially difficult for this type of alcoholic.

Craig et al. (1985) also assessed a group of drug abusers. In terms of the personality makeup, they described two clusters with the drug abusers. The first group, accounting for 31% of the sample, obtained elevated scores on the Narcissistic and Antisocial scales. This group was seen as characterologically similar to the second group of alcoholics described earlier. Perhaps Bartsch and Hoffman's (1985) argument that individuals belonging to this group use chemicals for "recreational" purposes can also be made for the drug abusers.

Additionally, Craig et al. (1985) reported a cluster made up of negativistic-avoidant patients who also tended to score highly on the Anxiety and Dysthymia scales. This group was seen by Craig et al. as being different from any of the alcoholic clusters. This group accounted for 28% of their sample. It was noteworthy that 40% of the drug abuse sample remained unclustered.

On the issue of whether alcoholic and drug-abusing patients are basically similar or different, the article by Craig et al. (1985) added new light to the debate. They pointed out that if one looks at the issue from the MCMI-I personality perspective, there are four describable types of alcoholics and two types of drug addicts. Both types of addiction have been found to appeal to narcissistic personality types who might also demonstrate histrionic or antisocial elements. Because this cluster may account for about 25% of the substance abuse population, it could be said that 25% of the two diagnostic groups is basically alike. When the treatment offered is engineered to reflect personality aspects, perhaps these patients could be treated together, regardless of the kind of addiction they have. From a characterological viewpoint, however, alcoholics and substance abusers are more different than they are alike. As sophistication increases in measuring characterological tendencies, the old debate seems obsolete because it becomes clear that, even within one of the addictive groups, the patients are not all alike.

In subsequent work, Craig and Olson (1990) investigated the similarities and differences between cocaine and opiate addicts using the MCMI-I. They reported that these two groups of drug abusers are more similar than different in terms of their personality styles. Nevertheless, they found that cocaine addicts demonstrated more features of an antisocial personality style, whereas the heroin addicts had significantly higher scores on the Alcohol Abuse, Anxiety, and Somatic Preoccupation scales.

Using multivariate procedures, Craig and Olson (1990) were also able to distinguish between two different types of cocaine abusers. The first cluster was dominated by high scores on the Narcissistic, Antisocial, Paranoid, and Drug Abuse scales. Those patients were described as "arrogant and self-centered" and "driven to act out because of fear or mistrust of others" (Craig & Olson, 1990, p. 235). In addition to elevated scores on the Narcissistic and Antisocial scales, the second cluster showed a very predominant Negativistic scale and elevations on the Paranoid, Avoidant, Drug and Alcohol Abuse, Anxiety, and Dysthymia scales of the MCMI-I. These individuals were seen as driven by their irritability, unpredictable moods, and pessimistic attitudes. They were characterized as suffering from a great deal of inner turmoil and feeling "cheated in life, misunderstood, and unappreciated" (Craig & Olson, 1990, p. 235).

Similarly, Craig and Olson (1990) described two kinds of heroin addicts using data from the MCMI-I. The first type was defined by elevations on the Narcissistic and Antisocial scales. They described these subjects as showing "arrogant traits of self-worth, an intimidating social manner, tendencies to exploit other people, [and] a lack of personal responsibility" (1990, p. 235). By contrast, the second cluster was characterized by elevated scores on the Negativistic scale, indicating erratic behaviors with a great deal of anger as well as guilt and remorse.

In addition to characterological problems, researchers have noted a prevalence of depression among alcohol abusers. McMahon and Davidson (1986b) showed that 66% of male alcoholics undergoing inpatient treatment obtained elevated scores on the Dysthymia scale of the MCMI. McMahon and his co-workers (McMahon & Davidson, 1986b; McMahon & Tyson, 1989, 1990) went on to demonstrate how the MCMI-I can be used to discriminate between the patients who will experience only transient depressive episodes and those for whom the depressive feelings may be more enduring and problematic. In their work, the enduring depression was associated with higher scores on the Passive-Aggressive and Avoidant scales and was negatively correlated with Compulsive scale scores. In other words, the more enduring depressive feelings tended to include a pattern of interpersonal ambivalence, low self-image, irritable affectivity or explosive anger, hypersensitivity to rejection, and social isolationism. On the other hand, the more transient episodes tended to be associated with excessive emotional control, fear of social disapproval, and psychological restraint (McMahon & Davidson, 1985a; McMahon & Tyson, 1989, 1990).

Alcoholics can also be differentiated in terms of the level of their social functioning on the basis of the MCMI. McMahon, Davidson, and Flynn (1986) found the low-social-functioning group of alcoholics to have a significantly higher mean score on the Schizotypal scale of the MCMI-I and a significantly lower mean on the Compulsive scale.

Additionally, the MCMI-I can be used to describe the pattern of drinking used by alcoholic patients. McMahon and his associates (McMahon & Davidson, 1989; McMahon, Gersh, & Davidson, 1989b) found that continuous drinkers tended to have higher scores on the Psychotic Thinking scale than episodic drinkers. A group of the alcoholics in the Craig et al. (1985) sample also demonstrated such elevations, a finding that was attributed to the possible development of an organic mental disorder that causes "disorganization of thinking, regressive behavior, confusion, and disorientation" (p. 159). McMahon et al. (1989b) found associations of lesser magnitude between continuous drinking and scores on the Drug Abuse, Paranoid, and Hypomanic scales. Episodic drinking, on the other hand, was associated with higher scores on the Compulsive scale. On the basis of their data, McMahon et al. characterized continuous drinkers as being more likely to be confused, agitated, and disorganized in their thinking than episodic drinkers; the former are also more likely to feel misunderstood and unappreciated and to be discontented and socially alienated. Although continuous drinkers are likely to be more stable in terms of their social and occupational functioning than episodic drinkers and to have greater prospects for controlled drinking, McMahon et al. cited data indicating that continuous drinkers are more psychologically disturbed and at greater risk for neuropsychological impairment and liver problems (McMahon & Davidson, 1989).

Finally, children of alcohol and substance abusers have also recently been studied with the MCMI. Hibbard (1989) examined whether adult children of alcoholics (ACOAs) had greater emotional and characterological problems than a matched control group of adults with nonalcoholic parents. The MCMI-I and Rorschach were administered; the Rorschach was scored with a specialized method purported to assess object relations. Results indicate that ACOAs were more pathological in their personality functioning and object relations. Post hoc comparisons of MCMI results demonstrated interactions between group and gender for several scales (Histrionic, Narcissism, Hypomania, and Dysthymia). ACOAs overall scored higher on the Cycloid and Negativistic scales and lower on the Compulsive scale than normal subjects. These results are only suggestive, however, and must be viewed with caution because of the extremely small sample size ($n = 15$ in each group).

Wife Abuse

James Hastings and L. Kevin Hamberger have done a substantial amount of work using the MCMI-I to characterize male patients who abuse their spouses. The subjects were participants in violence-abatement programs. In support of the contention that wife batterers often suffer from a personality disorder, Hastings and Hamberger (1988) were able to show marked differences in the MCMI personality elevations between the batterers and a control group of nonbatterers. The low number of subjects used did not allow them to characterize the abusers with confidence. Nevertheless, the data described the abusers as individuals who have difficulty regulating affective states and who also feel uncomfortable within intimate relationships; they were seen as being more alienated, more in need of approval, and more sensitive to rejection than the nonbatterers. According to the MCMI scores, the batterers were more prone to anxiety, depression, somatic complaints, and substance abuse than the members of the control group. The presence of alcohol abuse (Hamberger & Hastings, 1987; Hastings & Hamberger, 1988) was associated with an even greater tendency toward overall pathology.

Perhaps of even greater clinical value is the factor analysis that Hamberger and Hastings (1986, 1988a) carried out using the eight personality scales of the MCMI. This procedure led to the emergence of three factors of wife batterers in the MCMI. The findings allowed them to classify their subjects in a way that elucidated the psychodynamics behind the spouse abuse. Using the proposed system, three "pure" types are recognized: borderline-schizoid, narcissistic, and dependent.

The borderline-schizoid type typically had elevated scores on those two MCMI scales, whereas the rest of the personality scale scores remained below the cutoff. These people were characterized as withdrawn, moody, and hypersensitive to interpersonal slights. Using the conceptualizations of Elbow (1977) and Symonds (1978), Hamberger and Hastings (1986, 1988a) characterized such individuals as "Dr. Jekyll and Mr. Hyde" types who can be very calm and sociable one moment but then turn uncontrollably hostile the next because of the unpredictable lability. Theoretically, the subjects require a symbiotically supportive relationship that offers the external validation they need in order to feel that they have a defined existence. If the partner fails to recognize their worth, these individuals are devastated and express their anger physically. Once the incident is over, however, these individuals tend to express considerable guilt and remorse.

By contrast, the subjects obtaining elevated scores on the Narcissistic scale of the MCMI have self-centered approaches to life. Typically, these people feel that they are more important than others and demand their respect and admiration. A refusal to look at them with awe invites threat and aggression. Hastings and Hamberger (1986, 1988a) felt that, for these types of individuals, the abuse is like a punishment that is handled in a matter-of-fact manner because of the sense of superiority and entitlement that leads them to believe it is appropriate for them to show others the error of their ways.

Finally, the dependent type is an individual who lacks self-esteem and feels in dire need of support from others. It is the failure of other people to meet these individuals' needs that is eventually translated into rebellious and hostile feelings.

In addition to subjects who are "pure" types, Hastings and Hamberger (1986, 1988a) found many who represent a combination of the pure types as well as some individuals whose scores on the MCMI personality scales would not be indicative of any personality tendencies.

The usefulness of this information can readily be applied when evaluating a wife batterer who meets one of the described types. In that case, the clinician can readily use the MCMI, for instance, to predict the kind of situation that evokes the aggressive feelings within the context of the family system. Or, the information can be used in working with patients in order to make them aware of the personal issues that they are reacting to when they act in a hostile manner toward their wives.

Posttraumatic Stress Disorders

Psychologists in the VA system have used the MCMI repeatedly to diagnose posttraumatic stress disorder (PTSD) among Vietnam veterans. A study by Robert et al. (1985), for instance, compared the profiles of 25 veterans diagnosed as suffering from PTSD with a matched group of psychiatric patients. They found that the PTSD patients had significant elevations in 9 of the 20 MCMI scales and that profiles for the two groups were significantly different in shape and scatter. The PTSD mean profile included seven critically elevated scales: Avoidant, Negativistic, Borderline, Anxiety, Dysthymia, Alcohol Abuse, and Drug Abuse. A discriminant analysis accounted for 100% of the variance and correctly classified 88% of the patients (92% of the PTSD subjects and 84% of the comparison subjects). A comparison of coefficients for the discriminant function indicated that the Borderline, Schizoid, Dysthymia, and Schizotypal scales made a larger relative contribution to the discriminant score than did the other variables. Modified code types produced a correct PTSD identification rate of 60% with a 12% false-positive rate when comparison patients were misclassified as PTSD. The researchers noted that 4 of the 10 scales used in the discriminant function failed to emerge as discriminating variables when group means were subjected to univariate analysis. These researchers observed that the difference in classification accuracy based on discriminant function versus modified code types only reinforces the need "to determine whether the MCMI-I code types accurately identify PTSD subjects from other settings" (Robert et al., 1985, p. 229).

Consistent with these findings are the reports by Hyer and his co-workers (Hyer & Boudewyns 1987; Hyer, Woods, Boudewyns, Harrison, & Tamkin, 1990) of the PTSD veteran as one who is prone to score highly on the Negativistic and Avoidant scales of the MCMI, the so-called 8-2 profile. McDermott (1987) compared PTSD patients with other Vietnam combat veterans with non-PTSD psychiatric disorders and also found that the 8-2 profile characterized the PTSD group but not the comparison group. Like Robert et al. (1985), McDermott found that a high Borderline scale score was an additionally frequently occurring phenomenon, as were high scores on the Anxiety, Dysthymia, Alcohol Abuse, and Drug Abuse scales. The presence of all of these elevations, of course, suggests a pattern of emotional instability that is often part of the clinical picture in the case of PTSD patients (Hyer et al., 1990).

As helpful as these data may be, the findings do not exclusively identify individuals with PTSD because there may be individuals with other diagnoses who also fit the same pattern of scale elevations. In trying to fulfill the need to diagnose PTSD accurately, we attempted to develop a PTSD scale for the MCMI. Using a method of empirical keying, we compared the item answers obtained from patients judged to suffer from this disorder with the answers obtained from matched controls. This method led to 17 items that diagnosed the PTSD subjects in the derivation sample with accuracy. The scale was then tested against a second, cross-validating sample. The latter consisted of patients admitted into a PTSD inpatient unit for treatment; the control group was a matched sample of psychiatric inpatients without PTSD. Although the results were significant, we noted that the means and standard deviations of the two cross-validating groups were such that it was difficult to use the scale clinically (Choca, Shanley, et al., 1987).

It seemed to us that the MCMI does not, unfortunately, have enough items addressing the issues surrounding the PTSD diagnosis to provide a reasonable measure for this disorder. In terms of its inability to measure PTSD, the MCMI is in good company: Problems have been reported in the effective use of the clinical scales of the MMPI (Burke & Mayer, 1985; Fairbank, Keane, & Malloy, 1983; Keane, Malloy, & Fairbank, 1984; Keane, Wolfe, & Taylor, 1987) and Keane's experimental PTSD subscale for the MMPI (Gayton, Burchstead, & Matthews, 1986; Hyer et al., 1986).

Adjustment Disorders

While studying 68 patients requesting cancer evaluations at a breast clinic, Malec, Wolberg, Romsaas, Trump, and Tanner (1988) collected MCMI data before the diagnosis was made and on several occasions thereafter. The data showed how the MCMI-I reflects the emotional changes experienced by some of the subjects who turned out to have cancer, when compared with those whose growth proved to be benign. Although the MCMIs of the two groups were not statistically different on the initial evaluation, the cancer group had significant elevations on the clinical syndrome scales when compared with the noncancer group after the cancer was diagnosed. Specifically, 29% of the cancer patients obtained significant elevations on those scales, whereas only 7% of the noncancer group obtained such elevations. The elevations were mostly obtained on the Anxiety, Dysthymia, and Somatic Preoccupation scales. These elevations were observed even though the subjects did not meet the *DSM–III* criteria for a major depressive episode. Malec et al. also reported that, judging from the MCMI-I, the psychological disturbance shown by the cancer group has disappeared 16 months after the diagnosis was made.

Problem-Solving Deficits

Gilbride and Hebert (1980) examined the MCMI characteristics of good and poor interpersonal problem solvers. The measure of problem-solving ability used was the Means Ends Problem Solving Procedure (MEPS), which requires the subject to finish a story that presents some sort of problem. Black subjects who were poor problem solvers showed significant elevations in the Paranoid and Psychotic Delusions scales when compared with good problem solvers of the same race. For White subjects, the poor problem solvers had higher means on the Schizoid and Schizotypal scales.

Suicide Potential

Clinicians are often faced with evaluating the suicidal risk that a particular patient may present. Joffe and Regan (1989a) provided some evidence that depressed patients showing borderline traits on the MCMI-I are more likely to make a suicide attempt than those who do not. This finding has a certain amount of face validity because many of the suicidal items included in the test are keyed into the Borderline scale.

McCann and Suess (1988) found that 85% of their psychiatric inpatients with elevation scores on the Schizoid, Avoidant, Dependent, and Negativistic scales of the MCMI-I demonstrated suicidal ideation and that 65% had made a suicide attempt. Similar results were reported by McCann and Gergelis (1990), possibly indicating that this personality profile is a bit of a suicide marker. In the latter article, McCann and Gergelis noted that the findings are consistent with the stress–vulnerability model of suicidal ideation because the model emphasizes the likelihood that individuals who feel alienated, depressed, and unable to cope will experience suicidal thoughts.

Attempts to find a definite MCMI suicide marker, however, have been unsuccessful. Joffe and Regan (1989b), for instance, failed to find any difference on the frequency of MCMI-I personality scale elevations of suicide attempters and nonsuicide attempters. The only significant difference found by McCann and Gergelis (1990) between individuals having suicide ideation and those who had attempted to kill themselves was in the scores on the Desirability scale of the MCMI-II, on which the attempters obtained a higher score.

8 Case Reports

In this chapter we offer some of our own testing reports as concrete examples of how the MCMI can be integrated with historical information or data obtained from projective measures into a descriptive and useful narrative. Although the test data are reported without any alterations, we have tried as much as possible to change all of the identifying information in order to protect the client's confidentiality.

In writing reports it is often useful to have a scheme around which to organize them. This idea has been further explained elsewhere (Choca, 1988) and involves the use of one of four different organizational strategies that we label *personality, developmental, motivational, and diagnostic.*

The typical report using a *personality scheme* starts with a description of the individual's basic personality style. Once the personality has been described, the rest of the data can be presented as they relate to the personality style. If there was a clear precipitant to the onset of the symptomatology, the importance of that event can often be discussed in terms of the values and assumptions of the individual's personality style. The psychopathology can be explained, following this model, as exaggerations of the basic personality style, as maladjustments caused by the interaction between that personality style and the environment, or as some reflection of the personality traits.

The common thread in the different parts of the report in the *developmental scheme* is the tracing of the client's history to explain how the client developed the way he or she did. This scheme may involve speculations about the etiological underpinnings of the personality style, a description of the personality style per se, and a review of the effect that the personality style might have had during the different stages of development in order to bring about the experiences that the individual had at that stage. The psychopathology is then understood in terms of a failure to achieve developmental tasks along the way.

The *motivational scheme* is particularly useful when the client's life has revolved around striving toward a particular conscious or unconscious goal. In such cases, the report can be organized around the client's striving. The personality may then be seen as resulting from such a striving (e.g., the person who resolved early in life that he or she would avoid making any mistakes and developed a compulsive personality style) or as influencing the different attempts that the client has made to reach his or her goal. The psychopathology can then be explained as reactions the person had to difficulties in striving for the goal.

Finally, with cases presenting a difficult differential diagnosis question, it may be useful to follow what we call a *diagnostic organizational scheme*. Such a report would revolve around the issues involved in the differential diagnosis, perhaps discussing the different criteria for the diagnoses under consideration and offering the evidence that the testing has provided in support of or against each of the criteria. This system may be used for the Axis I syndromes first and then repeated for the Axis II personality structure.

These schemes should be thought of as a way of conceptualizing and organizing the report and should not inhibit readers from developing some of their own. In addition, the manner of presentation can be varied for any one of the schemes; in other words, a report following the personality scheme does not always need to begin with a description of the personality as suggested earlier because one could do it just as well in the reverse order. The schemes could also be intermixed (e.g., the report of a schizophrenic using the diagnostic organizational scheme could switch, at some point, into the developmental scheme and discuss how the psychotic episodes have prevented the individual from accomplishing various developmental tasks in his or her life).

We chose the cases that follow to represent the different kinds of pathology rather than to exemplify the different diagnostic schemes, but readers may be able to see more than one organization being used in the reports.

Thought Disturbance in a Schizoid Personality Disorder

Patient History

Mr. Donald Green is a 26-year-old Black male who was admitted into the psychiatric unit while he was in a psychotic state. The patient had come to believe that he could control the weather with his thoughts. He placed tapes across his chest in response to the request of "voices" that he heard. Four days prior to admission, the patient shaved his head because he believed there were "things" living in his head and that he could get rid of them by doing that. Mr. Green admitted feeling that he was "more than one person" and could hear "two voices," one male and one female, when he spoke. He also tended to be somatically preoccupied: Reportedly he had been suffering from headaches and abdominal pain for some time and was currently complaining of a cracking noise in his left shoulder.

The present evaluation was requested in order to help with the differential diagnosis. In particular, the issue was whether Mr. Green was suffering from a schizophrenic disorder. At the time of the testing, Mr. Green was being treated with Stelazine (10 mg three times/day).

Psychiatric History
This is the first time that the patient has received psychiatric treatment. Mr. Green also denied abusing alcohol or drugs and knew of no member of his family who had a history of psychiatric problems.

Medical History
Mr. Green was hospitalized at a medical hospital in July 1985 with complaints of headaches and abdominal pain. That was the only other time he had been in the hospital. During the present admission, a computerized tomography (CT) scan of the brain and an electroencephalogram were taken and found to be within normal limits.

Family History
Mr. Green had considerable difficulty giving his history. Very often he claimed not to know what different members of the family did for a living or other important pieces of information. At other times, his answers were very confusing and it took much effort to clarify what he was trying to say.

Mr. Green was born in New York City and raised in the Brooklyn area. He is the oldest of six children who were raised together, but he has three younger stepsisters who were not raised with him. Mr. Green was born out of wedlock. His biological father is a 53-year-old machinist whom the patient sees on a yearly basis. His father left the relationship with Mr. Green's mother very early, married someone else, and has three daughters from that marriage.

Mr. Green's mother is a 51-year-old woman employed by a hospital in Brooklyn. The patient talked about her as being a very religious person and seemed to have positive feelings toward her. She married when Mr. Green was very young but is now divorced.

The ex-husband, Mr. Green's stepfather, is a man in his 50s to whom the patient refers to as his "father" because he was the male figure in the home through most of Mr. Green's childhood. The stepfather used to work as a mail carrier but quit his job some time ago and moved out of state. As a result, Mr. Green does not see him frequently at this time.

The patient was the oldest among the siblings and was followed by William. William is 25 years old, single, and living in the streets because he does not have a place to stay. Gwen is a 24-year-old sister who is single and lives with the patient. He characterized her as a "pain" because she has a "big mouth." Like her mother, Gwen works at the same Brooklyn hospital. David is a 22-year-old Marine stationed elsewhere. The 21-year-old brother, Rodney, obtained a college degree on a football scholarship and lives in California. Brenda, aged 9, is the last of the siblings who were raised together. She is still living with her mother.

Mr. Green was married in 1983. The marriage lasted 2 years. His ex-wife is still single and they see each other fairly often. She was characterized as a straightforward sort of woman. They have a 2-year-old daughter who has not been a problem.

Mr. Green readily admitted that he had no friends. For his social enjoyment, he goes out dancing, but he picks different partners and does not have a steady companion.

Educational History

While he was in high school in Brooklyn, Mr. Green did just enough work to get by. He was never placed in a special education program, but he was always a below-average student. The patient attended a technical school for 2 years, but he ended up feeling "wiped out" and dropped out to go to work.

Occupational History

Mr. Green worked at a freight company for 9 years until that company was purchased by a trucking company. For the last 6 months, he has been employed as a dispatcher by the latter company and apparently has had no problems with his job.

Mental Status Examination

At the time of this evaluation, Mr. Green was alert, oriented, verbal, and coherent. His speech and language functions were intact. The other intellectual functions examined (e.g., memory, figure reproductions, mental control, abstractions) were also within normal limits. His ability to perform calculations could not be tested because he refused to cooperate: He stated that he never calculated anything and would not make the necessary effort. His thought processes were jumbled at times, and his thought content was marked by delusions and auditory hallucinations. He was quite evasive and superficial. Affective responses were often inappropriate in that he sometimes joked constantly and refused to take the testing seriously; at other times, he seemed angry with the examiner. His mood was within normal limits and had a good range of emotions. Anger, however, was prevalent in his comments and sarcastic remarks. There was no suicidal or homicidal ideation. He was mildly restless and needed to stand up or walk around several times during the testing. Although he tried to appear relaxed, he seemed tense and apprehensive about the testing. He had no insight and claimed that there was nothing wrong with him, even when he spoke of fairly severe psychiatric symptoms. Mr. Green was only minimally cooperative; he often tried to avoid having to give information and completed the entire procedure rapidly.

Discussion

Unfortunately, all of the data obtained was consistent with the presence of a schizophrenic process. About the only requirement that did not appear to be met for a schizophrenic disorder was that of duration: Mr. Green had not been in a psychotic state for 6 months at the time of the evaluation.

Specifically, Mr. Green showed a defective contact with reality, which was clinically obvious in his auditory hallucinations, deluded thinking, and possible somatic delusions. His Rorschach results, on the other hand, uncovered vague and confused thinking as well as occasional illogical reasoning. As seen on this test, his communications were often so egocentric that they seemed not to be intended to share information: His thinking frequently could only be understood after repeated questioning to clarify all of the steps in the chain of associations that he had not communicated.

Mr. Green seemed bizarre, both inside and outside of the testing. Often this effect was created by the content of his responses, as was the case when he made several inappropriate sexual responses on the Rorschach. At other times, the bizarre quality was produced by the lability of the affect and by the defenses that he was using. The lability left the examiner off balance, not knowing what to expect next. On the Rorschach, a constriction and an inability to share his feelings and use his psychic resources was intermixed with an uncontrolled expression of emotions. On the surface, the mood lability materialized in the following manner. It seemed as if Mr. Green first attempted to deny troublesome thoughts through humor. He repeatedly made humorous discounting remarks about the testing or to the examiner, not taking the diagnostic procedure seriously. This defense did not hold for long and he eventually projected his discomfort through a sarcastic remark or a mildly insulting comment about the procedure or the examiner.

Practically all of the MCMI pathology scale scores were elevated, showing that, even by his own assessments, Mr. Green was having many emotional problems and functioning poorly. In fact, the scores were so elevated that they probably constituted a "cry for help," an attempt on Mr. Green's part to communicate that things were not well with him.

As far as the personality structure was concerned, Mr. Green's scores on the MCMI were characteristic of individuals with predominant passive-aggressive, avoidant, and dependent traits. Individuals with similar scores tend to be moody and to change their overall feelings without any obvious reason. At times, they may be very friendly and engaging; they then become angry and resentful; later yet, they may feel guilty and contrite. The cycle is completed when they again become friendly and cooperative. A different substyle of the same basic personality makeup can be observed in individuals who vent their resentment through obstructionistic maneuvers that allow them to dissipate their anger without threatening their interpersonal support.

Most of these individuals have considerable feelings of insecurity. They tend to feel that others are more gifted, more capable, or more worthy. They feel, however, that if others get to know them, their own lack of value would be recognized and they would be rejected. Such individuals also tend to be nervous and uncomfortable when relating to others; they often feel that the other person does not really like them and that they are imposing. They frequently avoid some of the discomfort of relating by avoiding social relationships altogether. As a result, these people tend to lead lonely lives, fairly distant from others, whom they view as untrustworthy and judgmental.

Individuals with scores similar to those obtained by Mr. Green are sensitive: They would like to be appreciated by others and wish they could relate better than they do. They are caught, however, between wanting to depend on others but feeling that if they trust others, they will be hurt in the end. The emotional changes and other possible maladaptive developments are simply the surface behaviors that their basic conflict brings about.

All of Mr. Green's personality findings were consistent with what was known about his premorbid functioning. For example, Mr. Green admitted having no friends and his mother apparently described him as a "sensitive" individual who was "a loner, given to daydreaming." Thus, he seemed to have a schizoid personality disorder that preceded the psychotic episode.

The psychological strengths uncovered by the evaluation included the absence of a cognitive or memory impairment and at least average intellectual abilities. The patient has also had a good work history and seemed to function, even if at a marginal level, prior to the onset of the psychosis. Therefore, it is possible that when the patient recovers from his psychotic episode, he may be able to return to his previous level of functioning.

Mr. Green's stories on the Thematic Apperception Test (TAT) were quite varied and did not suggest that he was preoccupied with any interpersonal issue. As a result, it was difficult to identify any troublesome situations in his life. Because he had several inappropriate sexual responses on the Rorschach and because the story evoked by the heterosexual intercourse card of the TAT involved the murder of the woman probably indicated difficulty with that kind of sexual closeness.

Diagnostic Assignments and Recommendations

    I   Schizophreniform disorder (295.40)

   II   Schizoid personality disorder (301.20)

 III   No known contributing medical problems

Continued evaluation for the use of psychotropic medications seems indicated. In addition, the formation of a therapeutic alliance would be beneficial. The problem with the latter recommendation is that any kind of close relationship will be threatening to Mr. Green and therefore difficult to establish.

Test Results

The Millon Clinical Multiaxial Inventory-II

Personality Style Scales		BRS
1–Schizoid	=	99
2–Avoidant	=	92
3–Dependent	=	88
4–Histrionic	=	69
5–Narcissistic	=	64
6A–Antisocial	=	65
7–Compulsive	=	30
8A–Negativistic	=	105

Clinical Symptom Scales		BRS
A–Anxiety	=	109
H–Somatic Preoccupations	=	81
N–Hypomania	=	119
D–Dysthymia	=	94
B–Alcohol Abuse	=	94
T–Drug Abuse	=	97
SS–Psychotic Thinking	=	101
CC–Psychotic Depression	=	88
PP–Psychotic Delusion	=	114

Severe Personality Scales		BRS
6B–Aggressive	=	45
8B–Self-Defeating	=	61
S–Schizotypal	=	85
C–Borderline	=	81
P–Paraphrenic	=	108

Modifier Indices		BRS
X–Disclosure	=	35
Y–Desirability	=	65
Z–Debasement	=	35
V–Validity	=	0

Rorschach Protocol

1. Card I	Reaction time:	16 seconds	
SCORE → W F	A	P	Z1
bee			
INQUIRY: prongs, wings			

2. Card I	Reaction time:	19 seconds	
SCORE → W vF	Art		Z1
blotches on a blot folded in half			
INQUIRY: just the way they looked			

3. Card I	Reaction time:	39 seconds	
SCORE → W F	A	(P)Psv	Z1
bat			
INQUIRY: same thing, wing			

4. Card I	Reaction time:	9 seconds	
SCORE → W vF	u Art		
somebody sat in some ink on something			
INQUIRY: it just looks look like the mark that would be left if you sat on some paint			

5. Card II   Reaction time: 333 seconds
   SCORE → D F   Ad
   butterfly
   INQUIRY: tail end, long tail sticking out, something doesn't make sense
   LOCATION: Bottom central detail

6. Card II   Reaction time: 201 seconds
   SCORE → Dd F   Ls   Per
   Positions, church steeple
   INQUIRY: I've seen church steeples shaped like that
   LOCATION: midcenter

7. Card III   Reaction time: 57 seconds
   SCORE → D M   a (2)(H).Sx   P   Z3
   two ladies beating the drums; the titties are together, though.
   Two ladies or two men, I don't know
   INQUIRY: Heads, breasts, kettle; mixing ups some kind of potion.
   Two witches.

8. Card III   Reaction time: 12 seconds
   SCORE → D F   Cg
   Bow tie
   INQUIRY: looks like one

9. Card III   Reaction time: 5 seconds
   SCORE → D vF   u (2)An   Incom.Dv   Z3
   Two hearts joined together
   INQUIRY: shape
   I don't understand why you are showing me such pictures

10. Card IV   Reaction time: 4 seconds
    SCORE → W vm   pu Hh   Z2
    A bell
    INQUIRY: The Liberty Bell. Shape, little hanger in the middle. It's hung by here

11. Card IV   Reaction time: 61 seconds
    Score → W M.FD   p– H.Sx   P   Z2
    A guy laying on his back with his feet up and his dick between his legs
    INQUIRY: laughs
    Laying on his back? you are looking at his feet first

12. Card V   Reaction time: 5 seconds
    SCORE → W F   A   P
    A bat
    INQUIRY: wings

13. Card VI   Reaction time: 19 seconds
    SCORE → D FC'   — Hh.Bl   (P)Contam   Z2.5
    A blood stain on a fur rug, a bear skin rug
    INQUIRY: the whole thing could be a blood stain
    rug? the way it looks
    Bl? this spot here (darker center)
    LOCATION: bottom D

14. Card VI   Reaction time: 24 seconds
    SCORE → Reject
    Blood stain
    INQUIRY: part of #13, does not want by itself.

15. Card VII   Reaction time: 4 seconds
    SCORE → W vF   u Art   Z2.5
    Black ink spot
    INQUIRY: just the way it looks

16. Card VIII   Reaction time: 15 seconds
    SCORE → D F   (2)A   P
    Pair of lions, like the Lowenbrau bottle with the two lions on it
    INQUIRY: two cats on side

17. Card IX   Reaction time: 29 seconds
    SCORE → DW —m   — Fi
    A solar flare
    INQUIRY: Shooting out. It can reach way over here too (expanding the gray D on top of W)

18. Card X   Reaction time: 4 seconds
    SCORE → DW —CF   — An.Sx   DV
    Picture of the ovaries and stuff like that
    INQUIRY: Two blue spots reminds me of a picture I drew in grammar school. I saw three
    levels, too.
    ? (can't explain)
    LOC? wants W

19. Card X   Reaction time: 5 seconds
    SCORE → D F   Ls
    Could be the Eiffel Tower, too.
    INQUIRY: the shape

Rorschach Score Sequence

Card	No.	Time	Scoring					
I	1	46	W	F		A	P	Z1
I	2	19	W	vF		Art		Z1
I	3	39	W	F		A	(P)Psv	Z1
I	4	9	W	vF	u	Art		
II	5	333	D	F		Ad		
II	6	201	Dd	F		Ls	Per	

Rorschach Score Sequence

Card	No.	Time	Scoring					
III	7	57	D	M	a (2)(H).Sx	P		Z3
III	8	12	D	F	Cg			
III	9	5	D	vF	u (2)An		Incom.Dv	Z3
IV	10	4	W	vm	pu Hh			Z2
IV	11	61	W	M.Fd	p− H.Sx	P		Z2
V	12	5	W	vF	A	P		
VI	13	19	D	FC′	− Hh.Bl	(P)Contam		Z2.5
VI	14	24	Reject					
VII	15	4	W	vF	u Art			Z2.5
VIII	16	15	D	F	(2)A	P		
IX	17	29	DW	−m	− Fi			
X	18	4	DW	−CF	− An.Sx	DV		
X	19	5	D	F	Ls			

Rorschach Structural Summary

Global	n	%	Location	n	%	Determinants	n	%	Contents	n	%	Quality	n	%
R	18		W	8	44	M	2	11	CONT	10	OF ALL			
Rejects	1		D	7	39	FM	0	0			+		0	0
			Dd	1	6	m	2	11	H	1	5	o	10	56
P	5	28	DW	2	11	FT	0	0	(H)	1	5	u	4	22
(P)	2	11	S	0	0	TF	0	0	Hd	0	0	−	4	22
						T	0	0	(Hd)	0	0			
(2)	3	17				FY	0	0	A	4	18	OF F		
Fr	0	0	POSITION			YF	0	0	(A)	0	0	+	0	0
rF	0	0	^	18	100	Y	0	0	Ad	1	5	o	9	75
3 r+ (2)		17	<	0	0	FV	0	0	(Ad)	0	0	u	3	25
			>	0	0	VF	0	0	Ab	0	0	−	0	0
RT Ach	23		V	0	0	V	0	0	Al	0	0			
RT Ch	74					FC′	1	5	An	2	9			
						C′F	0	0	Art	3	14	DV	1	6
AFR		29	DEV QUAL			C′	0	0	Ay	0	0	Incom	1	6
			+	0	0	FC	0	0	Bl	1	5	Fabcom	0	0
			o	11	61	CF	1	5	Bt	0	0	Alog	0	0
			v	5	28	C	0	0	Cg	1	5	Contam	1	6
Zf	10		−	2	11	Cn	0	0	Cl	0	0	Ag	0	0
ZSum	18					FD	0	0	Cp	0	0	Cp	0	0
						F	12	63	Fi	1	5	Mor	0	0
									Fd	0	0	Per	1	6
						Blends	1		Ge	0	0	Psv	1	6
									Hh	2	9	DR	0	0
			RATIOS			RATIOS			LS	2	9			
			W	8		a	1	6	Na	0	0			
			M	2		p	2	11	Sc	0	0			
									Sx	3	14			
			W	8		M	2		Vo	0	0			
			D	7		wtd C	1.0		Xy	0	0			
						M+wtd C	3							
						FM+m	2							
						Y+T+V+C′	1		RATIOS					
									H+HD	2				
						ΣFMmYTVC′	3		A+AD	5				
						FC	0		H+A	6				
						CF+C	1		HD+AD	1				
									A%		23			

TAT Stories

1. A little boy sitting in a dark room wishing he had a violin and according to the picture he has got his violin and now he has to learn to read the music. I don't see no future there.

2. I see a girl going to school and she is watching her parents fixing the yard or planting seeds for next summer. (Oh, there are two ladies.) One is going to school and one is watching the man work. The horse and the man be serious. I hope he will get good crops.

3BM. It looks like someone is praying, or either hurting, in pain, or they are looking for their keys and they are right by their foot and they don't see them. The lady is sitting in an awkward position hoping that she can find her keys and they are right next to her feet and she hasn't found them yet, but according to this picture she should see them.

4. I see a man and a woman standing outside of a doorway or a window. He is fixing to go get in some trouble he ain't got no business getting into and she is saying, "Baby, will you please wait and think about it?" He just froze there so he didn't go.

6BM. I don't see nothing in this one, just a lady and a man. The woman is looking out of the window, the guy is grabbing his hat or something, I don't know. It looks like half of this part was cut out. Maybe somebody died and they are both sad about it.

7BM. Father and son, the son is trying to do what he wants to do and the father is saying, "Look, would you listen? I got the gray hair here." Hopefully the guy will get wise.

8BM. It looks like somebody got shot and the doctor is trying to remove the bullet and the woman is walking away with the gun. I wouldn't come near. I don't know, he might die.

10. A mother and daughter—I couldn't tell you what is happening in this picture. It looks like they are knee-deep in trouble for sure. It looks like she is whispering in her ear. I don't know what will happen.

12M. I can't tell if her eyes are open or closed. Are her eyes open or closed? Someone is laying on the bed and somebody came and knelt beside them in the bed, maybe he is trying to hypnotize her and showing his right hand. I don't know. The outcome of that is she should wake up.

13MF. Well, it looks like she did not wake up. He just killed her. Now he is upset at what he has done. The outcome of that is straight to jail. Do not pass go. You now collect $200.

16. Spades. Those who went bowling before would have wished they hadn't. This reminds me of space because the paper is blank, or a full moon because the paper is blank, that is about it.

17BM. It looks like somebody is climbing a rope. They are pulling on a serious bill or coming down a rope and looking somewhere else as they do it. It is a fireman coming down a rope and he is trying to get to the squad before it becomes more than just a one alarm fire, so he is in a hurry. He forgot his clothes though. He was in a real hurry.

18BM. This I couldn't tell you nothing about. It looks like a fat man with a nice jacket. He has got hands all in his back. Somebody is grabbing him from behind. It looks like he is trying to get shook up real good there. No maybe he is going to jail. He is handcuffed and the cops got their hands on him taking him away.

Affective Disorder With a Dependent Personality Style

Patient History

Mr. Paul D'Angelo is a 32-year-old White man who was admitted into the psychiatric ward after becoming paranoid at his place of employment. The patient explained that when a wallet belonging to another employee was stolen, a supervisor threatened to fire all of the employees unless the wallet was found. Even though he had nothing to do with the incident, he felt the need to openly deny that he had done anything wrong and thought that others were talking about him behind his back. He became tense and somewhat agitated and was not able to sleep well. He became insecure and indecisive and believed that he was unable to cope with the demands of his daily life.

On admission into the unit, Mr. D'Angelo was described as guarded and agitated and was said to be preoccupied with his genitals. Flight of ideas and ideas of reference were also noted. He was diagnosed as having an agitated depression. At the time of the testing, he was on Navane (5 mg 3 times/day) and Norpramine (150 mg every evening).

Psychiatric History

Mr. D'Angelo was seen by a physician on consultation during a medical hospitalization in August 1986. At the time he complained of labile emotions and mood swings that had been bothering him for several months. The physician felt that the patient was depressed and prescribed antidepressants. Mr. D'Angelo received follow-up treatment from another physician and was continued on antidepressants. According to the patient, his emotional difficulties started after his wife and his mother quarreled; he had taken his wife's side and had not been on speaking terms with his mother prior to this admission.

Mr. D'Angelo admitted having a problem with excessive drinking in the past but has only had an occasional beer since he was started on medication last August.

The family history is remarkable in that Mr. D'Angelo's father reportedly has a bipolar affective disorder and is maintained on Thorazine. His mother and three of his brothers were alleged to be alcoholics.

Medical History

Patient's medical history is unremarkable except for a bout of pneumonia that required hospitalization when he was 15 years old. A medical evaluation by a physician at a hospital last August led to negative findings. A CT scan of the brain taken during this latest admission was also within normal limits.

Family History

Mr. D'Angelo was born and raised in the Los Angeles area in a Catholic Italian family. He is the youngest of five siblings. His father is a 65-year-old man who was in and out of hospitals all of his life. He was a building inspector who worked for the city until 4 years ago. The father was characterized as a mild-mannered individual who was always "weak," so his mother was very much the head of the family. One of the issues that led to the falling out with his mother was Mr. D'Angelo's disapproval of her decision to put his father in a nursing home. In spite of the patient's feeling that the nursing home is the best place for his father, he resents that the decision was made only on the basis that the mother was "tired of him." The father has been in the nursing home since last July.

Mr. D'Angelo's mother is a 57-year-old woman. Although she used to work as a clerk at a community center, she is not employed at this time. The patient talked about her as having been a "good mother" but someone who drank six beers every day. He characterized all family members as inclined to ignore any problem or issue that may be bothering them. It was apparently this characteristic that led to the fight between his wife and his mother a year ago: His wife reportedly confronted her mother-in-law about the fact that many of the siblings were drinking excessively, an issue that the mother allegedly did not want to face.

The oldest of the siblings is Tom (age 39). Tom is an alcoholic and was also an inpatient in the psychiatric ward at the same hospital where the patient is now; Tom was in detox at the time of the testing. A plumber, Tom has had difficulty finding work during the last 5 years, perhaps as a result of his alcohol abuse, but he is gainfully employed at this time. Tom is married and has two children. As an adult, the patient has been closer to Tom than to any of the other brothers. The frequency of their contacts, however, varies considerably, depending on whether their wives are getting along well.

The second brother is 38-year-old Danny. Danny lives in Texas with his new wife. He is an epileptic on anticonvulsant medication and is also thought to be an alcoholic. Danny is a driver for a major beer company.

Frank (age 37) is disabled with a left-sided partial hemiparesis. He was hurt when he dove into the shallow end of a swimming pool. Frank has never been married and is cared for by his mother.

The brother immediately preceding the patient is Tony, a 35-year-old handyman who lives in Montana. Tony is married and has two children, one of his own and one born from his wife's first marriage. One of the children has a defect in the spinal cord that caused paralysis in the lower extremities.

Mr. D'Angelo was married to his present wife 9 years ago. The wife is a 33-year-old housewife. She was characterized as a beautiful woman who is outgoing, straightforward, energetic, and thought to be very good to him.

The D'Angelos have two children. Tiffany is 7 years old and Chip is 5. Both are doing well and have presented no problems.

Educational History

Mr. D'Angelo went to a Catholic elementary school and graduated from a public high school in Los Angeles. He was an "average" student and never posed any significant difficulties in school.

Occupational History

After his high school graduation, Mr. D'Angelo went to work for a car dealership. He was first employed unloading new cars but was able to learn the repair work and is now an assistant mechanic. He has worked for this employer for 12 years, is very satisfied with his present position, and feels that his supervisor has been happy with his work.

Mental Status Examination

At the time of the evaluation, the patient was alert, oriented, verbal, and coherent. His speech and language functions were intact. The other intellectual functions examined—including memory, calculations, figure reproductions, mental control, and abstractions, were also within normal limits. His thought processes were orderly and effective. Thought content was unremarkable. The presence of paranoid delusions, ideas of reference, and preoccupation with his genitals were noted on admission. His affective responses were always appropriate. Mood was within normal limits and demonstrated a good range of emotions, but this apparently constituted a change from his previous dysphoria. There was no suicidal or homicidal ideation. Psychomotor activity was within normal limits by the time of the testing, although the patient reportedly was in an agitated state originally. Mr. D'Angelo was anxious, asked how he was doing on several occasions, and showed a fine hand tremor when he was required to draw figures. He associated this tremor with his being tense and claimed that he did not have it the rest of the time. He was friendly and cooperative and posed no problems during the test administration.

Discussion

Mr. D'Angelo obtained scores on the MCMI suggesting that he has a dependent personality style. Similar individuals assume that they are not very capable of taking care of themselves and must find someone who is benevolent and dependable and would support them, at least emotionally. They tend to form strong attachments to people who would then take a dominant role in decision making. They are followers rather than leaders and are often submissive in interpersonal affairs, shying away from highly competitive situations. Concerned with losing friends, they hide their feelings, especially when such feelings are aggressive or objectionable. These are unconceited people who try to be as congenial as possible to the people around them. Mr. D'Angelo is probably well liked but may be occasionally considered wishy-washy because he never takes a strong position on controversial issues. Similar individuals could be criticized for their inclination to be submissive, their lack of self-esteem, and their constant looking outside of themselves for help.

 Mr. D'Angelo has been able to establish himself well, both socially and occupationally, and leads a fairly independent life. As a result, his personality style cannot be considered dysfunctional or to constitute a personality disorder. Nevertheless, the dependent personality style can explain the kind of stress that Mr. D'Angelo has been under. It seemed that his mother was the all-powerful figure in his childhood home, the "stronghold" of the family on whom the patient had learned to depend. Although his loyalties have shifted to his wife and his acquired family, it seems that he still needs the support of his mother in order to feel comfortable. Thus, when the quarrel ensued between his mother and wife, Mr. D'Angelo's insecurities increased and he started having emotional problems. It is interesting that the issues at work revolved around the possible loss of support from another authority figure, a supervisor, and that the patient strongly wished to reassure everyone of his innocence so that there would be no chance that this support would also be compromised.

At the time of testing, Mr. D'Angelo was not actively psychotic. Nevertheless, several of his Rorschach responses showed faulty reality contact. Although the number of such responses was not extreme, it was significantly higher than the normal range. In addition, the patient often saw "eyes" as an important part of his responses and was reminded of a "mask" on many of the cards, both of which are thought to be associated with paranoid defenses.

The presence of anxiety and depression was repeatedly seen throughout the testing. To mention just one indication, most of the TAT stories revolved around negative or depressive events such as a car accident, a man who is about to leave his wife, a son who leaves his mother, a dying father, a man who is emotionally distressed after having sex with a prostitute, and so on. Consistent with the preoccupation with his genitals that he demonstrated at the beginning of the hospitalization, his MCMI scores also indicated the presence of somatic concerns. Finally, there were indications that Mr. D'Angelo abuses alcohol as a way of defending against his anxieties.

On the positive side, there were no signs of cognitive deficits in the mental status examination. The impression was that Mr. D'Angelo had average intellectual capacities. The fact that he has also achieved all of the major developmental milestones of the past is impressive. Thus, Mr. D'Angelo has established himself independently, has a good family and a good job, and has no great conflicts in his life. Once he has been able to reconstitute the sources of support that he needs, he may be able to return to his premorbid level of functioning.

Diagnostic Assignments and Recommendations

     I   Major depression with psychotic features (296.34)

    II Dependent personality style with no personality disorder

  III No known medical problem contributing

Continued evaluation for the use of psychotropic medications to control the symptomatology seems indicated. In addition, Mr. D'Angelo may benefit from psychotherapy. Given his personality style, he will obtain support from a therapeutic relationship that is protective and guiding in a parentallike manner.

Test Results

The Millon Clinical Multiaxial Inventory-II

Personality Style Scales		BRS	Clinical Symptom Scales		BRS
1–Schizoid	=	51	A–Anxiety	=	84
2–Avoidant	=	60	H–Somatic Preoccupations	=	92
3–Dependent	=	80	N–Hypomania	=	4
4–Histrionic	=	65	D–Dysthymia	=	84
5–Narcissistic	=	28	B–Alcohol Abuse	=	70
6A–Antisocial	=	18	T–Drug Abuse	=	49
7–Compulsive	=	64	SS–Psychotic Thinking	=	58
8A–Negativistic	=	24	CC–Psychotic Depression	=	47
			PP–Psychotic Delusion	=	9

Severe Personality Scales		BRS
6B–Aggressive	=	0
8B–Self-Defeating	=	61
S–Schizotypal	=	72
C–Borderline	=	78
P–Paraphrenic	=	22

Modifier Indices		BRS
X–Disclosure	=	60
Y–Desirability	=	65
Z–Debasement	=	26
V–Validity	=	0

Rorschach Protocol

1. Card I   Reaction time: 0
SCORE → W F   A   P   Z1
Wasp or bee
INQUIRY: Tail, wide wing span

2. Card I   Reaction time: 22 seconds
SCORE → W S FT   (Ad)   Z1
Mask
INQUIRY: Of a wolf, outline, two sets of eyes, whiskers (?) shaggy outline; face of a wolf

3. Card I   Reaction time: 7 seconds
SCORE → W m   a Hh
Glider plane
INQUIRY: Flying over. They build them in such weird shapes these days

4. Card II   Reaction time: 4 seconds
SCORE → D FC   (2)H   P   Z3
Two women, old
INQUIRY: In black dress and red faces. They could be two chickens too with the beaks

5. Card II   Reaction time: 3 seconds
SCORE → D SvFC'   Hh   Z4.5
A night light in the blackness.
INQUIRY: Imprint of a lampshade in the middle of the dark
LOCATION: black and white center

6. Card II   Reaction time: 10 seconds
     SCORE → D FM   a (2)(A)   (P)   Z3
     Two chickens touching hands
     INQUIRY: Looking at each other, from a cartoon

7. Card III   Reaction time: 10 seconds
     SCORE → D–F   – Ad   Z3
     Two people looking at each other
     INQUIRY: The looks. Some kind of animal face or something
     At a distance; nostrils, eyes
     LOCATION: the usual P including orange center D. Patient is only seeing two faces

8. Card III   Reaction time: 3 seconds
     SCORE → D M   a H   P
     Two women
     INQUIRY: the way they look

9. Card III   Reaction time: 4 seconds
     SCORE → D vF   u (Ad)
     Two eyes in a mask
     INQUIRY: Mask of a wasp or something, face. It's a very ugly creature.
     Head of a wasp

10. Card IV   Reaction time: 15 seconds
     SCORE → W F   (A)   P
     A giant monster with a long tail hanging down the middle. Two big feet, two small claws
     INQUIRY: Head, pinhead

11. Card V   Reaction time: 5 seconds
     Score → W FC'   A   Incom   Z1
     Butterfly with a woman's face, maybe
     INQUIRY: In the fine blackness you can see two eyes and a nose

12. Card V   Reaction time: 1 second
     SCORE → D M   p (2)Hd   Z2.5
     Two heads looking down
     INQUIRY: Forehead, nose and mouth

13. Card VI   Reaction time: 9 seconds
     SCORE → W vm   (A)   Z2.5
     A cat flattened out on the pavement after it got run down by a steamroller

14. Card VI   Reaction time: 5 seconds
     SCORE → D M   (2)Hd.Cg   Z6
     Two opposing faces looking out
     INQUIRY: King with a crown, long beard, nose

15. Card VI   Reaction time: 4 seconds
      SCORE → W vF   u An   Z2.5
      The inside anatomy of something
      INQUIRY: The amoebas or something, like that in somebody's body

16. Card VII   Reaction time: 4 seconds
      SCORE → D M   p (2)Hd   P   Z3
      Two women looking at each other
      INQUIRY: Faces, hats

17. Card VII   Reaction time: 4 seconds
      SCORE → D FM   p (2)(Ad)   Z3
      Two pigs looking away from each other
      INQUIRY: Round nose, something you might see in a cartoon, eye

18. Card VII   Reaction time: 2 seconds
      SCORE → D FM   p A   Z1
      Upside down butterfly
      INQUIRY: Body, wings spread out
      LOCATION: bm D

19. Card VIII   Reaction time: 6 seconds
      SCORE → DdS-F   – (Ad)   Z4
      Mask of a wasp or something
      INQUIRY: I see a face in here somewhere
      LOCATION: circular area taking the center part of both of the top Ds (green & blue)

20. Card VIII   Reaction time: 7 seconds
      SCORE → D -F   – Hd.Cg   Z3
      Face of a man with a hat
      LOCATION: top & center D (green and blue)

21. Card VIII   Reaction time: 2 seconds
      SCORE → Dd m   p (2)Hd
      Maybe a couple of legs fused together
      INQUIRY: Couldn't find at first
      LOCATION: tiny projections at center bm of blue D

22. Card IX   Reaction time: 12 seconds
      SCORE → W –F   – Ad   V Z5.5
      Some kind of insect's face, upside down
      INQUIRY: Eyes, stinger, nose

23. Card IX   Reaction time: 20 seconds
      SCORE → Dd vF   u Na
      Map of river with tributaries
      INQUIRY: Lake, river and tributaries
      LOCATION: inside darker edge of orange D

24. Card IX   Reaction time: 5 seconds
    SCORE → Dd M   p (2)Hd   Z4.5
    Two faces looking away on the green part
    INQUIRY: Nose, eyes
    LOCATION: outside edge

25. Card X   Reaction time: 7 seconds
    SCORE → D S+F   + Hd
    Two faces, one on bottom, one on top
    INQUIRY: Eyes (yellow), nose (green center), mustache (green)
    LOCATION: white space with defined by pink in bm

26. Card X   Reaction time: 3 seconds
    SCORE → D FM   ao (2)A   P   Z4.5
    Two crabs meeting at top
    INQUIRY: claws (green)
    LOCATION: blue D

27. Card X   Reaction time: 13 seconds
    SCORE → DdS − F   − (Hd)   Z6
    Face
    INQUIRY: eyes (tiny circular s defined by blue D in center and pink D)
    LOCATION: circular area bound by the pink D, the wishbone on top & the green D on bm

28. Card X   Reaction time: 3 seconds
    SCORE → Dd F   Hd
    Three sets of eyes
    LOCATION: tiny details in three different places of the blot

29. Card X   Reaction time: 11 seconds
    SCORE → D FM   a (2)A   Z4
    Butting heads here (top gray)
    INQUIRY: like 2 animals butting heads

Rorschach Score Sequence

Card	No.	Time (in seconds)	Scoring				
I	1	0	W F		A		Z1
I	2	22	W FT		(Ad)	P	Z1
I	3	7	W m	a	Hh		
II	4	4	D FC		(2)H		Z3
II	5	3	D SvFC'		Hh	P	Z4.5
II	6	10	D FM	a	(2)(A)		Z3
III	7	10	D −F	−	Ad	(P)	Z3
III	8	3	D M	a	H		
III	9	4	D vF	u	(Ad)	P	
IV	10	15	W F		(A)		
V	11	5	W FC'		A	P	Z1
V	12	1	D M	p	(2)Hd	Incom	Z2.5
VI	13	9	W vm		(A)		Z2.5

Rorschach Score Sequence

Card	No.	Time (in seconds)	Scoring				
VI	14	5	D M	(2)Hd.Cg			Z6
VI	15	41	W vF	u An			Z2.5
VII	16	4	D M	p (2)Hd	P		Z3
VII	17	4	D FM	p (2)(Ad)			Z3
VII	18	2	D FM	p A			Z1
VIII	19	6	DdS–F	– (Ad)			Z4
VIII	20	7	D –F	– Hd.Cg			Z3
VIII	21	2	Dd m	p (2)Hd			
IX	22	12	W –F	– Ad		V	Z5.5
IX	23	20	Dd vF	u Na			
IX	24	5	Dd M	p (2)Hd			Z4.5
X	25	7	D S+F	+ Hd			
X	26	3	D FM	ao (2)A	P		Z4.5
X	27	13	DdS–F	– (Hd)			Z6
X	28	3	Dd F	Hd			
X	29	11	D FM	a (2)A			Z4

Rorschach Structural Summary

Global	n	%	Location	n	%	Determinants	n	%	Contents	n	%	Quality	n	%
R	29		W	8	28	M	5	17	CONT	6		OF ALL		
Rejects	0		D	15	52	FM	5	17				+	1	3
			Dd	6	21	m	3	10	H	2	6	o	20	69
P	6	21	DW	0	0	FT	1	3	(H)	0	0	u	3	10
(P)	1	3	S	5	17	TF	0	0	Hd	8	26	–	5	17
						T	0	0	(Hd)	0	0	OF F		
(2)	10	34				FY	0	0	A	6	19			
Fr	0	0	POSITION			YF	0	0	(A)	3	10	+	1	8
rF	0	0	^	28	97	Y	0	0	Ad	2	6	o	3	25
3 r+ (2)		34	<	0	0	FV	0	0	(Ad)	4	13	u	3	25
			>	0	0	VF	0	0	Ab	0	0	–	5	42
RT Ach	10		V	1	3	V	0	0	Al	0	0			
RT Ch	7					FC'	2	7	An	1	3			
						C'F	0	0	Art	0	0	DV	0	0
AFR		61	DEV QUAL			C'	0	0	Ay	0	0	Incom	1	3
			+	1	3	FC	1	3	Bl	0	0	Fabcom	0	0
			o	18	62	CF	0	0	Bt	0	0	Alog	0	0
			v	5	17	C	0	0	Cg	2	6	Contam	0	0
Zf	22		–	5	17	Cn	0	0	Cl	0	0	Ag	0	0
ZSum	72					FD	0	0	Ex	0	0	Cp	0	0
						F	12	41	Fi	0	0	Mor	0	0
									Fd	0	0	Per	0	0
						Blends	0		Ge	0	0	Psv	0	0
									Hh	2	6	DR	0	0
			RATIOS			RATIOS			Ls	0	0			
			W	8		a	5	17	Na	1	3			
			M	5		p	6	21	Sc	0	0			
									Sx	0	0			
			W	8		M	5		Vo	0	0			
			D	15		wtd C	5		Xy	0	0			
						M+wtd C	6							
						FM+m	8							

Rorschach Structural Summary

Global		Location		Determinants		Contents		Quality	
n	%	n	%	n	%	n	%	n	%
				Y+T+V+C'	3	RATIOS			
						H+HD	10		
				ΣFMmYTVC'	11	A+AD	15		
				FC	1	H+A	11		
				CF+C	0	HD+AD	14		
						A%		48	

TAT Stories

1. This is a little boy looking at a violin. He looks kind of sad. The violin could be broken or something. It looks like before he wanted to play the violin and now that he has got the violin he doesn't know if he can play it. In the future he will be a great violinist.

2. This looks like a guy plowing the field getting ready to plow some corn with the fork. It could have been the winter snows. There is a lady looking on with a book. It looks like it is going to be a good harvest in the future, although he is doing it by hand. It is like winter and now it is spring where the guy is plowing the field and in the fall it will be a good harvest.

3BM. This is a picture of a man or woman sobbing over something. It looks like I see a set of keys lying on the floor. Maybe she was in a car accident or something and she is crying about what happened, but in the future she will learn not to drink and drive. Maybe she was drunk when she was driving, caused an accident. She will quit drinking from the picture.

4. It kind of reminds me of a [sic] old Navy World War II movie star and actress. They are all talking on the porch, maybe before they were in dancing or something. It looks like maybe she said something to make him mad and he is getting ready to leave. He will be leaving her. She is trying to hold him back. It looks like she said something to make him mad and he is leaving, either that or he is going off to war or something.

Substance Abuse in a Borderline Personality Disorder

Patient History

Mrs. Janet Olsen is a 35-year-old woman who was admitted into a chemical abuse program for detoxification and treatment. The patient stated that in addition to her drinking, she had been feeling lonely and isolated and had been having crying spells. She felt abused by the other family members and feared that she "couldn't" trust anybody. Finally, she felt that she was "falling apart" and was "losing control" of her life.

Among the recent stressors that may be associated with the presenting complaints is that the family had moved into their present area recently and the patient felt that she did not have any good friends. Mrs. Olsen claimed to have heard rumors that her husband was having an affair and explained that her husband is an amphetamine abuser. She has had trouble controlling her 15-year-old daughter and is concerned about facial scars that her 13-year-old daughter received in an accident. The family has financial difficulties and is still involved in a legal suit in order to recover their losses from the accident in which the daughter was injured.

The course of treatment during the present admission was marked by obvious symptoms of alcohol withdrawal during the first few days, including hand tremors. The present evaluation was requested in order to learn more about the patient, particularly whether she was suffering from an affective disorder.

Psychiatric History

This is the second psychiatric admission for Mrs. Olsen. The first admission took place when she was 20 years old and her first husband "sent [her] away." At the time, she spent 2 weeks at a hospital in Nashville, Tennessee. The patient recalled that in 1973, she attempted to kill herself and her children by turning on the gas but then changed her mind and received no treatment for her depression. Mrs. Olsen has been drinking continuously for the last 8 months, during which time she has had amnesic episodes and two blackouts. There is also weekly abuse of marijuana and cocaine. Prior to admission she had been on Elavil and Xanax, which were given to her last April by a general practitioner at a university hospital.

Her family history is remarkable in that her mother suffered from a psychiatric disorder and was in an institution for 6 years. The father was an abusive alcoholic, a problem that one of her brothers and one of her sisters also have. In addition, the same sister was said to have emotional problems and to be under psychiatric care.

Medical History

Mrs. Olsen has never had any major medical problems or serious accidents. She had a dilation and cutterage procedure about 8 years ago.

Family History

Mrs. Olsen was born and raised in Nashville. Both of her parents reportedly abused the children physically and the patient explained that she was sexually abused by her father and two of her brothers. She remembers her childhood as being quite difficult and traumatic. Her father, who was referred to as a "jerk" and was an alcoholic, died of liver failure when the patient was an adult. The mother had to be psychiatrically hospitalized for 6 years when Mrs. Olsen's father went into the military and was said to have lived a "rough" life. The mother lives with the youngest sister in Nashville and is apparently dying of complications of her diabetes.

Mrs. Olsen was the fourth of five children. Her older sister died of diabetes before she was 40 years old. The rest of the siblings are still living in Nashville. Her older brother, Joe, is in his 40s and works as a plumber. He is married to a blind and physically challenged woman. David (aged 37) is an alcoholic who abuses his wife, according to the patient. Mrs. Olsen came next and was followed by Nancy (aged 27), who is an alcoholic with additional emotional problems. Nancy has led a tragic life in that her boyfriend killed her children when "they would not stop wetting the bed."

Mrs. Olsen moved to Kentucky 14 years ago while she was still married to her first husband. She married him when she was 18 in order to get out of the house. She claimed that he abused her physically. Her first hospitalization took place, however, when they were not getting along and he sent her back to Tennessee. The couple were apart for perhaps a year, during which time Mrs. Olsen had a boyfriend and lived in Virginia. She eventually went back to her first husband, but the marriage ended in divorce 9 years ago.

After separating from her first husband, Mrs. Olsen went to live with her present husband and his girlfriend. It was at that time that she tried to kill herself and the children. Three years ago, however, after the girlfriend left, Mrs. Olsen married her present husband.

Her husband, Kevin, is a 35-year-old appliance salesman. He is an outgoing man who seems to love attention in public but is quiet at home. Her husband is reportedly bothered by his wife's inability to "carry on an intelligent conversation," something that suggests to her that she is not the "right" woman for him and makes her feel guilty. She, in fact, thinks about going back to school as a way to remedy this situation. The husband is addicted to amphetamines and recently changed jobs.

Mrs. Olsen has a 15-year-old daughter by her first husband. Eleanor was described as "confused" and occasionally suicidal. Recently, she was brought into a hospital emergency room alleging that she had been raped. There have been conflicts between the patient and Eleanor because Mrs. Olsen has disapproved of Eleanor's friends. Other problems involving Eleanor have been poor school performance and her being injured when she was struck by a car and having to be hospitalized on two occasions as a result.

The second of Mrs. Olsen's daughters, Cathy, was born from the relationship the patient had with a boyfriend during her first marriage. Cathy is 14 years old and has been a poor student. She was hurt 4 months ago when a store's plate glass window shattered as she was standing next to it waiting for a bus. Cathy was left with facial scars. The family hopes to get plastic surgery for Cathy with money they hope to win in a lawsuit against the store owner.

Angela (aged 11) was fathered by the patient's first husband during the period they were back together. Angela is a quiet child who is involved in church activities and is doing better in school than her siblings. However, Angela has experienced emotional problems, perhaps as a result of her feeling responsible for her parents' divorce. She has seen a psychiatrist at a mental health center in order to try to work through this problem.

Finally, Mrs. Olsen has a fourth child by her present husband. Donald was born before the couple was married and has another last name. He has had a difficult time in school and is currently in special education. In addition, he has allergies and has to take a medication that tends to slow him down.

Educational and Occupational History

Mrs. Olsen finished eighth grade before dropping out of school. She explained that she "failed a few years" and has been told that she reads at a fourth-grade level. The patient has been a housewife most recently but was employed as a file clerk intermittently throughout her adult life.

Mental Status Examination

At the time of the evaluation, the patient was alert, oriented, verbal, and coherent. Her speech and language functions were intact. Most of the other intellectual functions examined showed mild deficits. In terms of the memory, for instance, the patient could only remember one out of three words after a 5-minute delay. She had trouble doing simple subtractions, even when she was allowed to use paper and pencil; the patient was never able to do a simple multiplication task accurately. She had trouble thinking of different meanings for the same word and proverb interpretations were concrete. The figure reproductions were within normal limits. Her thought processes were disordered, confused, and circumstantial. Mrs. Olsen often blocked on information in that she would not offer information unless asked directly. At times, she talked as if she took for granted that the examiner knew something that she had not yet disclosed. There were also several instances in which she stated that she did not want to talk about something or seemed uncomfortable and asked questions about who would have access to that information. No delusions or hallucinations seemed present. Her affective responses were always appropriate. Mood was within normal limits and she demonstrated a good range of emotions. There was no suicidal or homicidal ideation. The psychomotor activity and anxiety levels were within normal limits. The patient was friendly and cooperative.

Discussion

According to the responses that Mrs. Olsen gave on the MCMI, the central traits in her personality makeup are introversiveness, a fear of rejection, feelings of inadequacy, and a tendency toward mood changes. The scores suggested that she wants very much to be liked by others but expects that her social approaches will be rejected. As a result, Mrs. Olsen is likely to be apprehensive when relating to others. Probably perceived as a nervous individual, she tends to feel uncomfortable in social situations. This type of person is often caught in a bind: On one hand, she would like very much to interact with others and to be liked and appreciated. On the other hand, she tends to avoid social situations in order to avoid the anxiety that these situations evoke.

The psychic conflict may be seen behaviorally in a vacillation or ambivalence that Mrs. Olsen may have. At times, she may be more open and friendly and at other times she will seem aloof, distant, abrasive, moody, or disinterested in others. Occasionally, similar individuals may also project the feelings created by the frustration engendered by their basic conflict. In such instances, they may be even more distrusting or become hostile and prone to blame others for their failures. This pattern, however, will be short-lived and eventually the individuals come back to feeling inadequate and blaming themselves for everything that happens to them.

Mrs. Olsen is probably a dependent and cooperative individual. People with similar personality profiles usually underestimate themselves: When they compare themselves with others, they feel that they are less capable or less worthy. They tend to be unassertive and seldom demand anything from others, although they can be controlling in a dependent, submissive manner. Similar individuals seem more comfortable when they can rely on others to make the important decisions and offer them guidance and protection. Mrs. Olsen's feelings of inadequacy are consistent with the fear of rejection because she seemed likely to assume that people will develop uncomplimentary views about her and would not want to relate to her.

All of the indications were that Mrs. Olsen's personality had developed only to a borderline level of functioning. The history, for instance, showed the affective instability, the tendency toward sexual acting-out, the suicide attempts, and the problems with her self-image that are hallmarks of this disorder according to the *DSM–III*. The clinical picture would even meet previous definitions of the borderline because significant problems with her thought processes were found.

The testing was most informative because it offered a rare glimpse of the dynamics that were possibly connected with the borderline personality disorder. It seemed as if she did not feel appreciated by either of her parents and might have had a poor relationship with all of her siblings. Her own self-esteem was not enhanced by her school experiences either, as her intellectual abilities were low enough that she was seen as "retarded." The one area in which she probably felt valuable was sexually. Unfortunately, she was sexually abused by her father and brothers, which caused her to be sexually conflicted and confused. Ultimately, she became "ashamed" of her lack of education and potential and obtained gratification in life mainly through her ability to please men sexually. In what seemed like a replay of her childhood home situation, the picture she has of herself is negative and unrewarding.

Consistent with all of these dynamics, two themes were prevalent in the TAT stories: shame, which was often associated with a lack of education, and problems in her romantic relationships.

The shame theme started on the first TAT card, with the boy being afraid to "take the chance of trying to learn how to play the violin." It continued on with the following comments obtained on Card 2: "It is quite possible that she is ashamed of her mother. Maybe her mother is not well educated and she is getting a more proper education. Look at the difference of clothing. Look at how nice she looks and look at mama."

Although her response to Card 2 betrays a concern that her children would be ashamed of her, the most prevalent preoccupation involved her husband, as indicated in the following statements: "He just had sex with her and after he is done, he is ashamed of her and he is hiding [his face]. 'Aw, I'm ashamed of you! It's done and over! I got what I wanted!'. . . . That's [what] aggravates me about men, honestly! Because, you know, that irritates me, it really aggravates me. Everything is fine and dandy until after they have sex and then they are done with the woman. [Then] they say 'I'm ashamed of you.' They got what they wanted. So rather than deal with saying 'goodbye' they say 'I'm ashamed of you.' " Notice that the issue is often deeper than abandonment. It is not that the men leave her after they have sex (although she restates this in her response to Card 4) but that they abuse her again: It seems that her men bolster their own self-esteem by denigrating hers.

The theme of being taken advantage of in her romantic relationships was recurrent: The "husband" on Card 3GF was said to be an "alcoholic" and was "cheating" on his wife. In response to Card 4, she stated that the husband "can't even look at her face," he is a "jerk" who will "end up leaving her." Finally, it was noteworthy how she responded to Card 10, which portrays two people in a gentle embrace: "It looks like someone is hugging somebody. It looks like a father hugging his son. It sure don't look like no woman, no young girl! You know how I've seen on TV, I've also seen it here, you know how a priest leans over and kisses the forehead of a woman. Catholic people, that's what it reminds me of! It looks like they are showing caringness, you know, feelings. You know how even though you don't love that person, you may want to hug them as a friend." It was striking how far Mrs. Olsen had to remove the feeling of love before she could conceive of it: First, the exchange was not between a man and a woman; it then became a feeling shared only between people different from herself ("Catholic people"); and finally, it became a hug between "friends," devoid of much meaning.

The patient's low self-esteem, her shame, probably dates back to a childhood sense of deprivation as suggested in the excerpt that follows: "It reminds me of me. But I never had any dolls. I never had nice clothes either! You know what they used to say about me, my sisters and brothers? Because I was quiet and shy and I wasn't doing any good in school. They told my mother that I was retarded, deformed in the mind. It wasn't that. It was just that it did no good to speak. It did no good. . . . The little girl is in pain. She has buried herself."

In addition to the characterological problems discussed so far, the testing generated concerns about the presence of other kinds of psychopathology. Mrs. Olsen, for example, had significant problems with her thinking processes, which was evident in the faulty reality contact on her Rorschach responses and the disturbed thought processes observed during the interview. Given that she has apparently never been delusional, these problems could be blamed on the combination of the borderline personality disorder and low intellectual abilities. However, the indications would be that she has some propensity toward thought disturbances during stress. Finally, there were also signs that she experiences periods of despondency and depression and a high level of anxiety. The presence of an alcohol abuse disorder was also indicated.

Diagnostic Assignments and Recommendations

I   Alcohol intoxication (303.00)
     Alcohol abuse disorder (305.01)
II   Borderline personality disorder (301.83)
III No known medical problems contributing

Mrs. Olsen needs to take her drinking problem seriously and to commit herself to actively participating in Alcoholics Anonymous. That her husband is also a substance abuser presents further difficulties; an effort should probably be made to have the two of them treated during the same period of time if permanent gains are to be made. The use of family therapy in order to evaluate and improve the relationships at home is also recommended.

Mrs. Olsen would also benefit from individual psychotherapy. It would be helpful if she could gradually learn to develop closeness and positive feelings for another person. An exploration of her low sense of self and her feeling of being abused by others could lead to growth-producing insights.

Test Results

The Millon Clinical Multiaxial Inventory-II

Personality Style Scales	BRS	Severe Personality Scales	BRS
1–Schizoid	= 115	6B–Aggressive	= 42
2–Avoidant	= 109	8B–Self-Defeating	= 76
3–Dependent	= 96	S–Schizotypal	= 63
4–Histrionic	= 0	C–Borderline	= 92
5–Narcissistic	= 26	P–Paraphrenic	= 60
6A–Antisocial	= 54		
7–Compulsive	= 62		
8A–Negativistic	= 87		

Clinical Symptom Scales	BRS
A–Anxiety	= 107
H–Somatic Preoccupations	= 87
N–Hypomania	= 70
D–Dysthymia	= 112
B–Alcohol Abuse	= 78
T–Drug Abuse	= 59
SS–Psychotic Thinking	= 81
CC–Psychotic Depression	= 73
PP–Psychotic Delusion	= 72

Modifier Indices	BRS
X–Disclosure	= 50
Y–Desirability	= 65
Z–Debasement	= 55
V–Validity	= 0

Rorschach Protocol

1. Card I   Reaction time: 0
   SCORE → D −F   − (2)A
   Butterfly
   INQUIRY: flares out, four butterflies
   LOCATION: top outside D and the outside D

2. Card I   Reaction time: 5 seconds
   SCORE → D −F   − (2)A
   (Second set of butterflies from response 1)

3. Card I   Reaction time: 5 seconds
   SCORE → W −F   − A   Z1
   Like the nest of bats, queen and family, getting closed in for protection or food. This one is
   saying I'm the king, I'm under control. Vampire, because I saw a vampire movie last night.
   INQUIRY: we would kill them when we were kids

4. Card II   Reaction time: 6 seconds
   SCORE → D M   a (2)H   P   Z3
   This is kind of silly. Reminds me of a cartoon, clapping hands, dancing. Could be regular
   dancers, too.

5. Card III   Reaction time: 3 seconds
   SCORE → D M   a (2)H   P   Z3
   Reminds me of waiters for some reason. It's like they are wearing tuxedos. The are holding
   their hats. It looks like they are gentlemen (laughs). It could also be dancers because of the
   heels and the different positions.

6. Card IV   Reaction time: 28 seconds
   SCORE → W F   (A)   P   Z2
   Monster, something evil. I don't like this one at all. Makes me feel fear. I do not like it.
   INQUIRY: tail

7. Card V   Reaction time: 6 seconds
   SCORE → W F   A   P   Z1
   Butterfly
   INQUIRY: wings and body

8. Card V   Reaction time: 5 seconds
SCORE → W M   p H.Cg   Z1
A dancer in Vegas wearing a costume.
INQUIRY: the dancer is here in the middle and this is the custom.
Is got the arms spread out like this

---

9. Card V   Reaction time: 18 seconds
SCORE → Dd F   Hd   Per
Reminds me of something ugly. It looks like my mother becasue she was . . . I don't want to look at it.
INQUIRY: the face. The face she used to look at me. (Talks about the last time she saw her mother).
LOCATION: face in Dd center top below the "ears"

---

10. Card VI   Reaction time: 13 seconds
SCORE → W vm   au Na   Z2.5
Earthquake, ground is cracking, ear is opening up.

---

11. Card VI   Reaction time: 4 seconds
Score → W vm   au Na.Ex   Z2.5
Could be a volcano
INQUIRY: this part over here and here is the lava coming out

---

12. Card VI   Reaction time: 6 seconds
SCORE → W vm   au Fi   Z2.5
Fourth of July with flares going up

---

13. Card VI   Reaction time: 2 seconds
SCORE → D vF   u Hd
Evil face
LOCATION: top center inner detail

---

14. Card VII   Reaction time: 7 seconds
SCORE → W vM   a (2)H.Hh   (P)   Z2.5
Oh, goodness. See saw in the park with pony tails. That's cute.
INQUIRY: two girls here

---

15. Card VII   Reaction time: 23 seconds
SCORE → D vFM   u A.Hh   Per   Z1
We have dogs. They really surprise you. Dogs: Sandy and Bandit on top of the picnic table.
INQUIRY: Picnic Table with our dogs
LOCATION: picnic table = bm D; dogs = mid D; top D not included

---

16. Card VII   Reaction time: 21 seconds
SCORE → D M   a (2)Hd   Ag   Z3
Two people staring at each other, like a contest of outstaring. Or full of anger.
LOCATION: top D, head only

17. Card VIII   Reaction time: 33 seconds
    SCORE → W vCF   u Na   Per   Z4.5
    Oh, at least this one has some color, more cheerful. Like Christmas colors. Tree with birds on
    the side of the tree. I love going into the forest preserve. I only see nice things on this.

18. Card IX   Reaction time: 11 seconds
    SCORE → W vm   au Hh   Z5.5
    Fountain, middle part shooting up. Water going in separate directions

19. Card IX   Reaction time: 4 seconds
    SCORE → D M   a (2)(H)   Z4.5
    Sword fighting up here
    INQUIRY: 2 creatures fighting with swords
    LOCATION: orange D

20. Card X   Reaction time: 13 seconds
    SCORE → D F   (2)A
    Clams or crabs, different kinds of fish
    INQUIRY: it looks like a clam with something sticking out
    LOCATION: side brown D

21. Card X   Reaction time: 2 seconds
    SCORE → D F   (2)A   Per
    Goldfish
    INQUIRY: we used to have a couple of aquariums.
    LOCATION: yellow D with red circle in midfield

22. Card X   Reaction time: 5 seconds
    SCORE → D −F   − A
    Lobster
    INQUIRY: it looks like one
    LOCATION: blue D

23. Card X   Reaction time: 17 seconds
    SCORE → D F   (2)A
    Worms. Pretty colors, a pleasure to look at, no fear
    LOCATION: green bm

Rorschach Score Sequence

Card	No.	Time	Scoring				
I	1	0	D −F	− (2)A			
I	2	5	D −F	− (2)A			
I	3	5	W −F	− A			Z1
II	4	6	D M	a (2)H	P		Z3
III	5	3	D M	a (2)H	P		Z3
IV	6	28	W F	(A)	P		Z2
V	7	6	W F	A	P		Z1
V	8	5	W M	p H.Cg			Z1
V	9	18	Dd F	Hd		Per	
VI	10	13	W vm	au Na			Z2.5

Rorschach Score Sequence

Card	No.	Time	Scoring					
VI	11	4	W vm	ɑu	Na.Ex			Z2.5
VI	12	6	W vm	ɑu	Fi			Z2.5
VI	13	2	Dd vF	u	Hd			
VII	14	7	W vM	ɑ	(2)H.Hh		(P)	Z2.5
VII	15	23	D vFM	u	A.Hh		Per	Z1
VII	16	21	D M	ɑ	(2)Hd		Ag	Z3
VIII	17	33	W vCF	u	Na		Per	Z4.5
IX	18	11	W vm	ɑu	Hh			Z5.5
IX	19	4	D M	ɑ	(2)(H)			Z4.5
X	20	13	D F		(2)A			
X	21	2	D F		(2)A		Per	
X	22	5	D −F	−	A			
X	23	17	D F		(2)A			

Rorschach Structural Summary

Global	n	%	Location	n	%	Determinants	n	%	Contents	n	%	Quality	n	%
R	23		W	10	43	M	6	26	CONT	7		OF ALL		
Rejects	0		D	11	48	FM	1	4				+	0	0
			Dd	2	9	m	4	17	H	4	15	o	12	52
P	4	17	DW	0	0	FT	0	0	(H)	1	4	u	7	30
(P)	1	4	S	0	0	TF	0	0	Hd	3	11	−	4	17
						T	0	0	(Hd)	0	0			
(2)	10	43				FY	0	0	A	9	33	OF F		
Fr	0	0	POSITION			YF	0	0	(A)	1	4	+	0	0
rF	0	0	^	23	100	Y	0	0	Ad	0	0	o	6	55
3 r+ (2)		43	<	0	0	FV	0	0	(Ad)	0	0	u	1	9
			>	0	0	VF	0	0	Ab	0	0	−	4	36
RT Ach	10		V	0	0	V	0	0	Al	0	0			
RT Ch	10					FC'	0	0	An	0	0			
						C'F	0	0	Art	0	0	DV	0	0
AFR		44	DEV QUAL			C'	0	0	Ay	0	0	Incom	0	0
			+	0	0	FC	0	0	Bl	0	0	Fabcom	0	0
			o	11	48	CF	1	4	Bt	0	0	Alog	0	0
			v	8	35	C	0	0	Cg	1	4	Contam	0	0
Zf	17		−	4	17	Cn	0	0	Cl	0	0	Ag	1	4
ZSum	46					FD	0	0	Ex	1	4	Cp	0	0
						F	11	48	Fi	1	4	Mor	0	0
									Fd	0	0	Per	4	17
						Blends	0		Ge	0	0	Psv	0	0
									Hh	3	11	DR	0	0
			RATIOS			RATIOS			LS	0	0			
			W	10		ɑ	9	39	Na	3	11			
			M	6		p	1	4	Sc	0	0			
									Sx	0	0			
			W	10		M	6		Vo	0	0			
			D	11		wtd C	1.0		Xy	0	0			
						M+wtd C	7							
						FM+m	5							
						Y+T+V+C'	0		RATIOS					
									H+HD	8				
						ΣFMmYTVC'	5		A+AD	10				
						FC	0		H+A	15				
						CF+C	1		HD+AD	3				
									A%		37			

TAT Stories

1. This reminds me of a young boy looking at a violin. He is trying to figure out can I play it or should I take that chance of trying to learn how to play it. The way his eyes look it doesn't look like he really wants to learn how to play according to his eyes, because they look awfully uninterested in it. They look sad and down and his mouth looks sad. It doesn't look like he wants to play it.

2. This reminds me of farmers living out in the country. It looks like a man is plowing, fixing the field for corn and this looks like the mother leaning against the tree. This looks like the daughter looking back at her mother. It looks like she is going to school or to church the way she is dressed. It looks like that to me. That could be a Bible or it could be a schoolbook of some kind. It looks like the woman is pregnant with child unless she is overweight. It just looks like a family, a farmer. It looks like there is water out in the back. That's what it looks like to me. If you look at it from my point of view, I'd like to be where they are. I envy them, I honestly do because it doesn't look like they are really pleased by their mouths. This woman looks like she is contented. He looks like he is strong. He is healthy but she doesn't look too happy the way her mouth is, down. It is quite possible that she is ashamed of her mother. Maybe her mother is not well educated and she is getting more proper education. Look at the difference of clothing. Look at how nice she looks and look at mama. Mother doesn't have her hair fixed up nicely and you can see that mama is plain but it looks like the daughter has some makeup on. It looks like to me she is just going to take off and leave her mother.

3GF. It looks like she is crying. It looks like she is upset. She is trying to decide if she should walk out of that door or shouldn't I? Should I go get help or shouldn't I? She looks very unhappy, very unhappy and as for myself the way she is trying to force herself out I think she will make it. She could be unhappy about anything. She could find that her husband is an alcoholic. She could find out that her husband is cheating on her. It looks like to me she wants to go and get help.

4. It looks like she is really in love with him and he is turning away from her. He is turning his head away. He can't even look her in the face, look her in the eye. That is terrible. What a jerk. Look at the love in her face. He is going to end up leaving her and she is going to have a broken heart and she is going to cry.

6GF. It looks like they are having some kind of discussion or something. He said something and she looked back. He is looking at her and saying, "Do you understand what I am saying?", and her eyes are going, I understand what he is saying but I don't really want to tell him how I feel because if I tell him how I feel it is just going to cause problems and why should I do that? She just keeps it to herself.

7GF. That doesn't remind me of a mother; it looks like a house maid. It is a child and the child looks lonely. He is holding a little doll. The woman looks sad. She wants to communicate with the child because she can tell the child is, you know. You know what that reminds me of? But I never had any dolls. It reminds me of me. But I never had any dolls. I never had nice clothes either. You know what they used to say about me, my sisters and brothers, because I was quiet and shy and I wasn't doing good in school? They told my mother that I was retarded, deformed in the mind. It wasn't that. It was just that it did no good to speak out. It did no good. That is what it reminds me of. The little girl is in pain. She has like buried herself. I hope that woman can reach her. She has a book in her hand. Maybe she is trying to read something to the child. Maybe communication wasn't doing too good so she got a book to read to the child to see if she could communicate with the child like that or maybe the child is supposed to be listening—you know you could look at this at a different angle, honestly, if you think about it. Maybe my mind was just in a depressing way, right. Because it is possible that the woman, she is no mother, I can see that according to her clothing and maybe she is trying to help the child with remembering things. She could be reading to the child. Like myself, if someone reads to me or if I read out loud, I remember better.

9GF. It looks like they are at the beach, the ocean; trees, water, waves. It looks like this young woman is going down the beach and this one is like spying on her, watching her. This one isn't quite as pretty as this one. This one looks more intelligent. This one looks more prettier. Maybe she envys her because she is prettier. The problem does not get solved. The women do not really communicate to understand why they have these feelings towards each other. They will stay away from each other.

10. It looks like someone is hugging somebody. It looks like a father hugging his son. It sure don't look like no woman, no young girl. You know how I've seen on TV, I've also seen it here, you know how a priest leans over and kisses the forehead of a woman, Catholic people, that's what it reminds me of too. It looks like they are showing caringness, you know, feelings. You know how even though you don't love that person, you just want to hug them as a friend.

13MF. You know what this reminds me of. He just had sex with her and after he is done he is ashamed of her and he is hiding, "Aw, I'm ashamed of you." It's done and over. I got what I wanted. I'm not trying to be nasty but I got to tell you what is on my mind. That's the reason it aggravates me about men, honestly, because you know, that irritates me, it really aggravates me. Everything is fine and dandy until after they have sex and then they are done with the woman. They say I'm ashamed of you. They get what they wanted. So rather than deal with saying goodbye they say I'm ashamed of you.

16. I can tell you right away because this is what I want. I want it bad. I want to go visit Florida and see the white sand, the beautiful waves, the sail boats, people surfing, and way out there, see Pensacola is a Navy town, and when you look way, way out, well way back, well it has been years. I don't know if they have the ships out in the Gulf again. That's what I see. I see Pensacola Beach on the Gulf side. I go back not so much to visit my friends but I want to visit the town because the town then I disliked because it has too many memories. I want to go back and see it as something beautiful, something I can say yes, it has changed. I see happiness. I don't have to look at Pensacola as something ugly and disgusting.

17GF. This is like a bridge of some kind. That could be the sun or the moon. This is the water and the boats. This is like a shed of some kind. This woman is looking down at the water. It looks like fishermen. Not really, not fishermen. It looks like they are carrying some heavy packages of some kind. Have you ever seen those old-fashioned potato sacks? Well, that is what it reminds me of, some kind of grain of some kind. I don't really see a story, to tell you the truth. It is a young girl just looking down in the water watching the people. Well, she was all alone and now she is happy they are back so she won't have to be alone anymore.

Anxiety Disorder in an Avoidant Personality

Patient History

Ms. Wolcott is a 62-year-old single White woman who was admitted into the psychiatric ward with complaints of intense anxiety, panic attacks, and depression. The patient had been sleeping and eating poorly, was experiencing a low energy level and a lack of motivation, and was anhedonic. She was unable to stay home alone or function independently. Ms. Wolcott also had several somatic complaints such as a strange feeling on the back of her neck, shortness of breath, a tingling sensation on the head, and stomach aches. Among the stressors noted was the death of her mother a month before, her being withdrawn from the chronic use of a minor tranquilizer, and a lack of social contacts.

The course of treatment during the hospitalization was marked by many requests from the patient to be placed back on Ativan. Sinequan was given for a day or so, but it was discontinued when the patient complained about the amount of sedation she experienced. At the time of the testing, Ms. Wolcott was kept on Tolectin (400 mg, 3 times/day) and Buspar (5 mg, 3 times/day).

Psychiatric History

Ms. Wolcott explained that she had been "nervous" all of her life. She was admitted into the medical ward of a hospital 20 years ago, and it was at that time that she was placed on benzodiazepam. She continued taking this drug as prescribed by her family physician until recently. Last November, already suffering from the problems that led to the present admission, Ms. Wolcott spent a week in a medical ward at the same hospital she had been in 20 years before. A history of psychiatric problems in the family was denied.

Medical History

Ms. Wolcott had a tonsillectomy at the age of 9 and had gallbladder surgery 6 years ago. Laboratory tests during the present admission were said to indicate subclinical hypothyroidism. However, she was evaluated by a physician, who concluded that she did not have any significant medical illness.

Family History

Ms. Wolcott was born and raised in the Madison, Wisconsin, area. Her father died 15 years ago at the age of 72. He worked for a heating and air conditioning company and was characterized as a wonderful man who was liked by everyone. Ms. Wolcott always had a good relationship with him; her father was fond of telling her that, no matter how old she was, she would "always be his baby."

As close as Ms. Wolcott was to her father, she had an even closer relationship with her mother. The patient explained that she had lived with her mother all of her life and that when her mother had to be placed in a nursing home before her death, her absence left the patient feeling very lonely. The mother worked for 20 years as a bookkeeper in an office supply store. She is remembered as "the best" of mothers but the patient recalled how her mother unfortunately tried to shelter her from the world.

Ms. Wolcott never married. She is the youngest of two siblings. Her 66-year-old brother is an aerospace engineer in California. At this time, however, he has accepted a job at the University of Louisville and is in the process of moving to Kentucky. Her brother is married and has a daughter. He is expected to live with the patient on a temporary basis until he can find a place for himself and his family.

Ms. Wolcott explained that she has always been shy and "never went out to make friends." In fact, the patient admitted that she seldom went out with anyone outside of the family. As long as she was employed, she had a group of acquaintances at work. However, she lost those contacts when she retired and has been very isolated, especially after her mother went into the nursing home.

Educational History

Ms. Wolcott recalled that after graduating from grammar school, she was sent to a boarding school for 2 years. She went to the boarding school on the advice of her grammar school principal, who felt that she needed to be "away from the home." She apparently never adjusted to the boarding school and felt lonely and homesick. Thus, at the end of 2 years, she was allowed to return home and continued her studies in a local business school. Ms. Wolcott was an average student and never presented any academic difficulties.

Occupational History

Ms. Wolcott retired 4 years ago from the company where she did bookkeeping work for 37 years. She explained that at the end of her tenure there, she was expected to do tasks (e.g., moving files from one room to another) that she was not physically able to do anymore. Up until that time, however, she had apparently performed her functions well. Because the patient's mother became sick right after the patient's retirement and has since died, Ms. Wolcott has not enjoyed her retirement. At this time, she feels she needs some activities and some way to structure her life.

Mental Status Examination

At the time of the evaluation, the patient was alert, oriented, verbal, and coherent. Her speech and language functions were intact; the other intellectual functions examined were also within normal limits. These functions included memory, calculations, figure reproductions, mental control, and abstractions. Her thought processes were orderly and effective. Her thought content was remarkable only in that she was originally concerned about getting her medication on time. She talked about the death of her mother several times but did not seem unduly preoccupied with that loss. There were no indications of delusions or hallucinations. The affective responses were always appropriate. Although her mood was within normal limits, it tended to be serious. There was no verbalized suicidal or homicidal ideation. The psychomotor activity and anxiety levels were within normal limits. Ms. Wolcott was very anxious at the beginning, repeatedly asking questions while taking the paper-and-pencil questionnaire, and wondering whether she could do an adequate job in the testing. As time went on, however, she seemed to become more comfortable and relaxed. The patient was friendly and cooperative and presented no significant problems during the test administration.

Discussion

The test results were consistent with the presence of a generalized anxiety disorder. In addition, the indications were that Ms. Wolcott's was mildly depressed. Her Rorschach responses, for instance, were somewhat unproductive and constricted, and her TAT stories often alluded to the death of someone in the family, as in the following story obtained on Card 3GF: "It looks like somebody is in the depths of despair. Looks like she is crying, very sad about something. She could have been happy before this happened. I would say someone close to her died and her future would be that she will get over her grief."

Among the other stories with similar depressive themes, the one that is noteworthy is her response to the story on Card 14, on which the protagonist commits suicide by jumping out of a window.

Judging from her MCMI scores, at the basis of Ms. Wolcott's problems is a personality style with dependent and avoidant components. Individuals with similar scores tend to have low self-esteem; they see others as being more capable or worthy than they are. They are followers rather than leaders, often taking a passive role in interpersonal affairs. They would like to seek the emotional support and protection of others but, together with that wish, they experience discomfort.

The discomfort comes from the assumption that if others get to know them as well as they know themselves, these people would develop the same uncomplimentary views that they have of themselves. As a result, Ms. Wolcott is guarded and apprehensive in social situations. Similar people try to put their best foot forward and have a tendency to cover up their true feelings, especially when these feelings are aggressive or otherwise objectionable. They may seem tense, nervous, and distant. Because they feel ill at ease in social situations, they often avoid such affairs and are frequently lonely and isolated as a result.

Thus, one way in which Ms. Wolcott defends against the insecurity that her low self-esteem may bring is by counting on the guidance and protection of others. The second defense mechanism that she uses is thinking that if she manages to avoid making a mistake, she can always expect the outcome to be a positive one. Individuals with a similar compulsive bent are orderly and plan for the future. They prepare in a conscientious manner and do the work on schedule. They try to be efficient, dependable, industrious, and persistent. Often these individuals relate in an overly respectful and ingratiating manner. They may be somewhat perfectionistic and self-disciplined. They tend to be indecisive, especially when they have to make a decision by themselves. The compulsive inclination may also serve to strengthen the feelings of inadequacy that are beneath it in that, whenever bad events take place, Ms. Wolcott will be inclined to look for what mistakes she made that might have led to the undesirable outcome.

The extent to which this dependent, anxiously shy, and compulsive personality style was caused by an overprotective mother is debatable. What seems undeniable, however, is that it fits in very well with the relationship that the patient had with her mother. The mother was the protective figure who was the only real safe relationship that she had.

Perhaps as a result of this good fit, the indications were that the personality style was exaggerated enough to be dysfunctional. Very early in the evaluation it was clear the patient was someone who could not relate socially outside of the family. Her MCMI scores suggested that she is isolated and has few real relationships. Individuals obtaining similar scores are somewhat eccentric. They may have a rich fantasy life and may mix their own personal idiosyncrasies with other material in their conversations; they appear anxious and apprehensive and may have flat affect.

Finally, her responses to the projective measures depict a fairly immature and infantile individual who is not well developed psychologically. The impression was that the personality structure is impaired enough to constitute a personality disorder.

Encumbered with this personality disorder, Ms. Wolcott has been able to make only a somewhat marginal adjustment in her adult life. She was never able to establish significant relationships outside of the family and seemed to cope psychologically only with the help of her family; even with that support, she became dependent on a tranquilizer as the only way to control the anxieties that she experienced. The loss of her job a few years ago and the recent death of her mother have further jeopardized the kind of adjustment that she was able to make.

Regarding psychological strengths, Ms. Wolcott is very personable and shows no evidence of intellectual or memory deficits. She also had some insight into her problems and seemed well motivated.

Diagnostic Assignments and Recommendations

  I Generalized anxiety reaction ⁷⁶
   Sedative dependence
   Uncomplicated bereavement   85   94
  II ⁸⁵Avoidant personality disorder with schizoid, dependent, and compulsive elements
  III No known medical problems contributing

Continued evaluation for the use of psychotropic medications to reduce the patient's anxiety is indicated. In addition, Ms. Wolcott may benefit from a period of psychotherapy. Given her personality style, she can be expected to experience as supportive a relationship in which the therapist has a benevolent and protective attitude toward her. Feeling that the therapist is a powerful expert who will advise and guide her appropriately will be reassuring for Ms. Wolcott. The patient's fear of rejection may require frequent reaffirmation and promise of support.

Test Results

The Millon Clinical Multiaxial Inventory-II

Personality Style Scales	BRS
1–Schizoid	= 85
2–Avoidant	= 85
3–Dependent	= 94
4–Histrionic	= 3
5–Narcissistic	= 24
6A–Antisocial	= 35
7–Compulsive	= 95
8A–Negativistic	= 7

Clinical Symptom Scales	BRS
A–Anxiety	= 76
H–Somatic Preoccupations	= 84
N–Hypomania	= 0
D–Dysthymia	= 75
B–Alcohol Abuse	= 35
T–Drug Abuse	= 0
SS–Psychotic Thinking	= 68
CC–Psychotic Depression	= 44
PP–Psychotic Delusion	= 70

Severe Personality Scales	BRS
6B–Aggressive	= 32
8B–Self-Defeating	= 52
S–Schizotypal	= 80
C–Borderline	= 53
P–Paraphrenic	= 74

Modifier Indices	BRS
X–Disclosure	= 55
Y–Desirability	= 57
Z–Debasement	= 37
V–Validity	= 0

Rorschach Protocol

---

1. Card I   Reaction time: 2 seconds
   SCORE → W FM.FC'   o A   P   Z1
   butterfly
   Flying bat, more than a butterfly
   INQUIRY: It's black. Wing spread, the body and the feet

---

2. Card II   Reaction time: 4 seconds
   SCORE → W vFM.FC   au A   Z4.5
   Oh my God, two colors! Could be a flying insect but it's so big. Here is the body and these
   are the wings
   INQUIRY: wings, 2 different colors, this glow is like the end lights up.

---

3. Card III   Reaction time: 9 seconds
   SCORE → D M   o (2)H   P   Z3
   2 people stirring up a pot
   INQUIRY: repeats

---

4. Card III   Reaction time: 3 seconds
   SCORE → D FC   A   Contam
   a butterfly between them
   INQUIRY: the wings, the color, the shape

---

5. Card IV   Reaction time: 8 seconds
   SCORE → W F   (A)   P   Z2
   Oh my! Some kind of a monster from a creepy show
   INQUIRY: Big feet, floppy arms. Like King Kong.

---

6. Card V   Reaction time: 7 seconds
    SCORE → W F   A   P   Z1
    They are all very similar, they would have to be.
    Some kind of butterfly, the legs sticking out
    INQUIRY: the wings, the legs, the thing coming out on top.

7. Card VI   Reaction time: 8 seconds
    SCORE → W vF   u (2)(A)   Z2.5
    These are all very similar. Wings sticking out. Some kind of a creepy character. Some kind of
    a monster. Head there, there are a couple of eyes there.
    INQUIRY: I don't know what kind of a monster would have 2 sets of wings.

8. Card VII   Reaction time: 5 seconds
    SCORE → D F   (2)Ad   Z1
    That don't look like nothing. Too much space in between. There is a face on each one of these.
    INQUIRY: 2 faces on each side. The eye, the nose, the mouth. The ear and the snout.
    LOCATION: 2nd D from top, below the usual girl's face

9. Card VII   Reaction time: 9 seconds
    SCORE → D F   A   Z1
    butterfly
    INQUIRY: the wings with the body in the middle
    LOCATION: bottom D

10. Card VII   Reaction time: 10 seconds
    SCORE → D vF   u A   V Z1
    a long tail
    INQUIRY: a tail, a body and the head. It's kind of an animal.
    LOCATION: top D with card upside down

11. Card VIII   Reaction time: 18 seconds
    Score → D F   (2)A   P   Z3
    This is different. I see 2 rats on each side.
    INQUIRY: long tail, head

12. Card VIII   Reaction time: 3 seconds
    SCORE → D FC   A
    butterfly
    INQUIRY: the wings, the color, the body.
    LOCATION: bottom D

13. Card VIII   Reaction time: 2 seconds
    SCORE → D vFM   au (2)A   Z3
    2 insects
    INQUIRY: they are getting together.
    LOCATION: uppermost green D

14. Card IX   Reaction time: 7 seconds
    SCORE → D F   A   Z2.5
    They get worse. That looks like a big butterfly.
    INQUIRY: the wings and the body
    LOCATION: midsection

15. Card IX   Reaction time: 10 seconds
    SCORE → Reject
    The line going down the middle makes you think that it is the body of an insect. Maybe more
    than one kind because of the different colors
    INQUIRY: (cannot find and rejects)

16. Card X   Reaction time: 7 seconds
    SCORE → D F   A   P   Z4
    An animal with a lot of feet
    INQUIRY: the feet. It's a crab or something
    LOCATION: upper blue D

17. Card X   Reaction time: 6 seconds
    SCORE → D FC   (2)A
    2 rats
    INQUIRY: black rats. There are 2 of them
    LOCATION: top gray D

18. Card X   Reaction time: 6 seconds
    SCORE → Dd vF   u Xy   Z4
    An x-ray of the inside of a body.
    INQUIRY: this part coming down here
    LOCATION: center bottom up to the blue D

Rorschach Score Sequence

Card	No.	Time	Scoring				
I	1	2	W	FM.FC′	a	A	P	Z1
II	2	4	W	vFM.FC	au	A		Z4.5
III	3	9	D	M	a	(2)H	P	Z3
III	4	3	D	FC		A		
IV	5	8	W	F		(A)	P	Z2
V	6	7	W	F		A	P	Z1
VI	7	8	W	vF	u	(2)(A)		Z2.5
VII	8	5	D	F		(2)Ad		Z1
VII	9	9	D	F		A		Z1
VII	10	10	D	vF	u	A		V Z1
VIII	11	18	D	F		(2)A	P	Z3
VIII	12	3	D	FC		A		
VIII	13	2	D	vFM	au	(2)A		Z3
IX	14	7	D	F		A		Z2.5
IX	15	10	Reject					
X	16	7	D	F		A	P	Z4
X	17	6	D	FC		(2)A		
X	18	6	Dd vF		u	Xy		Z4

Rorschach Structural Summary

Global			Location			Determinants			Contents			Quality		
	n	%		n	%		n	%		n	%		n	%
R	17		W	5	29	M	1	5	CONT	3		OF ALL		
Rejects	0		D	11	65	FM	3	16				+	0	0
			Dd	1	6	m	0	0	H	1	6	o	12	71
P	6	35	DW	0	0	FT	0	0	(H)	0	0	u	5	29
(P)	0	0	S	0	0	TF	0	0	Hd	0	0	−	0	0
						T	0	0	(Hd)	0	0			
(2)	6	35				FY	0	0	A	12	71	OF F		
Fr	0	0	POSITION			YF	0	0	(A)	2	12	+	0	0
rF	0	0	^	16	94	Y	0	0	Ad	1	6	o	7	70
3 r+ (2)		35	<	0	0	FV	0	0	(Ad)	0	0	u	3	30
			>	0	0	VF	0	0	Ab	0	0	−	0	0
RT Ach	7		v	1	6	V	0	0	AI	0	0			
RT Ch	6					FC'	1	5	An	0	0			
						C'F	0	0	Art	0	0	DV	0	0
AFR		70	DEV QUAL			C'	0	0	Ay	0	0	Incom	0	0
			+	0	0	FC	4	21	BI	0	0	Fabcom	0	0
			o	12	71	CF	0	0	Bt	0	0	Alog	0	0
			v	5	29	C	0	0	Cg	0	0	Contam	0	0
Zf	14		−	0	0	Cn	0	0	Cl	0	0	Ag	0	0
ZSum	34					FD	0	0	Ex	0	0	Cp	0	0
						F	10	53	Fi	0	0	Mor	0	0
									Fd	0	0	Per	0	0
						Blends	2		Ge	0	0	Psv	0	0
									Hh	0	0	DR	0	0
			RATIOS			RATIOS			LS	0	0			
			W	5		a	4	24	Na	0	0			
			M	1		p	0	0	Sc	0	0			
									Sx	0	0			
			W	5		M	1		Vo	0	0			
			D	11		wtd C	2.0		Xy	1	6			
						M+wtd C	3							
						FM+m	3							
						Y+T+V+C'	1		RATIOS					
									H+HD	1				
						&FMmYTVC'	4		A+AD	15				
						FC	4		H+A	15				
						CF+C	0		HD+AD	1				
									A%		88			

TAT Stories

1. That looks like a boy studying his lesson. He looks like 5 or 6 years old and that would be before his school days, I would say. Well, he will go on to have a career in his life, whatever he wants to do in his life.

2. This looks like a farm. A man is working with a horse. This might be his wife and daughter. He's probably been a farmer all his life. His daughter is going to school and his wife is standing here and he's working with a plow horse. The girl looks like she is going to school with books in her hand. She will go on to do better things, too. If she continues with her studies she will make something out of her life.

3GF. It looks like somebody is in the depths of despair, looks like she's crying, very sad about something. She could have been happy before this happened. I'd say somebody close to her died and in her future she will get over her grief. Just like me when my mother died.

4. Looks like two movie stars in two movies that I saw not too long ago. These people remind me of a musical I saw. They fell in love with each other. He left her and never came back to her. Looks like he's pulling away from her. He's a riverboat gambler but he left her and finally came back after he found out she had a child and it was his.

6GF. This woman is talking to a man standing behind her and turning around. The look on her face, he must have startled her. Well, she might have been married and is falling in love with him, both nice looking people and that's what will happen in the future.

7GF. That's a mother talking to her daughter who is holding a doll, both sitting on a couch talking about something. She looks like she's got a book in her hand. She must be reading to her but she doesn't look like she is paying any attention to her. If she was paying any attention to her mother she would get something out of it. They are all cooking out there.

9GF. This girl is running away for some reason. This one is standing behind a tree with something in her hand. I can't make it out. She is watching her run away wondering where she is going but she looks frightened. This is water, maybe she sees someone in the water that needs help and she is running to help that person. See, she's got a towel in her arms and she will save the person that needs help.

10. This is two middle-aged people that have been married for a long time and they still love each other. He is kissing her on the forehead. It looks like they are married for almost 50 years and will be married for the rest of their life.

13MF. The man is in despair over the death of his wife. She is not already gone. She will die and that will be it.

14. It looks like he's ready to jump out the window. A small picture, looks like somebody is jumping out the window in a dark room. Either he's thinking about doing himself in or trying to escape from something. Whoever is bothering or whatever is bothering him, maybe despondent over something.

15. Looks like a man in a graveyard, he's praying for something he's buried there. It's an old gravestone. He came to visit somebody's grave and he's praying for them. Nothing can happen if the person is dead there, then nothing can happen.

17GF. This looks like a house, but there's some people outside the house, or one person at least. It looks like there's other people too. There is somebody on the roof, another building here and the sun is shining. There's a boat here. They are getting out of the boat, in the water. Somebody's looking down on them. There's a high wall around the house, high windows. They can get out of the boat right there. The sun shining down and somebody's looking down. It almost looks like they are up to no good to me. They are bringing something to this house on the rafters by boat. This looks like a woman here and these are men. They look like smugglers and might hide it in this house here and if they get caught they will get thrown in jail.

18GF. This looks like a very sad woman. She is holding her daughter in her arms and she must be very ill. That's why she looks so sad, because her daughter is so ill. There is a staircase here. I don't know if somebody fell down the stairs and got hurt. She was laying there and she picked her up in her arms and she could have died or be seriously injured in the fall. Hopefully, she will recover if she is still living. You always hope for something better.

The MCMI and Other Psychological Instruments

The MCMI and the MMPI

The biggest competitor of the MCMI has been, of course, the MMPI. These two tests are used in the same settings and are both designed to measure patterns of emotional disturbance. There is evidence that they are indeed very similar from a global or structural viewpoint. Sexton, McIlwraith, Barnes, and Dunn (1987), for example, demonstrated that the MCMI and a short version of the MMPI (the MMPI-168) had conceptually identical factor structures and were equally useful in predicting discharge diagnosis in an inpatient psychiatric unit. Ownby, Wallbrown, Carmin, and Barnett (1991) conducted a canonical analysis on these two tests using data from 800 male criminal offenders. Ownby et al. reported that 29% of the MMPI variance was accounted for by the MCMI-I, whereas 36% of the MCMI-I variance was redundant with the MMPI scores of the same individual.

Smith et al. (1988) administered the MMPI and the MCMI-I to 106 consecutive new admissions to a private outpatient mental health clinic. Twelve of the 20 MCMI-I scales correlated highly with the MMPI, whereas 8 scales failed to show positive correlations with any scales of the MMPI.

In terms of the equivalence of specific scales, McNiel and Meyer (1990) reported a great deal of similarity between the weight factor (now called the Disclosure Index) of the MCMI-I and the F and K scale scores of the MMPI. Their investigation with correctional inmates and forensic inpatients revealed that the MCMI index was negatively correlated with the F scale score and positively correlated with the K score.

The depression scales of these two inventories appeared to be interchangeable. According to Millon (1987), the correlation between these two scales is .70 (p. 51). The Depression scale of the MMPI was also modestly correlated with the Cyclothymia and Dysthymia scales of the MCMI. In a study comparing depressed patients with patients with other psychiatric disorders, Wetzler et al. (1989) found that both of these scales were efficient in predicting the diagnosis of major depression. On the basis of their data, those authors argued that the scale to be used should be chosen with a specific goal in mind: If one wishes to rule out a major depression, the MMPI Depression scale would be the most useful; the strength of the MCMI, on the other hand, is in its higher overall accuracy (Wetzler et al., 1989).

Millon (1987) also reported that the Cyclothymia scale was modestly correlated with the Psychasthenia scale, whereas the Schizotypal and Thought Disorder scales were modestly correlated with the Schizophrenic scale of the MMPI. Otherwise, however, Millon's figures showed little or no relation between the scales of these two inventories, a finding that has been supported by others (Marsh et al., 1988).

On the other hand, at least with the Ownby et al. (1991) population of criminal offenders, the paranoid scales of the two inventories appeared to be measuring different aspects of paranoia and produced appreciably different results. The same conclusion was reached with regard to the Hysteria scale of the MMPI and the Somatic Preoccupation scale of the MCMI-I (Ownby et al., 1991).

McCann (1989, 1991) has provided confirmatory data from studies on the concurrent, convergent, and discriminant validities of the MCMI-I, MCMI-II, and MMPI personality disorder scales. McCann (1989) reported strong support for the concurrent validity of MMPI personality disorder scales when they were compared against the criterion of the personality disorder scales of the MCMI-I. The 11 personality disorder scales of the MMPI developed by Morey et al. (1985) have been demonstrated to have had adequate levels of internal consistency. These scales were also shown to be moderately congruent with the clustering of the *DSM–III* personality disorders (Morey, 1986). Some of these MMPI personality disorder scales had also been validated against the external criterion of clinicians' judgments of personality disorders (Morey, Blashfield, Webb, & Jewell, 1988). McCann (1989, 1991) reported that 8 of the 11 MMPI-based overlapping personality disorder scales were highly correlated with their corresponding MCMI-I scales: Schizoid, Avoidant, Dependent, Histrionic, Narcissistic, Passive-Aggressive, Schizotypal, and Borderline.

McCann (1991) examined the convergent and discriminant validities of the MCMI-II and the MMPI personality disorder scales using multitrait–multimethod procedures and factor analyses. Using both overlapping and nonoverlapping scales, he was able to determine the effects of item overlap. He concluded that item overlap did not have a general impact on validity but that some MCMI-II scales demonstrated better validity in nonoverlapping form (Passive-Aggressive and Borderline scales in particular) and that some scales (Paranoid in particular) performed best in the overlapping form. He concluded that the convergent and discriminant validities of these scales were generally established by the results of his study done on 80 psychiatric inpatients. His findings also indicated that the Antisocial and Passive-Aggressive scales of the MCMI-II performed better and represented significant improvements over the original MCMI-I scales. In the factor-analytic studies performed, he found that the MMPI factors reflected the *DSM–III–R* personality disorder clusters, whereas the MCMI-II scales yielded a factor structure that reflected Millon's (1969) dimensions of personality.

A different approach to that of examining the similarities between the MMPI and the MCMI is to determine how these two inventories may complement each other. A series of articles by Antoni and other Millon associates suggested that the MCMI can add to the information derived from the MMPI. Their investigations were based on data collected by approximately 175 clinicians on more than 3,000 patients. Their reports revealed a number of personality patterns that commonly occur with people obtaining particular MMPI profiles.

Patients who obtained an MMPI 28/82 code type (elevations on the Depression and Schizophrenia scales), for instance, can be characterized as depressed people who have difficulties being assertive. They are often stubborn, irritable, resentful, and moody and are typically thought to be in a state of inner turmoil. They are conflictual people who tend to feel guilty whenever their conflicts are externalized. Prone to depression, such individuals may additionally be anxious or agitated or demonstrate psychomotor retardation (Dahlstrom, Welsh, & Dahlstrom, 1972; Graham, 1977; Greene, 1980; Lachar, 1974).

A somewhat similar MMPI profile is the 24/42 code type (elevations on the Depression and Psychopathic Deviance scales). Like people with a 28/82 code type, these individuals are prone to have periods of guilt and depression. In contrast, however, these patients' depression commonly results from their being "caught" in some way (e.g., were fired from a job because of dishonesty) so that they are seen as "psychopaths in trouble." By nature, these subjects tend to be impulsive, unable to delay gratification, and have little respect for the norms of society. Substance abuse is a common problem (Dahlstrom et al., 1972; Graham, 1977; Greene, 1980; Lachar, 1974).

For both of these two "depressed" MMPI profiles, three main MCMI styles have been reported (Antoni, Tischer, Levine, Green, & Millon, 1985a, 1985b). The *interpersonally acting-out* group has elevated MCMI scores on the Antisocial and Narcissistic scales (Scales 5 and 6A). People in this group are characterized as arrogant, aggressive, and self-centered individuals who may drift toward paranoidlike behaviors if they are repeatedly unable to secure support and reinforcement. The *interpersonally acting-in* group has elevated scores on the Schizoid scale of the MCMI. In addition to the MMPI characterization, these individuals can be further described as people who think of themselves as weak and ineffectual and tend to become alienated from both themselves and others. Decompensation for this group is expected to take the form of a schizotypal personality pattern with behavioral eccentricities and cognitive slippage. Finally, the *emotionally acting-out* group has elevations on the Negativistic, Dependent, and Histrionic scales of the MCMI (Scales 8A, 3, and 4). They can be described as having a labile affect and being inclined to vacillate between depressive moods and euphoric or hostile episodes.

Another common MMPI profile that is associated with a depressed affect is the 27/72 (elevations on the Depression and the Psychasthenia scales). Individuals who obtain such a profile are usually described as anxious worriers and indecisive, insecure people with a dependent personality style. They have very high expectations of themselves and feel guilty when they fail to accomplish their personal goals. Their depression typically involves a pessimistic view of their problems, a tendency to brood and ruminate, and complaints of tiredness and exhaustion (Dahlstrom et al., 1972; Graham, 1977; Greene, 1980; Lachar, 1974).

In terms of the MCMI, three different styles of the MMPI 27/72 profile have been noted (Levine, Tischer, Antoni, Green, & Millon, 1985). The *fearful dependent* group has elevated scores on the Avoidant, Schizoid, and Dependent scales of the MCMI (Scales 2, 1, and 3). These individuals typically have strong dependency needs and would like to be accepted by others, but their fear of rejection makes them apprehensive. As a result, they are usually loners who withdraw from others so as to defend against the possible rejection. The *conforming-dependent* group is characterized by elevations on the Compulsive and Dependent scales of the MCMI (Scales 7 and 3). These people react to the risk of rejection by submitting to the wishes of others and conforming to societal norms rather than avoiding interpersonal relationships. Finally, Levine et al. noted a third group defined by elevations on the Negativistic and the Dependent scales of the MCMI (Scales 8A and 3). These *ambivalent dependent* individuals deal with interpersonal risks by becoming conflictual, vacillating in their moods, and acting out their frustrations.

Individuals characterized by MMPI code 78/87 are introspective worriers. Harboring feelings of inferiority, such people are likely to interact in a passively dependent manner and to be nervous when they are with others. They typically have rich fantasy lives and spend a great deal of time daydreaming. The diagnosis of a schizoid personality or a schizophrenic reaction is commonly assigned (Dahlstrom et al., 1972; Graham, 1977; Greene, 1980; Lachar, 1974).

With the 78/87 MMPI group, Antoni, Levine, Tischer, Green, and Millon (1987) found three patient groups that were distinguishable in terms of their MCMI scores. The *interpersonally acting-in* group has elevated scores on the Schizoid and Avoidant scales of the MCMI. In addition to the inferiority feelings and passive dependence described by the MMPI scores, these individuals can be characterized by withdrawal and lack of interpersonal relationships; their insecurities surface as a lack of assertiveness and an inability to act in a decisive and self-initiating manner. In contrast, Antoni et al. uncovered two other groups that tend to dissipate their issues in emotional ways. The *emotionally acting-out* group has elevations on the Negativistic, Histrionic, and Avoidant scales of the MCMI. Caught in a conflict between their dependency and strivings toward autonomy, these individuals tend to have labile affect and to vacillate between angry defiance and feelings of guilt accompanied by inner turmoil. Finally, there was a group with primary elevations on the Avoidant and Dependent scales of the MCMI that was labeled the *emotionally acting-in* group. The authors conceptualized such individuals as struggling with a conflict between taking the risk of relating interpersonally or leading a life of loneliness and isolation. In the authors' minds, these are people who not only feel inadequate about their own abilities but have a great fear of rejection so that they find it difficult to establish dependent relationships with others.

Finally, the MMPI code type 89/98 (elevations on the Schizophrenia and Hypomania scales) has also been examined (Antoni, Levine, Tischer, Green, & Millon, 1986). This profile is usually characterized by a lability of mood, confusion, disorientation, restlessness, indecisiveness, and hyperactivity. Typical individuals are fearful of relating to others and engage in excessive daydreaming instead of developing strong social ties. Their reality testing may be marginal, and autistic thinking and hallucinations or delusions may be present. They are self-centered and infantile, often demanding a great deal of attention and becoming resentful and hostile when their demands are not met. Although these individuals have a need to achieve, feelings of inferiority and inadequacy often contribute to a mediocre performance. Projection, regression, and inappropriate affect are common. Diagnostically, they are mostly seen as either schizophrenic or manic (Graham, 1977; Greene, 1980; Lachar, 1974).

Data collected by Antoni et al. (1986) showed a set of six MCMI profiles that appeared most frequently with people obtaining the 89/98 MMPI profile. These groups were further refined such that the individuals were characterized as primarily narcissistic (elevation on Scale 5 of the MCMI), antisocial (elevation on Scale 6), or dependent/negativistic (elevations on Scales 3, 8, or both).

The information from the MCMI was then used to further explain the individual's style. In the case of the narcissist, the manic and schizophreniclike clinical picture was seen as being fueled by feelings of grandiosity and a disregard for social constraints. When their charm is not impressive to others and their arrogant presentation does not obtain the needed support, these individuals respond with the defensive picture drawn by the MMPI or by acting-out behaviors such as substance abuse.

Subjects with a primarily antisocial personality style composed the largest group. The psychopathology was said to be driven by a mistrust of others and an angry rejection of social norms. In their view of the world as cruel and competitive, these individuals feel that they have to compensate for their inner sense of weakness by avoiding close relationships and projecting blame.

Finally, the dependent/negativistic personality substrate was thought to explain the clinical syndrome described by the MMPI as a response to conflicts over dependency. Anticipating disillusionment in their desperate need for closeness and support, such individuals become suspicious of others and fearful of their domination. The inner turmoil caused by their unresolvable conflict is eventually translated into the social, thought process, and mood disturbances described by the MMPI.

The MCMI and the SCL-90

There has also been some interest in looking at the Symptom Checklist-90 (SCL-90; Derogatis, 1983) and the MCMI. According to Millon (1982), only four of the SCL-90 scales are modestly related (correlations in the 60s) to scales of the MCMI. Of these, the Depression scale is again noteworthy, having commonalities with the Psychotic Depression, Dysthymia, Negativistic, and Cyclothymia scales of the MCMI. The investigation by Wetzler et al. (1989) also demonstrated similarities in that they found the Dysthymia scale of the MCMI and the Depression scale of the SCL-90 to be equally efficient in diagnosing major depressions.

Additionally, Millon (1982) reported modest correlations between the SCL-90's Interpersonal Sensitivity scale and the Avoidant, Negativistic, Schizotypal, Cyclothymia, Psychotic Thinking, and Psychotic Depression scales of the MCMI. Anxiety, as measured by the SCL-90, seemed similar to the Anxiety, Psychotic Depression, and Cyclothymia scales of the MCMI. Finally, the Psychotic Thinking and Psychoticism scales were modestly related (Millon, 1982).

The MCMI and the Profile of Mood States (POMS)

Correlations between the MCMI-I and the POMS are also available. For example, associations have been found between the Avoidant and Negativistic scales of the MCMI and the Depression and Confusion scales of the POMS (McMahon & Davidson, 1985b). The Anxiety, Dysthymia, and Psychotic Depression scales were found to be related to the Tension, Depression, Fatigue, and Confusion scales of the POMS (McMahon & Davidson, 1986a). All of the reported relationships, however, were modest: The best correlation was .56.

The MCMI and the California Psychological Inventory (CPI)

Because the MCMI provides measures of personality styles, it should be related to other personality trait inventories, such as the CPI. Holliman and Guthrie (1989) administered both the MCMI-I and the CPI to 237 college students. As expected, they reported a significant overlap in the variance between the two tests so that about 40% of the variance of either test could be accounted for by the other.

The measures of social withdrawal and detachment of the MCMI-I were predictably related to low scores on the interpersonal interaction scales of the CPI. Specifically, the Schizoid, Avoidant, and Dependent scales of the MCMI-I negatively correlated with the Class I scales of the CPI (the Dominance, Capacity for Status, Sociability, Social Presence, Social Acceptance, and Sense of Well-Being scales). The Histrionic, Narcissistic, and Antisocial scales, on the other hand, were positively correlated with these Class I scales of the CPI. Another significant finding was that the MCMI-I Compulsive scale was associated with higher scores on the Class II scales of the CPI (Responsibility, Socialization, Self-Control, Tolerance, Good Impression, and Communality). It was felt that the Compulsive scale may be a measure of good adjustment to some degree, at least with a college population. Finally, the Negativistic scale of the MCMI-I showed its highest correlations with scales related to delinquency and criminal behavior (negatively correlated with Responsibility, Socialization, Achievement via Conformance, and Intellectual Efficiency).

The MCMI and the 16PF

Hyer et al. (1990) gave both the MCMI and the 16PF to a group of veterans diagnosed with PTSD. Their findings were always consistent with Millon's (1977) conceptualizations of the different MCMI scales. For instance, the Schizoid and the Avoidant scales were inversely related to the Assertiveness scale and positively related to the Self-Sufficiency scale of the 16PF. Additionally, the Avoidant scale was related to the Anxiety scale. The Dependent scale was positively related to the Sensitivity scale but inversely related to the Self-Sufficiency scale. Patients scoring highly on the Histrionic scale also tended to score highly on the Intelligence, Assertive, Happy-Go-Lucky, Boldness, Extraversion, Tough Poise, and Independence scales of 16PF. Both the Narcissistic and the Antisocial scales appeared to be associated with assertiveness and independence; the Narcissistic scale was additionally correlated with the Happy-Go-Lucky, Boldness, and Extraversion scales, whereas the Antisocial scale was found to be associated with the Tough Poise scale and negatively related to the Sensitivity scale. Correlating positively with the Conformity and Self-Discipline scales, the Compulsive scale of the MCMI was negatively related to the Tension, Anxiety, and Tough Poise scales. Finally, judging from these two inventories, subjects with negativistic personality styles tend to be tense, anxious, and uninclined to be warm, emotionally stable, happy-go-lucky, conforming, bold, and self-disciplined. Correlations for the Schizotypal, Borderline, and Paranoid scales of the MCMI are also included, along with the correlations obtained by the symptom formation scales on the traits of the 16PF (Hyer et al., 1990).

The MCMI and the NEO Personality Inventory

The NEO Personality Inventory (Costa & McCrae, 1985) was designed to measure personality in accordance with the five-factor model (Neuroticism, Extraversion, Openness to Experience, Agreeableness, and Conscientiousness). In terms of that model, Costa and McCrae reported the Schizoid scale was negatively related to the Extraversion scale, specifically showing low warmth, gregariousness, positive emotions, assertiveness, and openness to feelings. In addition to being negatively related to Extraversion scores, avoidants in Millon's (1969) typology scored highly on the Neuroticism scale, showing problems with self-consciousness, depression, and vulnerability. Dependent scale scores were related to low Openness to Experience scores and to high Agreeableness scores in terms of the five-factor model. Histrionic individuals obtained positive correlations with the Extraversion scale and negative correlations with the Conscientiousness scale. The high Extraversion scores were thought to be due to histrionic individuals' gregariousness, positive emotions, assertiveness, and excitement seeking. Individuals who scored highly on the Narcissistic scale were found to score highly on the Extraversion scale and low on the Agreeableness scale. These people were high in assertiveness and saw themselves as being low in self-consciousness and vulnerability. The Antisocial scale was also negatively correlated with Agreeableness scores. Compulsive individuals were found to score very highly on the Conscientiousness scale. Finally, scores on the Negativistic scale have been correlated with Neuroticism scores (Costa & McCrae, 1990).

The MCMI and Other Measures of Narcissism

The MCMI has received some attention for its ability to measure narcissism, a relatively new concept in psychology that is not easily measured by other instruments. Prifitera and Ryan (1984) administered both the MCMI and the Narcissistic Personality Inventory (NPI), which was developed by Raskin and Hall (1979), using a counterbalanced design and psychiatric patients.

Prifitera and Ryan reported a correlation of .66 between the Narcissistic scale of the MCMI and the NPI. They also found significant correlations between the NPI and the Histrionic and Negativistic scales of the MCMI. They explained the latter correlations on the basis of the similarities between the narcissistic personality prototype and the prototypes for the histrionic and negativistic individuals. Finally, Prifitera and Ryan used the two scales to classify their sample into low and high narcissism and found that the instruments agreed on the classification 74% of the time.

In a similar study done with undergraduates, Auerbach (1984) showed a statistically significant correlation of .55 between the Narcissistic scale of the MCMI and the NPI. This author found it troublesome, however, that the coefficient of homogeneity for the MCMI Narcissistic scale was low, thus suggesting that the scale may be measuring more than one concept in the case of college students. Moreover, neither the Narcissistic scale nor the NPI correlated significantly with the Marlowe-Crowne Social Desirability Scale (Crowne & Marlowe, 1964), possibly pointing out that the concept of narcissism may not be related to a wish to be perceived as being socially desirable.

The MCMI and Projective Techniques

To our knowledge, there is no published material on how the MCMI scores relate to any of the projective techniques. We would like to offer some suggestions, however, on the basis of our own clinical experience in administering the MCMI and projective tests together.

Information about a particular person obtained from different sources can be used to either support the finding from another source or add additional information about the patient. When scores on the Dysthymia scale of the MCMI are elevated, for instance, we would search for other evidence that can be used to confirm a diagnosis of depression. Perhaps the presenting complaints involved affective symptoms, the Rorschach was constricted and showed a repeated use of the blackness of the inkblot as a determinant, and the TAT stories betrayed a preoccupation with problematic or depressing situations. Having such confirmation from several sources of information increases our level of confidence on the relevance of our test findings and allows us to eventually decide, for instance, whether the patient meets DSM–III–R criteria for a particular disorder.

The fact that the projective measures can be used to gather evidence related to the clinical syndromes is well known and needs no further discussion. What we wish to emphasize here is that the patients' personality styles are often also reflected in the way they perform on projective measures. In the case of schizoid or avoidant personality styles, for example, we often look for signs of lack of social involvement such as a low number of human responses on the Rorschach or the portrayal of distant relationships on the TAT. A submissive and noncompetitive way of relating to others should be betrayed in the TAT stories of dependent individuals. Histrionic individuals typically have a great deal of color and movement on the Rorschach and dramatic and interesting TAT stories. The grandiosity of narcissists and their arrogant style of relating to others should also be apparent in the projective measures. From antisocial individuals, we often obtain competitive and somewhat sociopathic stories. The Rorschach of compulsive patients may be too constricted and will reveal a preoccupation with detail; their TAT stories may reveal the hierarchical or moralistic viewpoints for which they are known. Finally, with negativistic individuals, we have often obtained protocols with an excessive number of rotations or reversals of the figure–ground perspective and a great deal of emotion and anger.

We should emphasize that the suggestions just offered are an incomplete listing of how personality styles may be reflected on projective measures. If we looked at any of a number of dimensions of the testing, it would be possible to develop theoretical notions as to how particular styles can be expected to perform in that dimension. Take, for instance, the issue of "organization." All of the popular projective techniques can be used to characterize the ways in which individuals organize their perceptions of reality and whether their personality styles include a tendency to compulsively organize their worlds or to look at reality in a more disorganized way.

Moreover, determining what is the usual personality style of a particular individual can help us decide which of the feasible interpretations of a particular marker in the projective techniques is the most valid. Constriction on the Rorschach, for example, can be the result of personality traits or the reflection of an acute emotional state such as a depression. If the patient who had a constricted Rorschach protocol is, according to the MCMI, a very compulsive individual, we would still have to wonder to what degree the lack of determinants and the underproductivity were the result of the patient's compulsive bent as opposed to a reflection of the lack of energy and enthusiasm that often accompanies a despondent mood. If the patient were to have almost any other personality style, however, the constriction of the protocol could be confidently seen as indicating depression.

Similar considerations can be applied to evaluating patients' contact with reality. Blatantly psychotic responses are, of course, pathological regardless of patients' personality styles. Milder forms of thought disturbances, however, are probably much more likely to be present with histrionic or negativistic individuals than with compulsive individuals. Thus, in our experience, the protocols of histrionic patients are bound to contain personal references, boundary problems in terms of mixing one response with another, and color or movement responses that are not carefully linked to the form of the inkblot. Thus, we are much more prone to disregard mild lapses in thought processes when patients have a histrionic personality style than another style.

More generally, that a psychiatric inventory such as the MCMI can provide a good complement to the Rorschach and the TAT is attested to by the fact that such a combination represents the most popular clinical battery used with psychiatric patients. In such a battery, the Rorschach allows clinicians to evaluate the quality of patients' thought processes and their approaches to life. The psychiatric inventory typically provides a sophisticated way of looking at what patients think of themselves. TAT stories often reflect life problems that the individuals are facing and the way those issues play themselves out in their interpersonal relationships.

Psychotherapy and the MCMI

We hope that psychological assessment techniques are used not only to help diagnose and classify people reliably and validly but as an aid in choosing the most helpful methods of treatment. Ideally, the determination of certain diagnoses and personality profile types through personality testing should lead to logical prescriptions for a distinct type of psychotherapeutic treatment that is specific to that particular personality profile. This hope was guiding our therapeutic suggestions for the MCMI personality styles contained in chapters 4–7. However, as we discuss, we have relied primarily on a speculative application of personality theory and our own clinical experience in developing our ideas regarding the type of therapeutic relationship and techniques that would be most useful with the specific personality styles.

Psychological Testing and Treatment Recommendations

A priori objections to the notion that psychological testing can lead to useful therapy "prescriptions" include the argument that the information most germane to understanding and helping someone in psychotherapy can only be gathered through the face-to-face interpersonal contact of the therapy interview. It can also be argued that testing interferes with the developing therapeutic process. Paul Dewald (1967), writing from a psychoanalytic perspective, noted that the use of psychological tests "may have an impact on the developing therapeutic situation and relationship, since they tend to bypass the patient's conscious participation and suggest that the therapist may have semimagical means or methods of understanding the patient" (p. 297). Dewald also suggested that introducing psychological testing later in treatment can be complicated and problematic, as "the patient will have significant doubts about the therapist's confidence in himself and in the choice of treatment being undertaken, or they will indicate to the patient that the therapist has significant doubts about the patient's capacities and progress" (p. 297).

Others have argued that knowing a patient's psychological assessment makes no difference in subsequent therapy process or outcome. A variant of this second objection was discussed by Beutler (1989), who felt that "psychotherapies do not exert diagnosis-specific benefits" (p. 273) and that "psychiatric diagnoses have proved to be of little value either to the development of individual psychotherapy plans or to the differential prediction of psychotherapy outcome" (p. 271). Beutler instead sought to develop and understand nondiagnostic dimensions and factors that may lead to the best type of psychotherapeutic strategy. He called for improving therapist–patient matching, increasing the specificity of interventions, and clarifying treatment-setting decisions. It is interesting, however, that despite his reservations about the value of diagnosis for psychotherapy, Beutler did not fully disregard diagnosis as a potentially important variable to be taken into account, nor did he posit that a thorough assessment is not useful. He did not address explicitly the role of psychological testing in providing some of the information (other than a simple diagnostic label) that he felt is helpful in making treatment decisions.

A third argument against the use of psychological testing in psychotherapy is that its results actually bias or negatively skew the therapist's attitude toward the patient. In other words, it may be that the test results turn the relationship into an evaluative, pathologizing, or judgmental one. This is most often the objection of those from the humanistic, or client-centered, school, who tend to undervalue and even demean the usefulness of psychological testing.

For example, Carl Rogers (1951) was explicit in deemphasizing the use of the diagnostic process in psychotherapy. He was of the opinion that diagnosis, either through interviewing or psychological testing, "places the clinician in a god-like role which seems basically untenable from a philosophical point of view" (Rogers, 1951, p. 221). He felt that the use of diagnosis to determine treatment modalities or approaches "tends to be palliative and superficial, rather than basic" (Rogers, 1951, p. 221) and that "a diagnosis of the psychological dynamics is not only unnecessary but in some ways is detrimental or unwise" (Rogers, 1951, p. 223). The basic thrust of Rogers's objections is that diagnosis leads to the client losing a sense of responsibility for self-knowledge and that such assessment possibly leads to some form of social control "of the many by the few" (Rogers, 1951, p. 224).

This particular a priori criticism of the role of psychological assessment and diagnosis might also be an objection from someone who is a follower of Robert Langs's (1973) psychoanalytic viewpoint, wherein the use of psychological testing is construed as a "therapeutic frame" violation. For example,

Langs (1973) presented a case in his book *The Technique of Psychoanalytic Psychotherapy* that argues against the use of psychological testing. In that case, an adolescent boy who had been in treatment for 2 years (with one of Langs's supervisees?) was given psychological testing prior to going to college. This testing was done at the request of the boy's parents for unknown reasons. The boy responded poorly to the testing in that his subsequent behavior and fantasies in subsequent sessions were marked by paranoid concerns and withdrawal. Langs (1973) interpreted this scenario as follows:

> The implications of this vignette are clear: The therapist's use of testing evoked an iatrogenic regression and paranoid disturbance in the patient which was—on the patient's part—in keeping with his latent psychopathology. It is clear that the two-person ground rule should be followed without exception in almost all psychotherapies and that the infractions come primarily from the therapist's deficient understanding of proper principles of technique and from his countertransference difficulties. (p. 196)

Several points should be made regarding this example. First, few would disagree that giving psychological testing later in treatment has much different effects and meanings than does an early assessment. It is an empirical question whether the meanings of a later testing can be sufficiently discussed and worked through in a satisfactory way or whether there are so many problems that testing should only be reserved for early in treatment. Langs (1973) felt in his example that at termination "the therapeutic alliance remained compromised to the end" (p. 196). Second, it is unclear whether the adolescent in the example was upset about taking the psychological tests or whether he was more bothered by his parents' intrusion into his treatment. Finally, Langs generalized from this negative experience with one case of a disturbed adolescent to a prescription for all intensive therapies with all patients.

The issue of whether test results would make a difference in the therapy process or outcome is an empirical question. In order to answer the question, researchers would have to study two matched, roughly equivalent groups of therapists in which one group of therapists is given psychological testing data and the other group is not; the investigation would then have to include acceptable psychotherapy process and outcome measures. To simplify this type of study, one might have to circumscribe the problems studied or shorten the length of treatment, as Horowitz et al. (1984) have done. In this case, all patients were experiencing grief reactions from the death of a parent. To our knowledge, there is no study of this kind available.

Despite the a priori objections to using psychological testing to determine treatment method and strategy, numerous clinicians have attempted to do so, although the assessment methods and strategies have differed considerably. The question of the usefulness of test results in treatment planning was discussed by Meehl in 1960 and later reprinted in his 1973 book, *Psychodiagnosis: Selected Papers.* He wrote of a study with Bernard C.

Glueck in which they surveyed different therapists regarding the ultimate usefulness of "pretreatment personality assessment" (p. 118). Most groups, except followers of George Kelly, responded negatively. He wrote that "the over-all percentage who believe that such prior knowledge of the client's personality greatly speeds therapy is only 17 percent" (p. 118).

However, Meehl (1973) found that by using the Q-sort technique, therapists come to rapidly form a stable image of the patient. In fact, it appeared that "somewhere between the second and fourth therapeutic hour it has stabilized approximately to the degree permitted by the terminal sort-resort reliabilities" (p. 122). Of course, a stable view of the patient is not equivalent to the validity of the perception, but this finding does bear on the pragmatic or cost–benefit usefulness of testing and assessment. Summarizing these findings, Meehl (1973) wrote the following:

> Since the commonest justification for expenditure of psychometric time is the utility to the therapist of "advance knowledge," . . . the skepticism expressed by our sample of psychotherapists, taken in combination with the convergence curves for the therapist's perception of his patient, put this widely held belief badly in need of experimental support. (p. 132)

Unfortunately, Meehl and his colleagues never went on to test this belief (Meehl, personal communication, 1990).

Although Meehl's group of therapists in 1960 were quite skeptical about the value of psychological testing in psychotherapy, recent surveys of clinical psychologists demonstrate that a substantial number continue to do psychological testing (Berndt, 1983; Norcross & Prochaska, 1982; Wade & Baker, 1977) and apply their findings to their treatment recommendations. Moreover, articles continued to argue for the usefulness of psychological testing in making treatment recommendations (Honigfeld, 1971; Weiner, 1972; van Reken, 1981).

Most of the authors who discuss the actual application of psychological testing to treatment use projective tests and are primarily psychodynamically oriented. In many cases, the articles are anecdotal case reports. For example, Cerney (1978) wrote on the use of an entire test battery to predict outcome of psychotherapy, to function as an objective measure to assist in examining the process of treatment, and to point out possible pitfalls in psychotherapeutic treatment. Aronow and Reznikoff (1971) provided a case study of the application of projective tests in treatment. Walker (1974) noted the usefulness of the word association sentence method in predicting psychotherapy outcome. Lovitt (1988) provided support for his contention that "intensive study of each person's personality structure or coping style is necessary for a proper match between the patient and a treatment approach" (p. 518).

Mortimer and Smith (1983), from a psychodynamic perspective, wrote of the usefulness of psychological testing in three long-term treatment cases. Although their article was also anecdotal, its encouragement of explicit focus in treatment and clear case description is laudable. The test report of a battery of tests was used to provide explicit direction on a different focal point in each case. In one situation, the test report focused on the patient's ego deficits; in another, it focused on the centrality of a certain impulse-defense configuration; and in the third, it focused on a possible transference paradigm and core neurotic conflict. Mortimer and Smith (1983) noted that

> as psychotherapists, we have become convinced that an unfocused or inaccurately focused treatment may be a considerable disservice to the patient. . . . The test report is a useful tool to help establish a central focus initially and to regain it when the report is reviewed. . . . When we determine the relative centrality of the different facets which the patient presents to us in testing, we are able to help psychotherapists determine where to focus their efforts and attention. (p. 138)

Workers at the Menninger Foundation, long a bastion of the sophisticated use of psychological tests, continue to publish work on using projective testing in psychotherapeutic treatment. Colson, Pickar, and Coyne (1989) used the Rorschach to help predict possible patient factors leading to treatment difficulties in a long-term inpatient setting. There were some significant findings, although they cautioned that "the findings are few and of low magnitude. . . . Hence examiners should be cautious about using Rorschach findings to draw inferences about the course of hospital treatment" (Colson et al., 1989, p. 56). Schectman (1989) detailed how sensitive use of projective instruments can help therapists to better understand and deal with varying transference–countertransference dilemmas of borderline patients. In-depth use of such testing explicating countertransference possibilities can help clinicians to continue with such difficult patients: "What sustains us is our slow, but persistent, increased understanding of such patients, and of those dark parts of ourselves" (Schectman, 1989, p. 317).

Different from the traditional psychological testing instruments, Kiesler (1986a) used an interpersonalist assessment technique (either the Impact Message Inventory or Check List of Psychotherapy Transactions) prior to psychotherapy. He then formulated specific interventions and techniques to modify the interpersonal patterns if the patterns interfered with a person's life in or out of therapy. Kiesler's model is useful in that it highlights the inherently interactional basis of psychopathology and the therapeutic relationship. That is, Kiesler paid close attention to how the patient and the therapist reciprocally affect one another to produce any given dynamic moment in treatment. By conceptualizing treatment as interactional, the therapist can then begin to acknowledge his or her contribution to treatment and better understand how the patient's (or the therapist's) characteristic interpersonal style can be either an impediment or asset to therapeutic change.

Followers of George Kelly continue to value and publish articles and books on how their particular assessment methodology (the Role Construct Repertory Test) can be used to develop treatment strategies. Kelly defined constructs as "the axes of reference man contrives to put his psychological space in order and to plot his varying courses of action" (Kelly, 1969a, p. 36). Kelly's followers are convinced that use of their assessment methodology helps to alert the clinician to repetitive or limited constructs that patients bring to treatment. This could lead to explicit therapeutic strategies, including selecting other constructs, making constructs more explicit, testing constructs for their validity and consistency, and altering the range or meaning of a construct (Kelly, 1969b; Neimeyer, 1987).

There is one book by Butcher (1990) and at least one published article by Trimboli and Kilgore (1983) concerning the MMPI and treatment considerations. More directly germane to treatment issues, Trimboli (1979) offered unpublished material on ways in which the MMPI might be used to guide therapy. All of these authors discussed the ways in which the MMPI can be used in a psychodynamic manner to provide treatment implications. They also discussed each scale of the MMPI separately, making specific predictions about factors such as transference constellations, reasonable treatment goals, and issues of therapeutic timing and strategy.

Butcher (1990) recently wrote a comprehensive text on how the MMPI-2 can be used in objective assessment, treatment selection, and therapy planning. He provided methods for using each individual scale to predict treatment responsiveness, organized the material related to special scales of the MMPI and treatment evaluation, and addressed how to give feedback to patients who have taken the MMPI. One weakness of the book is that although Butcher claimed his treatment suggestions from high-point codes were "culled from the empirical literature on the MMPI in treatment contexts" (p. viii), he failed to cite any of those studies, which might lead readers to be skeptical of some of Butcher's suggestions.

There are few studies that have examined empirically the integration of psychological testing and psychotherapy outcome. W. Anderson and Bauer (1985), working with the MMPI, discussed how patients with a certain MMPI code type (2/4) present in psychotherapy and how successful treatment can be undertaken or altered to deal with the 2/4 personality characteristics. They contrasted successful and unsuccessful therapeutic work with these particular patients and provided rough guidelines for therapists working with "2/4" patients.

In another recent empirical study, Merbaum and Butcher (1982) examined the relation between therapists' ratings of patients' "likability," predictions of therapy benefit, and psychopathology as assessed by the MMPI. They found moderately strong associations between the patients rated by therapists as "difficult" and the patients' levels of self-reported pathology as reflected on the MMPI results. There were also strong associations between how "easy" patients were viewed as being by therapists and the estimated benefit from treatment. However, there were no differences between either easy or difficult patients and the actual number of therapy sessions completed. Merbaum and Butcher speculated that there is a relation between patients' pathology and their subsequent likability. Another interpretation may be that, because therapists tend to rate likable patients as having a superior prognosis, a self-fulfilling prophecy takes place. This has implications for the use of testing data early in treatment: It could be argued that therapists might become discouraged by a patient's pathological presentation on the testing and prematurely develop negative feelings about the eventual treatment outcome.

In a theoretical article related to concepts underlying the MCMI, Millon (1988) offered a new model of conceptualizing psychotherapy. He wrote of a model for interweaving diagnostic information and psychological treatment for those disorders. His "personologic psychotherapy" attempts to address environmental stressors, personality factors, and constitutional variables. He differentiated between "functional" and "structural" personality processes and highlighted particular combinations that lead to varying character pathology. Millon strongly supported the idea that assessment makes a difference in treatment technique but that simply making a diagnosis is not enough. Millon (1988) stated that "which attributes should be selected for therapeutic intervention is not, therefore, merely a matter of making 'a diagnosis,' but requires a comprehensive assessment, one that appraises not only the overall configuration of attributes, but differentiates their degrees of salience" (p. 215).

Millon was not specific in what treatment methods clinicians should apply, but he believes in basing interventions on empirically verified procedures that should be tailored to the patient's problem. He objected to application of the same therapy model to all emotional difficulties and hoped instead that clinicians combine techniques to achieve a whole that is greater than the sum of its parts. The foci of such therapy would vary, but, for example, it might involve simultaneous interventions at the level of interpersonal behavior a la Sullivan or modifications of dysfunctional beliefs or a faulty self-image through cognitive–behavioral modalities, a la Aaron Beck (Beck & Freeman, 1990). Others have argued that because the distinction between functional and dysfunctional personality traits is thought to lie in the extremeness and the rigidity of the traits, personality-oriented psychotherapy should attempt to help the patient become less extreme and less rigid with regard to the personality traits in question (Sim & Romney, 1990). Still others (Turkat, 1988, 1990; Turkat & Maisto, 1985) have offered specific guidelines and various techniques to use with personality disorders. However, such work is at a formative stage, and even the author of one "cookbook" admits that "scientific evidence to support or refute the validity of the approach is lacking" (Turkat, 1990, p. 16).

From an empirical viewpoint, the MCMI has been used in several studies to assess possible changes in personality that might occur as a result of varying treatment modalities. Clinical populations studied have included alcoholics and drug abusers (McMahon, Flynn, & Davidson, 1985b), private psychiatric inpatients (Piersma, 1986b), Vietnam veterans with PTSD (Hyer, Woods, Bruno, & Boudewyns, 1989), and spouse abusers (Hamberger & Hastings, 1988b). A consistent finding across these four studies is that, regardless of whether there was clinical improvement, personality style scales remained fairly stable from pre- to posttest assessments and were more stable than symptom scales (e.g., level of anxiety, depression).

Three other studies using the MCMI have briefly touched on the use of the MCMI in treatment contexts. Cantrell and Dana (1987) used the MCMI-I as a screening instrument with patients at a community mental health center. They demonstrated that the MCMI-I was poor at predicting premature termination of treatment, although there was evidence that dropouts scored significantly higher on the Dependent scale than patients who stayed in treatment long enough to be assigned a therapist. Moreover, there was a slight but significant correlation between total number of therapy sessions attended and scores on the Compulsive scale. These conclusions should be regarded as tentative because the sample size was relatively small ($N = 72$) and did not support the number of statistical tests performed on the data.

McMahon and Davidson (1986a) used the MCMI to examine depressed and nondepressed alcoholics treated in a VA inpatient unit. Patients were originally divided into the two groups on the basis of their scores on the Dysthymia scale. They demonstrated that these two groups could be differentiated on the basis of having a detached (schizoid or avoidant) personality style or because they were suffering from disorganized or distracted mentation (Schizotypal and Psychotic Thinking scale scores). Because the depressed alcoholics also had a longer history of alcohol abuse and more physical and psychological symptoms, McMahon and Davidson (1986a) recommended that this subgroup "would benefit most from an intensive, comprehensive, and long-term therapeutic program" (p. 183).

From a biological perspective, Joffe and Regan (1989a) examined patients who did and did not respond to tricyclic antidepressant treatment to determine whether there were personality differences between the two groups. The MCMI, Beck Depression Inventory, Hamilton Rating Scale for Depression, and Schedule for Affective Disorders and Schizophrenia were administered. In the remission phase, there were no significant differences between responders and nonresponders on the MCMI. In the depressed phase, responders scored higher on the Antisocial and Paranoia scales. The MCMI tended to overdiagnose personality disorders in the depressed phase. There was no difference in frequency of personality disorders between responders and nonresponders. The findings of this study are limited by the relatively small sample ($N = 42$).

One issue of concern involves the validity of the models presently used to generate treatment recommendations from test results. At least with the

MMPI, there is no shortage of automated programs (Graham, 1987). Many of these programs offer psychotherapeutic suggestions specific to a given code type. Unfortunately, these computerized services do not publish the method used in developing interpretations or therapy recommendations (Matarazzo, 1986). Moreover, they do not provide data on how accurate or helpful the suggestions were with given personality types. This is not to say, of course, that such a process of validating recommendations would be easy (Fowler & Butcher, 1986) but simply to highlight where current knowledge is in this area.

For example, one of the more publicized and favorably received computerized MMPI programs, the Caldwell Report, provides "treatment considerations" for the different MMPI code point types (Graham, 1977). These considerations include rough estimates of suicidal potential, possible indications for medications, predicted course of treatment, and suggestions of differing techniques that "have been beneficial in similar cases" (Caldwell, 1975, 1984). Caldwell has not, to our knowledge, published an explanation of how he obtained these results or data on their reliability and validity.

There have been many other attempts by computerized services to suggest treatment possibilities on the basis of MMPI results. To use another example, in the MMPI program by Strassberg, Cooper, and Marks (1987) available for use with personal computers, multiple treatment recommendations and suggestions are given. These include degree of psychological mindedness, potential transference constellations, and medication possibilities. Strassberg et al. mentioned in the report that their suggestions for treatment and diagnostic interpretation are based on their clinical experience and on the work of others. They cautioned that their information and suggestions are "suggestive and tentative" and "should be treated as hypotheses which are essentially untested outside of clinical work" (Strassberg et al., 1987, p. 1).

Graham (1987) believed that such caveats are not sufficient and cautioned that

> all of the studies that have tried to establish the validity of [computerized or automated] interpretive systems have had serious shortcomings. . . . No study to date has evaluated an entire interpretive system. The external criterion measures used in most studies have been limited in scope and of questionable reliability. (p. 242)

He further stated that it is essential that only qualified professionals use the reports and that other assessment data are integrated with the test findings. He concluded by saying that "the level of accuracy of the interpretive statements is at best modest, but in many cases it is no less than the accuracy of clinician-generated descriptions of clients based on MMPI data" (Graham, 1987, p. 242).

Thus, it is obvious that much work needs to be done to establish the validity and reliability of treatment suggestions, given certain test results. However, in lieu of such hard data and given that many clinicians already do make inferences for therapy on the basis of the testing they do with their patients or on even less reliable information, it might be useful to explore further what approaches could be used to generate treatment suggestions from MCMI results.

Using the MCMI in Psychotherapy: Supportive Versus Insight Orientations

What we can offer at this point are our own thoughts on how the results of the MCMI can be used to develop a treatment plan with psychotherapy patients.

We start by examining the issue of whether to recommend supportive or insight-oriented treatment. Dewald (1967, 1971) held that the vast majority of patients who seek psychotherapy actually are served best by supportive measures. He felt that insight-oriented, or exploratory, approaches are too anxiety-provoking and potentially overwhelming for most patients. Dewald appeared to feel that most patients have ego weakness or flawed self-identities that need "bolstering" or rebuilding rather than "deconstruction" or "reconstruction." He provided some clinical examples of how to generate supportive interventions for certain character types, such as giving a compulsive patient a less time-consuming substitute symptom. Unfortunately, Dewald failed to provide a comprehensive theoretical model of matching supportive techniques and treatment tactics with the patient's personality type.

Werman (1984), like Dewald, believed that many patients are better served by supportive rather than insight-oriented, or exploratory, methods. He also believed that many patients are too fragile to be able to handle interpretations of the unconscious, underlying dynamics, or even most aspects of the transference. Werman provided a rough cataloging of intervention strategies for supportive therapy, but he did not say much about the diagnoses of patients better suited for supportive treatment or about the results of psychological testing of such patients.

Kernberg (1984) differed from Werman and Dewald in his view of supportive psychotherapy. Kernberg felt that many patients can benefit more from an exploratory, expressive type of treatment. He tended to reserve supportive measures primarily for borderline patients with antisocial tendencies or for very focused, narrow goals when, because of financial or other constraints, a more leisurely expressive and exploratory approach is not possible.

A useful review of the supportive treatment literature is provided by Winston, Pinsker, and McCullough (1986). They summarized the major definitions, issues, and techniques of supportive psychotherapy. Of particular interest is the catalog and explanations they offered of the divergent techniques of supportive work. They concluded by urging better delineation of supportive treatment and encouraged those in training positions to supervise and teach supportive treatment with as much interest as they would in teaching the uncovering, or expressive, modalities. Winston et al. called for systematic research on the efficacy of such methods and readily acknowledged the dearth of empirical work in this area.

There is a tradition in psychoanalysis and in many forms of psychoanalytic therapy that discourages attempts to match therapy techniques to character patterns or constellations. Some might even object to a systematic method of choosing a given treatment modality or focus, particularly within expressive insight-oriented treatment. However, there are some notable exceptions. Alexander and French (1946), for instance, advocated briefer treatment methods wherein the therapist would attempt to provide whatever the patient had not been given by his or her original caretaker. For example, if the patient had been treated harshly and coldly as a child, the therapist would try to be as warm and nurturing as possible to ostensibly compensate for the deficits. This approach has met with a great deal of criticism and scorn, although some recent psychoanalytic writers (e.g., Levy, 1987; T. Shapiro, 1988, 1989) have seen the value in maintaining an explicit focus of the treatment strategy or aims in psychotherapy or psychoanalysis.

Levy (1987) argued that the analytical ideal of full neutrality, and the wait for the unfolding of the unconscious, is an artificial ideal. When being supervised on analytical treatment cases, Levy found that his supervisors would instruct him to focus on certain problems, ignore others, and, in general, adjust his technique to the patient's character type. He mentioned that such focusing and direction is a common part of the "unofficial" clinical lore of analytical therapists but that it is rarely discussed explicitly in the literature or in public forums.

Levy (1987) pointed out that one of the rare exceptions of strategic applications of technique on the basis of diagnosis or character pathology within the history of psychoanalytic literature is Glover (1955). In a chapter on the analyst's case list in his book *Psychoanalytic Therapy,* Glover (1955) discussed the numerous cases an analyst or analytically oriented therapist might encounter and generally divided the cases according to their "accessibility" or, as he put it, "the transference potential of the patient" (p. 185).

Within varying categories (e.g., anxiety hysteria, reactive depressions, obsessional neurosis, manic-depressive states), Glover (1955) speculated on the ultimate transference constellation, the most helpful and salient foci of the treatment, types of crises in treatment, and particular qualities of the termination process. He provided rough guidelines for the best "lines of approach" for each given case.

As a brief example of Glover's (1955) approach, he wrote of the paranoid patient:

> Of the three main character reactions manifested by the paranoiac ego, viz. suspicion, sensitiveness to contact and a defensive aggressiveness, the factor of suspicion calls for priority of attention. It should be ventilated from the first session of analysis; also from the first session the transference aspects should be raised in the slightly indirect form of ventilating the patient's reactions to treatment. . . . During these two early phases of analysis the delusional or near-delusional products of the patient should not be subject to interpretation but should be treated with non-committal receptivity. (p. 252)

Thus, it can be seen that Glover (1955) recommended specific technical maneuvers that take into account transference disposition, personality style, symptomatology, and timing within the treatment rather than the traditional analytical advice to remain more uniformly detached and silent, allowing the transference to unfold before making interpretations or providing direction.

More recently, other psychoanalytic clinicians have discussed explicitly the importance of needing to adapt the therapy technique to the differing psychopathology or character structure of the patient. Giovacchini (1984, 1987), Kernberg (1975), Kohut (1971, 1977), and D. Shapiro (1989), among others, have discussed in great detail the understanding and treatment of patients with borderline, narcissistic, or other character disorders. Those authors, to varying degrees, have developed particular techniques or guidelines for the specific treatment of the given character pathology. For example, Giovacchini (1987) wrote that "formulating a continuum of psychopathology based on the quality of object relations is useful for understanding patients and, to some extent, for anticipating transference development in treatment" (p. 314). Furthermore,

> the reason for making a diagnostic judgment—and some psychoanalysts doubt that there is any—is to help the clinician find dominant patterns of adaptations and defenses that permit conclusions about character structure and give some order and predictability to the treatment process. (Giovacchini, 1987, p. 322)

Thus, Giovacchini (1987) viewed diagnosis of character structure to be particularly useful in providing some broad outlines of possible transference manifestations so that there can be some planning of the therapeutic task ahead. He would probably emphasize assessment of the patient's history of object relations, as well as what led the patient to seek therapy. Although he did not mention it, psychological testing could also presumably be used to gain understanding into likely character traits and potential transference manifestations so that tentative treatment planning could occur.

Another recent contributor within psychoanalytic circles, T. Shapiro (1988, 1989) encouraged an intelligent integration of diagnostic classification and the methods and models of psychoanalysis. Shapiro wrote of the history of psychoanalytic or psychoanalytically informed diagnostic categorizations of the borderline patient. He, like Levy (1987), claimed that treatment of patients requires strategy, a strategy that is made more intelligible with firm diagnostic information. In the example of the borderline patient, he noted the following: "Of crucial importance for the conceptual soundness of borderline personality disorder or organization is the differentiation of therapeutic effect, with specific groups differentiated by the psychoanalytically guided techniques available" (T. Shapiro, 1989, p. 192). Although he did not mention psychological tests directly, presumably T. Shapiro (1989) would approve of the analytically informed usage of any psychological means to refine the "clinical truth" (p. 193) of clinical classifications so that wise treatment decisions can be made.

Along with the work done by those from a more classical analytical model, there has been a burgeoning of work from theorists within the interpersonalist camp that has examined treatment planning, predictions of process, and elucidation of strategies with differing personality styles. Kiesler (1977, 1979, 1982, 1986a, 1986b), McCullough (1984), and Van Denburg (1987), among others, have developed systematic methods to assess and direct treatment of patients with varying personality styles (e.g., borderline, passive-dependent, chronically dysthymic) from an interpersonal approach. The central assumptions of the interpersonalists' model were derived from Harry Stack Sullivan's (1953) seminal ideas that personality is "the relatively enduring pattern of recurrent interpersonal situations which characterize a human life" (pp. 110–111).

Kiesler's operationalization of Sullivan's ideas, following Leary's (1957) lead, was founded on the assumption that human interactions are a function of two basic motivations: the need for control (domination) and the need for affiliation (love, friendship). Kiesler (1983) constructed what he called the "interpersonal circle" to explain and classify the varying interactions that people engage in with one another. Kiesler posited that psychopathology is partially a function of rigid and extreme interpersonal behavior that is carried out across situations. Although the normal or healthy person is flexible and adaptable in his or her actions with significant others, the maladjusted person reenacts the same inflexible and limited roles with whomever he or she comes into contact. Kiesler extended these ideas to psychotherapy and theorized that patients will bring the same patterns to treatment, thus exerting the same interpersonal pulls in therapy that they exhibit in their outside lives. The therapist should be savvy enough to spot such interpersonal transactions and intervene accordingly in the treatment. Kiesler and his associates (Kiesler, 1982, 1986b; Kiesler, Van Denburg, Sikes, Larus, & Goldston, 1990) have demonstrated that *DSM–III* personality disorders can be reliably and validly described using interpersonal taxonomies and that there are beginnings of the application of such methodology to the treatment of specific disorders and styles (Andrews, 1984; Cashdan, 1982; Coyne, 1976; Kiesler, 1977, 1985, 1986a; Klerman, Weissman, Rounsaville, & Chevron, 1984; Young & Beier, 1982).

We think that one problem with the concept of "supportive" therapy is that the treatment is often unclear and poorly defined. Often what is meant by "supportive therapy" is simply that the therapist will be making an effort to be understanding, conciliatory, sympathetic, compassionate, and non-confrontative and that no demands will be made of the patient that the latter could find threatening or difficult. If those attributes are present in the relationship, it would generally be thought that the relationship would feel comfortable to the client and would contribute to the reduction of tension. This mode of therapy could possibly be prescribed for an individual who does not have the resources needed for a meaningful change, at least at the beginning of therapy. In spite of the merits of that general approach to therapy, the prescription of the same mode of interaction for every patient can be criticized as unduly simplistic and one that does not recognize the individual's uniqueness or the therapist's level of sophistication.

The results of the MCMI can provide one way of refining the system by allowing easy and effective consideration of the client's personality style. Knowing the individual's basic life assumptions and the cluster of traits that make up the client's personality structure allows the practitioner to set up an interpersonal environment during the session that is designed to be experienced by the client as ego syntonic and congenial to his or her own way of operating.

Table 7, borrowed from a training manual written by Choca (1988), offers some of the interpersonal characteristics that theoretically would lead to a supportive therapeutic experience with the different personality styles. Note the flexibility that this additional level of sophistication allows. Looking at any particular type of intervention (e.g., confrontation), the consideration of the personality style allows the practitioner to avoid such interventions with some individuals (i.e., avoidant or dependent clients) while using it with others (i.e., competitive clients). With most of our clients, the issues become more complex than the table would lead one to believe because most people have a combination of more than one personality style. Thus, the therapist would have to mix and integrate the recommendations that are given in the table in order to do justice to most patients.

Especially in the case of individuals whose personality traits are too extreme or too rigid and who may be considered to have a personality disorder, care should be taken not to emphasize the ego-syntonic recommendations to the point of fostering further pathology. For the supportive relationship to remain beneficial, the therapist has to operate at the client's level so that the relationship is comfortable without being antitherapeutic. With a dependent individual, for instance, if the therapist is to take responsibility for things that the client can handle by himself or herself, the interventions would be seen as encouraging the individual to become more dependent than he or she already is, a movement that would be regressive.

From our viewpoint, the issue of supportive versus insight-oriented therapy cannot involve the choice of one to the exclusion of the other. Most

Table 7

Supportive Interventions for the Different Personality Styles

Style	Supportive Attributes
1. Schizoid	Accept interpersonal distance Problem solve in practical matters Do not emphasize insight Do not emphasize relationships
2. Avoidant	Reassure Be careful with negative interpretations Be relaxed
3. Dependent	Be dominant Be protective
4. Histrionic	Allow patient to be center of attention Be emotionally demonstrative
5. Narcissistic	Allow patient to be dominant Be careful with negative interpretations
6. Competitive	Accept competitive assumption Show how the client is not competing well in terms of his or her psychological functioning Be firm when limits are tested
7. Compulsive	Be on time Be organized Accept a hierarchical view of the world
8. Negativistic	As much as possible, do not tell patient what to do (any controls will be used as an issue by the patient) Tolerate and interpret moods

Note.   Information contained in this table used by permission.

therapists adjust their treatment to fit patients' needs while attempting, at least to some degree, to increase their understanding of the way they function. The more capable, psychologically developed, functional, and motivated therapy candidates are, the more feasible it may be to emphasize the goal of raising their level of functioning or understanding.

Personality theory and the MCMI can also be useful with an insight-oriented treatment plan. In the majority of the cases we see, especially after the acute symptomatology diminishes, the client is left to struggle with cumbersome or pathological personality traits. Knowing what those traits are and having some understanding of the theoretical etiologies of those traits can provide invaluable help in designing the treatment strategies.

Using the MCMI in Psychotherapy: Brief Versus Long Term

The literature on brief therapy tends to pay more attention to ways in which psychotherapy can be altered or planned to appropriately deal with divergent personality types or diagnoses. This is no doubt about the need to be as judicious as possible, given either internally or externally imposed treatment length constraints.

Most, although not all, brief therapy theorists begin their therapeutic assessment procedure by limiting the patient populations that can be treated with their methods. Davanloo (1979), Sifneos (1972), Mann (1973), and Malan (1976) all attempted to screen patients for more serious psychopathology prior to attempting brief treatment. Thus, they would likely exclude personality types and disorders such as borderline, narcissistic, schizoid, schizotypal, and paranoid clients from being treated with their methods.

In contrast to the majority of brief therapists, Strupp and Binder (1984) reported that they "have seen that the range of patients thought to be treatable has been progressively extended" and that "the best available evidence [of when brief therapy is appropriate] remains clinical experience" (p. 56). Consistent with Strupp and Binder's perspective, Donovan (1987) wrote a very useful and insightful article on the ways in which brief therapy methods can be broadened to treat a wider variety of patient types and personality disorders. He postulated that all personality disorders can be traced to a nuclear conflict: the holding of a core pathogenic belief about the self. The belief can take on a variety of forms, but it usually pertains to issues involving the modulation of self-esteem. These problems with self-esteem, Donovan continued, are a direct derivative of interactions with early caretakers.

To help a patient in brief therapy using Donovan's (1987) ideas, the therapist must first do a focal inquiry of pathogenic convictions about the self. This requires "the taking of an empathic object relations history" (Donovan, 1987, p. 176). Along with this inquiry comes facing and dealing with potentially disorganizing and intense affect. However, the therapist should not make matters worse by prematurely confronting or interpreting in a manner that causes the patient to be retraumatized. Donovan seemed to be saying that if the patient can trust the relationship enough and be understood, powerful affect will emerge. Finally, an attempt is made to reframe the pathogenic belief about the self, and the therapist "must offer himself as an alternative self object" when "the patient is most vulnerable and most in need of this function" (Donovan, 1987, p. 176). By examining the patient's object-relations history and sensitively determining what the patient can bear to hear about himself or herself, Donovan would implicitly be taking into account the personality style of the patient, even though he did not use that exact language.

Horowitz et al. (1984), writing from within the brief treatment field, stated that

> the question of which kind of therapy is best for a particular person is unanswered by available research data. This is especially the case with reference to

character style or the nature of Axis 2 [*sic*] diagnosis [presence of personality disorders] in the American Psychiatric Association's *Diagnostic and Statistical Manual.* (p. 31)

Nonetheless, Horowitz et al. did attempt to provide explicit "roadmaps" and clinical landmarks for the psychotherapy of divergent personality types, including hysterical, compulsive, narcissistic, and borderline patients.

Horowitz et al. (1984) intentionally restricted their book and study to helping patients who were in the midst of a grief reaction caused by the death of a parent. They proposed that different personality styles have different defensive structures, varying cognitive patterns, and divergent interpersonal behavior. Because of these multiple variations, the reactions to the loss and grief differ. This necessitates that the therapist be flexible in his or her approach so that psychotherapeutic interventions can be best geared to the unique personality qualities of each patient.

Horowitz et al. (1984) described their use of a "configurational analysis" to examine all cases presented to their research group and used this analysis to order data in a more systematic manner than is often the case in ordinary case conferences and case studies. Factors such as *DSM–III* diagnosis, "states of mind," role relationships, and modes of information processing were considered, both within and outside of treatment. According to Horowitz et al. (1984), "case formulation may help a therapist to understand relationship problems based on individual personality styles" (p. 57). Treatment had to be uniquely tailored to the individual case because, in spite of the fact that each patient had a parent die shortly before beginning therapy, there were "individualized variations in response, resting in part on personality style" (Horowitz et al., 1984, p. 57). In the chapters covering the varying personality styles, the authors sought to "emphasize the difficulties in establishing a therapeutic alliance with persons who have different personality styles" and "describe the process in therapy by which this came about" (Horowitz et al., 1984, p. 67).

MCMI Personality Styles and the Therapeutic Relationship

As already mentioned, Lovitt (1988) argued that "intensive study of each person's personality structure or coping style is necessary for a proper match between the patient and a treatment approach" (p. 518). Although that suggestion may be ideal, in most settings clinicians generally have to accept patients as they are referred or assigned. In either case, in theory the MCMI results could help with the matching or at least could indicate the kind of relationship that would result between two specific individuals on the basis of their particular personality styles.

Such a pragmatic, real-world model was suggested by Sweeney, Clarkin, and Fitzgibbon (1987). They supported the use of the MCMI as a test that could profitably be used in initial screenings to make treatment recommendations within an acute inpatient setting. Sweeney et al. called for a more focused problem-oriented assessment method that is economically practical and backed by empirical support.

A number of studies have explored the relation between single personality traits and treatment parameters. For instance, Fry (1975) found that a directive and controlling therapist produced more satisfaction for patients who look outside of themselves for their locus of control. Canter's (1966, 1971) work indicated that the characteristic of authoritarianism was related to a patient's preference for different therapeutic approaches. The Intraception trait on the Edwards Personal Preference Schedule (Edwards, 1959) has been correlated with an orientation toward insight in therapy (Birch, 1976; Gibeau, 1975). In addition, numerous studies have examined the relation between "therapeutic behaviors" such as openness, empathy, and genuineness and the therapist's personality traits (S. Anderson, 1968; Bent, Putnam, Kiesler, & Nowicki, 1976; Beutler, Johnson, Neville, Workman, & Elkins, 1973; Brewer, 1974; C. Palmer, 1975; Wright, 1975).

It seems logical that an individual's personality style will exert a significant influence on the quality of the interpersonal relationship that he or she establishes. In a pilot study conducted at our medical center (Choca, Silverman, & Gerber, 1980; Silverman, 1979), we examined the quality of the kind of relationship that patients established with their therapists in terms of the strength, dominance, and conflictualness. As expected, the findings showed that schizoid individuals tended to establish relationships that were seen by the therapist as having low strength; an unpredicted significant correlation was found between Compulsive scale scores of the MCMI and the staff's strength rating. Our data suggested that histrionic and antisocial patients were inclined to play a more dominant role. Finally, the Antisocial and the Compulsive scale scores were significantly related to the amount of conflict that the patient perceived in the relationship.

Treatment Outcome Studies

The MCMI-I has also been occasionally used to document the effects of treatment. For instance, McMahon et al. (1985a) reported a reduction of the MCMI-I scores for a heterogeneous psychiatric population and two groups of substance abusers after 1–3 months of treatment. Similar results were reported by Piersma (1986a) for psychiatric inpatients.

Studying a more defined population and treatment, McMahon et al. (1986) found that high-social-functioning alcoholics made significantly greater gains on the MCMI-I as a result of a behaviorally oriented therapeutic community treatment than the low-social-functioning alcoholics. Although their findings may be plagued by the problem of distinguishing between the severity of the alcoholism and the level of social functioning, McMahon et al. saw their data as indicating that lower functioning alcoholics may need social skills training in addition to the conventional treatment for alcoholism.

Peniston and Kulkosky (1990) compared the effect of alpha–theta brainwave relaxation training with the use of group therapy and lectures in the treatment of alcoholics. The findings indicated that the group treated with the relaxation technique decreased their MCMI-I scores on 13 of the 20 scales. In contrast, the subjects receiving only group therapy and lectures obtained significant decreases on 2 scales and showed an increase on Compulsive scale scores.

Finally, at least judging from the MCMI-I, an intense 5-week inpatient treatment of veterans with PTSD did not lead to a reduction of the symptomatology (Hyer et al., 1989). They reported higher scores on 17 of the 20 scales after treatment, even though none of the changes were significant. Those authors tentatively concluded that chronic PTSD is resistant to short-term treatment.

Summary and Conclusion

There does not appear to be sufficient empirical evidence to support the rational "prescription" of specific therapeutic modalities or psychotherapeutic techniques given certain psychological test findings. Even attempts to do something as crude as predict through testing or other means who will and who will not remain in treatment has been problematic (Affleck & Garfield, 1961; Garfield & Bergin, 1978). Although there are some suggestions in the literature that individuals with certain personality constellations are more likely to terminate treatment earlier (e.g., Auld & Eron, 1953; Baekland & Lundwall, 1975; Lorr, Katz, & Rubinstein, 1958), rigorously controlled recent studies have failed to demonstrate that psychological tests (in this case the MMPI) or other methods can predict premature termination of psychotherapy (Dubrin & Zastowny, 1988). Thus, clinicians are forced to use theory, speculation, and clinical hunches to suggest treatment methods that might lead to successful process or outcome of treatment given certain testing findings.

This is essentially the approach we took in our suggested treatment recommendations with the Millon Clinical Multiaxial Inventory. Furthermore, we focused our attention and treatment advice solely on individual psychotherapy with a given patient. It is possible, of course, that the MCMI, and other test instruments, might be given when the patient is involved in family, marital, or group treatment in an outpatient or inpatient setting. It would be up to individual clinicians how they choose to apply our suggestions to varying therapeutic settings and situations. Moreover, as suggested by Graham (1987), we advocate the understanding and integration of other assessment materials and clinical case histories before any firm and definitive treatment methods are instigated. Finally, we firmly hold that only qualified professionals with full training in psychological testing, diagnosis, and psychotherapy use the MCMI as an instrument to guide treatment directions.

References

Abraham, K. (1927). The influence of oral eroticism on character formation. In *Selected papers on psychoanalysis* (pp. 393–406). London: Hogarth. (Original work published 1924)

Adams, W., & Clopton, J. (1990). Personality and dissonance among Mormon missionaries. *Journal of Personality Assessment, 54,* 684–693.

Adler, A. (1956). The style of life. In H. L. Ansbacher & R. R. Ansbacher (Eds.), *The individual psychology of Alfred Adler* (pp. 172–203). New York: Basic Books.

Affleck, D., & Garfield, S. (1961). Predictive judgments of therapists and duration of stay in psychotherapy. *Journal of Clinical Psychology, 17,* 134–137.

Alexander, G. E., Choca, J. P., Bresolin, L. B., DeWolfe, A. S., Johnson, J. E., & Ostrow, D. G. (1987, May). *Personality styles in affective disorders: Trait components of a state disorder.* Paper presented at the convention of the Midwestern Psychological Association, Chicago.

Alexander, G. E., Choca, J. P., DeWolfe, A. S., Bresolin, L. B., Johnson, J. E., & Ostrow, D. G. (1987, August). *Interaction between personality and mood in unipolar and bipolar patients.* Paper presented at the 95th Annual Convention of the American Psychological Association, New York.

Alexander, F., & French, T. (1946). *Psychoanalytic therapy.* New York: Ronald Press.

Alnaes, R., & Torgersen, S. (1990). MCMI personality disorders among patients with major depression with and without anxiety disorders. *Journal of Personality Disorders, 4,* 141–149.

American Psychiatric Association. (1980). *Diagnostic and statistical manual of mental disorders* (3rd ed.). Washington, DC: Author.

American Psychiatric Association. (1985). *DSM-IIIR in development: Draft.* Washington, DC: Author.

American Psychiatric Association. (1987). *Diagnostic and statistical manual of mental disorders* (3rd ed., rev.). Washington, DC: Author.

Anderson, S. (1968). Effects of confrontation by high and low-functioning therapists. *Journal of Counseling Psychology, 15*, 411–416.

Anderson, W., & Bauer, B. (1985). Clients with MMPI high D-PD: Therapy implications. *Journal of Clinical Psychology, 41*, 181–188.

Andrews, J. (1984). Psychotherapy with the hysterical personality. *Psychiatry, 47*, 211–232.

Anrig, G. R. (1987). "Golden rule": Second thoughts. *APA Monitor, 18*, p. 3.

Antoni, M., Levine, J., Tischer, P., Green, C., & Millon, T. (1986). Refining personality assessments by combining MCMI high-point profiles and MMPI codes, Part IV: MMPI 89/98. *Journal of Personality Assessment, 50*, 65–72.

Antoni, M., Levine, J., Tischer, P., Green, C., & Millon, T. (1987). Refining personality assessments by combining MCMI high-point profiles and MMPI codes, Part V: MMPI 78/87. *Journal of Personality Assessment, 51*, 375–387.

Antoni, M., Tischer, P., Levine, J., Green, C., & Millon, T. (1985a). Refining personality assessments by combining MCMI high-point profiles and MMPI codes, Part I: MMPI 28/82. *Journal of Personality Assessment, 49*, 392–398.

Antoni, M., Tischer, P., Levine, J., Green, C., & Millon, T. (1985b). Refining personality assessments by combining MCMI high-point profiles and MMPI codes, Part III: MMPI 24/42. *Journal of Personality Assessment, 49*, 508–515.

Aronow, E., & Reznikoff, M. (1971). Application of projective tests to psychotherapy: A case study. *Journal of Personality Assessment, 35*, 379–393.

Auerbach, J. S. (1984). Validation of two scales for narcissistic personality disorder. *Journal of Personality Assessment, 48*, 649–653.

Auld, F., & Eron, L. (1953). The use of Rorschach scores to predict whether patients will continue psychotherapy. *Journal of Consulting Psychology, 17*, 104–109.

Baekland, F., & Lundwall, M. (1975). Dropping out of treatment: A critical review. *Psychological Bulletin, 82*, 738–783.

Bagby, R. M., Gillis, J. R., Toner, B. B., & Goldberg, J. (1991). Detecting fake-good and fake-bad responding on the Millon Clinical Multiaxial Inventory-II. *Psychological Assessment: A Journal of Consulting and Clinical Psychology, 3*, 496–498.

Bartsch, T. W., & Hoffman, J. J. (1985). A cluster analysis of Millon Clinical Multiaxial Inventory (MCMI) profiles: More about a taxonomy of alcoholic subtypes. *Journal of Clinical Psychology, 41*, 707–713.

Bech, P., Shapiro, R. W., Sihm, F., Nielsen, B. M., Sorensen, B., & Rafaelsen, O. J. (1980). Personality in unipolar and bipolar manic-melancholic patients. *Acta Psychiatrica Scandinavica, 62*, 245–257.

Beck, A. T. (1983). Cognitive therapy of depression: New perspectives. In P. Clayton & J. E. Barrett (Eds.), *Treatment of depression: Old controversies and new approaches* (pp. 265–290). New York: Raven Press.

Beck, A., & Freeman, A. (1990). *Cognitive therapy of personality disorders.* New York: Guilford Press.

Benjamin, L. S. (1974). Structural analysis of social behavior. *Psychological Review, 81*, 392–495.

Benjamin, L. S. (1984). Principles of prediction using Structural Analysis of Social Behavior (SASB). In R. A. Zucker, J. Aronoff, & A. J. Rabin (Eds.), *Personality and the prediction of behaviors* (pp. 121–173). New York: Guilford Press.

Bent, R., Putnam, D., Kiesler, D., & Nowicki, S. (1976). Correlates of successful and unsuccessful psychotherapy. *Journal of Consulting and Clinical Psychology, 44*, 149.

Berndt, D. (1983). Ethical and professional considerations in psychological assessment. *Professional Psychology: Research and Practice, 14*, 580–587.

Bersoff, D. N. (1988). Should subjective employment devices be scrutinized? It's elementary, my dear Ms. Watson. *American Psychologist, 12*, 1016–1018.

Beutler, L. (1989). Differential treatment selection: The role of diagnosis in psychotherapy. *Psychotherapy, 26*, 271–281.

Beutler, L., Johnson, D., Neville, C., Workman, S., & Elkins, D. (1973). The A-B-therapy-type distinction, accurate empathy, nonpossessive warmth and therapist genuineness in psychotherapy. *Journal of Abnormal Psychology, 82*, 273–277.

Birch, W. (1976). The relationship between personality traits and treatment outcome in a therapeutic environment. *Dissertation Abstracts International, 37A*, 3508.

Blatt, S. J., & Auerbach, J. S. (1988). Differential cognitive disturbances in three types of borderline patients. *Journal of Personality Disorders, 2*, 198–211.

Bonato, D. P., Cyr, J. J., Kalprin, R. A., Prendergast, P., & Sanhueza, P. (1988). The utility of the MCMI as a DSM-III Axis I diagnostic tool. *Journal of Clinical Psychology, 44*, 867–875.

Brewer, B. (1974). Relationships among personality, empathic ability and counselor effectiveness. *Dissertation Abstracts International, 35A*, 6449.

Bryer, J. B., Martines, K. A., & Dignan, M. (1990). Millon Clinical Multiaxial Inventory Alcohol Abuse and Drug Abuse scales and the identification of substance abuse patients. *Personality Assessment, 2*, 438–441.

Burke, H. R., & Mayer, S. (1985). The MMPI and the posttraumatic stress syndrome in Vietnam era veterans. *Journal of Clinical Psychology, 41*, 152–155.

Buss, A. (1989). Personality as traits. *American Psychologist, 44*, 1378–1388.

Butcher, J. N. (1990). *MMPI-2 in psychological treatment.* New York: Oxford University Press.

Butcher, J. N., Braswell, L., & Raney, D. (1983). A cross-cultural comparison of American Indian, Black and White inpatients on the MMPI and presenting symptoms. *Journal of Consulting and Clinical Psychology, 51*, 587–594.

Butcher, J., & Owen, P. (1978). Objective personality inventories: Recent research and some contemporary issues. In B. Wolman (Ed.), *Clinical diagnoses of mental disorders: A handbook* (pp. 475–546). New York: Plenum Press.

Caldwell, A. (1975). *A handbook of MMPI personality types.* Unpublished manuscript.

Caldwell, A. (1984). *The Caldwell report: A sample.* Santa Monica, CA: Clinical Psychological Services.

Calsyn, D. A., Saxon, A. J., & Daisy, F. (1990). Validity of the MCMI drug abuse scale with drug abusing and psychiatric samples. *Journal of Clinical Psychology, 46,* 244–246.

Canter, F. (1966). Personality factors related to participation in treatment of hospitalized male alcoholics. *Journal of Clinical Psychology, 22,* 114–116.

Canter, F. (1971). Authoritarian attitudes, degree of pathology and preference for structured versus unstructured psychotherapy in hospitalized mental patients. *Psychological Reports, 28,* 231–234.

Cantrell, J. D., & Dana, R. H. (1987). Use of the Millon Clinical Multiaxial Inventory (MCMI) as a screening instrument in a community mental health center. *Journal of Clinical Psychology, 43,* 366–375.

Cash, T. F., Mikulka, P. J., & Brown, T. A. (1989). Validity of the Millon's computerized interpretation system for the MCMI: Comment on Moreland and Onstad. *Journal of Consulting and Clinical Psychology, 57,* 311–312.

Cashdan, S. (1982). Interactional psychotherapy: Using the relationship. In J. Anchin & D. Kiesler (Eds.), *Handbook of interpersonal psychotherapy.* New York: Pergamon Press.

Cattell, R. B. (1946). *The description and measurement of personality.* New York: World Book.

Cattell, R. B. (1965). *The scientific analysis of personality.* Chicago: Aldine.

Cattell, R. B. (1986). *Manual for the Sixteen Personality Factor Questionnaire.* Savoy, IL: Institute for Personality and Ability Testing.

Cerney, M. (1978). Use of the psychological test report in the course of psychotherapy. *Journal of Personality Assessment, 42,* 457–463.

Charney, D., Nelson, J. C., & Quinlan, D. M. (1981). Personality traits and disorder in depression. *American Journal of Psychiatry, 138,* 1601–1604.

Choca, J. (1988). *Manual for clinical psychology trainees* (2nd ed.). New York: Brunner/Mazel.

Choca, J., Bresolin, L., Okonek, A., & Ostrow, D. (1988). Validity of the Millon Clinical Multiaxial Inventory in the assessment of affective disorders. *Journal of Personality Assessment, 53,* 96–105.

Choca, J., Greenblatt, R., Tobin, D., Shanley, L., & Van Denburg, E. (1989, August). *Factor analytic structure of MCMI items.* Paper presented at the 97th Annual Convention of the American Psychological Association, New Orleans, LA.

Choca, J., Okonek, A., Ferm, R., & Ostrow, D. (1982, May). *The relationship of personality style and lithium efflux in affective disorders.* Paper presented at the convention of the American Psychiatric Association, Toronto, Ontario, Canada.

Choca, J. P., Peterson, C. A., & Shanley, L. A. (1986a). Factor analysis of the Millon Clinical Multiaxial Inventory. *Journal of Consulting and Clinical Psychology, 54,* 253–255.

Choca, J., Peterson, C., & Shanley, L. (1986b, August). *Racial bias and the MCMI.* Paper presented at the 94th Annual Convention of the American Psychological Association, Washington, DC.

Choca, J., Peterson, C., & Shanley, L. (1986c, March). *Racial bias and the MCMI: A factor analytic study.* Paper presented at the First Conference on the Millon Inventories, Miami, FL.

Choca, J., Shanley, L., Peterson, C., & Hong, J. (1987, August). *A PTSD scale for the MCMI.* Paper presented at the 95th Annual Convention of the American Psychological Association, New York.

Choca, J., Shanley, L. A., Peterson, C. A., & Van Denburg, E. (1990). Racial bias and the MCMI. *Journal of Personality Assessment, 54,* 479–490.

Choca, J., Shanley, L. A., Van Denburg, E., Agresti, A., Mouton, A., & Uskokovic, L. (in press). Personality disorder or personality style: That is the question. *Journal of Counseling and Development.*

Choca, J., Silverman, J., & Gerber, J. (1980). *The effect of the patient's personality style on the therapeutic relationship and therapy outcome ratings.* Unpublished manuscript.

Chodoff, P. (1972). The depressive personality. *Archives of General Psychiatry, 27,* 666–673.

Clarkin, J. F., Widiger, T. A., Frances, A., Hurt, S. W., & Gilmore, M. (1983). Prototypic typology and the borderline personality disorder. *Journal of Abnormal Psychology, 92,* 263–275.

Cohen, M. B., Baker, G., Cohen, R. A., Fromm-Reichmann, F., & Weigert, E. V. (1954). An intensive study of twelve cases of manic depressive psychosis. *Psychiatry, 17,* 103–137.

Colson, D., Pickar, D., & Coyne, L. (1989). Rorschach correlates of treatment difficulty in a long-term psychiatric hospital. *Bulletin of the Menninger Clinic, 53,* 52–57.

Comrey, A. L. (1978). Common methodological problems in factor analytic studies. *Journal of Consulting and Clinical Psychology, 46,* 648–659.

Costa, P. T., & McCrae, R. R. (1985). *The NEO Personality Inventory manual.* Odessa, FL: Psychological Assessment Resources.

Costa, P. T., & McCrae, R. R. (1990). Personality disorders and the five-factor model of personality. *Journal of Personality Disorders, 4,* 362–371.

Costello, R. M., Fine, H. J., & Blau, B. I. (1973). Racial comparisons on the Minnesota Multiphasic Personality Inventory. *Journal of Clinical Psychology, 29,* 63–65.

Costello, R. M., Tiffany, D. W., & Gier, R. H. (1972). Methodology issues and racial (black-white) comparisons on the MMPI. *Journal of Consulting and Clinical Psychology, 38,* 161–168.

Coyne, J. (1976). Toward an interactional description of depression. *Psychiatry, 39,* 28–40.

Craig, R. J., & Olson, R. E. (1990). MCMI comparisons of cocaine abusers and heroin addicts. *Journal of Clinical Psychology, 46,* 230–237.

Craig, R. J., Verinis, J. S., & Wexler, S. (1985). Personality characteristics of drug addicts and alcoholics on the Millon Clinical Multiaxial Inventory. *Journal of Personality Assessment, 49,* 156–160.

Cronbach, L. J. (1975). Five decades of public controversy over mental testing. *American Psychologist, 30,* 1–14.

Crowne, D., & Marlowe, D. (1964). *The approval motive.* New York: Wiley.

Dahlstrom, W. G., Lachar, D., & Dahlstrom, L. E. (1986). *MMPI patterns of American minorities.* Minneapolis: University of Minnesota Press.

Dahlstrom, W. G., Welsh, G. S., & Dahlstrom, L. E. (1972). *An MMPI handbook: Clinical interpretations* (Vol. 1). Minneapolis: University of Minnesota Press.

Davanloo, H. (1979). Technique of short-term psychotherapy. *Psychiatric Clinics of North America, 2,* 11–22.

Davis, W. E., Beck, S. J., & Ryan, T. A. (1973). Race-related and educationally-related MMPI profile differences among hospitalized schizophrenics. *Journal of Clinical Psychology, 29,* 478–479.

Davis, W., & Greenblatt, R. (1990). Age differences among psychiatric inpatients on the MCMI. *Journal of Clinical Psychology, 46,* 770–774.

Davis, W. E., Greenblatt, R., & Choca, J. (1991, August). *Racial bias and the MCMI-II.* Paper presented at the 99th Annual Convention of the American Psychological Association, San Francisco.

Davis, W. E., Greenblatt, R. L., & Pochyly, J. M. (1990). Test of MCMI black norms for five scales. *Journal of Clinical Psychology, 46,* 175–178.

DeJong, C. A. J., van den Brink, W., Jansen, J. A. M., & Schippers, G. M. (1989). Interpersonal aspects of the DSM-III Axis II: Theoretical hypotheses and empirical findings. *Journal of Personality Disorders, 3,* 135–146.

Denton, L. (1988). Board votes to oppose Golden Rule technique. *APA Monitor, 19,* p. 7.

Derogatis, L. (1983). The Symptom Checklist-90 Manual II. Towson, MD: Clinical Psychometric Research.

Dewald, P. (1967). Therapeutic evaluation and potential: The psychodynamic point of view. *Comprehensive Psychiatry, 8,* 284–298.

Dewald, P. (1971). *Psychotherapy: A dynamic approach.* New York: Basic Books.

DeWolfe, A., Larson, J. K., & Ryan, J. J. (1985). Diagnostic accuracy of the Millon test computer reports for bipolar affective disorders. *Journal of Psychopathology and Behavioral Assessment, 7,* 185–189.

Dohrenwend, B. S., & Dohrenwend, B. P. (1981). Life stress and illness: Formulation of the issues. In B. S. Dohrenwend & B. P. Dohrenwend (Eds.), *Stressful life events and their contexts* (pp. 1–27). New York: Prodist.

Donat, D. (1991, August). *Personality (MCMI) subtypes among public psychiatric inpatient admissions.* Paper presented at the 99th Annual Convention of the American Psychological Association, San Francisco.

Donnelly, E. F. (1976). Cross-sectional and longitudinal comparisons of bipolar and unipolar depressed groups on the MMPI. *Journal of Consulting and Clinical Psychology, 44,* 233–237.

Donovan, J. (1987). Brief dynamic psychotherapy: Toward a more comprehensive model. *Psychiatry, 50,* 167–183.

Door, D., Barley, W., Gard, B., & Webb, C. (1983). Understanding and treating borderline personality organization. *Psychotherapy: Theory, Research and Practice, 20,* 397–404.

Dubrin, J., & Zastowny, T. (1988). Predicting early attrition from psychotherapy: An analysis of a large private practice cohort. *Psychotherapy, 25,* 393–408.

Dubro, A. F., Wetzler, S., & Kahn, M. W. (1988). A comparison of three self-report questionnaires for the diagnosis of the DSM-III personality disorders. *Journal of Personality Disorders, 2,* 256–266.

Duthie, B., & Vincent, K. R. (1986). Diagnostic hit rates of high point codes for the Diagnostic Inventory of Personality and Symptoms using random assignment, base rates, and probability scales. *Journal of Clinical Psychology, 42,* 612–614.

Edwards, A. L. (1959). *Edwards Personal Preference Schedule.* San Antonio, TX: The Psychological Corporation.

Elbow, M. (1977). Theoretical considerations of violent marriages. *Social Casework, 58,* 515–526.

Endler, N. S., & Edwards, J. M. (1988). Personality disorders from an interactional perspective. *Journal of Personality Disorders, 2,* 326–333.

Endler, N. S., & Magnusson, D. (1976). Toward an interactional psychology of personality. *Psychological Bulletin, 83,* 956–974.

Eysenck, H. J. (1976). *The measurement of personality.* Baltimore, MD: University Park Press.

Fairbank, J. A., Keane, T. M., & Malloy, P. F. (1983). Some preliminary data on the psychological characteristics of Vietnam-era veterans with posttraumatic stress disorders. *Journal of Consulting and Clinical Psychology, 51,* 912–919.

Finn, S. E. (1982). Base rates, utilities, and the DSM-III: Shortcomings of fixed rule systems of psychodiagnosis. *Journal of Abnormal Psychology, 91,* 294–302.

Flynn, P. M., & McMahon, R. C. (1983). Indicators of depression and suicidal ideation among drug abusers. *Psychological Reports, 52,* 784–786.

Flynn, P. M., & McMahon, R. C. (1984). An examination of the factor structure of the Millon Clinical Multiaxial Inventory. *Journal of Personality Assessment, 48,* 308–311.

Fowler, R. D., & Butcher, J. N. (1986). Critique of Matarazzo's views on computerized testing: All sigma and no meaning. *American Psychologist, 41,* 94–96.

Fry, D. (1975). Interaction between locus of control, level of inquiry and subject control in the helping process: A lab analogue study. *Journal of Counseling Psychology, 22,* 280–287.

Garfield, S., & Bergin, A. (1978). *Handbook of psychotherapy and behavior change: An empirical analysis.* New York: Wiley.

Gayton, W. F., Burchstead, G. N., & Matthews, G. R. (1986). An investigation of the utility of an MMPI posttraumatic stress disorder subscale. *Journal of Clinical Psychology, 42,* 916–917.

Genther, R. W., & Graham, J. R. (1976). Effect of short term public hospitalization for both black and white patients. *Journal of Consulting and Clinical Psychology, 44,* 118–124.

Gibeau, E. (1975). An exploratory study of selected relationships among counseling orientations, theoretical orientations, personality and counselor effectiveness. *Dissertational Abstracts International, 36A,* 1303–1304.

Gibertini, M., Brandenburg, N. A., & Retzlaff, P. D. (1986). The operating characteristics of the Millon Clinical Multiaxial Inventory. *Journal of Personality Assessment, 50,* 554–567.

Gibertini, M., & Retzlaff, P. D. (1988a). Factor invariance of the Millon Clinical Multiaxial Inventory. *Journal of Psychopathology and Behavioral Assessment, 10,* 65–74.

Gibertini, M., & Retzlaff, P. D. (1988b, August). *Personality and alcohol use patterns among inpatient alcoholics.* Paper presented at the 96th Annual Convention of the American Psychological Association, Atlanta, GA.

Gilbride, T. V., & Hebert, J. (1980). Pathological characteristics of good and poor interpersonal problem-solvers among psychiatric outpatients. *Journal of Clinical Psychology, 36,* 121–127.

Giovacchini, P. (1984). *Character disorders and adaptive mechanisms.* Northvale, NJ: Jason Aronson.

Giovacchini, P. (1987). *A narrative textbook of psychoanalysis.* Northvale, NJ: Jason Aronson.

Glover, E. (1955). *The technique of psychoanalysis.* London: Bailliere, Tindall & Cox.

Goldberg, J. O., Segal, Z. V., Vella, D. D., & Shaw, B. F. (1989). Depressive personality: Millon Clinical Multiaxial Inventory profiles of sociotropic and autonomous subtypes. *Journal of Personality Disorders, 3,* 193–198.

Goldberg, J. O., Shaw, B. F., & Segal, Z. V. (1987). Concurrent validity of the Millon Clinical Multiaxial Inventory depression scales. *Journal of Consulting and Clinical Psychology, 55,* 785–787.

Graham, J. R. (1977). *The MMPI: A practical guide.* New York: Oxford University Press.

Graham, J. R. (1987). *The MMPI: A practical guide* (2nd ed.). New York: Oxford University Press.

Green, C. J. (1982). The diagnostic accuracy and utility of MMPI and MCMI computer interpretive reports. *Journal of Personality Assessment, 46,* 359–365.

Green, S. B., & Kelley, C. K. (1988). Racial bias in prediction with the MMPI for a juvenile delinquent population. *Journal of Personality Assessment, 52,* 263–275.

Greene, R. L. (1980). *The MMPI: An interpretative manual.* New York: Grune & Stratton.

Greenblatt, R. L., Mozdzierz, G. J., Murphy, T. J., & Trimakas, K. (1986, March). *Nonmetric multidimensional scaling of the MCMI.* Paper presented at the conference on the Millon Clinical Inventories, Miami, FL.

Guilford, J. P. (1936). *Psychometric methods.* New York: McGraw-Hill.

Guilford, J. P. (1952). When not to factor analyze. *Psychological Bulletin, 49,* 26–37.

Gutmann, D. L. (1980). The post-parental years: Clinical problems and developmental possibilities. In W. H. Norman & T. H. Scaramella (Eds.), *Midlife developmental and clinical issues* (pp. 38–52). New York: Brunner/Mazel.

Gutmann, D. L. (1987). *Reclaimed powers: Towards a new psychology of men and women in later life.* New York: Basic books.

Gynther, M. D. (1972). White norms and black MMPIs: A presentation for discrimination? *Psychological Bulletin, 78,* 386–402.

Gynther, M. D. (1981). Is the MMPI an appropriate assessment device for blacks? *Journal of Black Psychology, 7,* 67–75.

Gynther, M. D. (1989). MMPI comparisons of blacks and whites: A review and commentary. *Journal of Clinical Psychology, 45,* 878–883.

Gynther, M. D., & Green, S. B. (1980). Accuracy may make a difference, but does a difference make for accuracy? A response to Pritchard and Rosenblatt. *Journal of Consulting and Clinical Psychology, 48,* 268–272.

Hamberger, L. K., & Hastings, J. E. (1986). Personality correlates of men who abuse their partners: A cross-validation study. *Journal of Family Violence, 1,* 323–341.

Hamberger, L. K., & Hastings, J. E. (April, 1987). *The male batterer and alcohol abuse: Differential personality characteristics.* Paper presented at the meeting of the Western Psychological Association, Long Beach, CA.

Hamberger, L. K., & Hastings, J. E. (1988a). Characteristics of male spouse abusers consistent with personality disorders. *Hospital and Community Psychiatry, 39,* 763–770.

Hamberger, L. K., & Hastings, J. E. (1988b). Skills training for treatment of spouse abusers: An outcome study. *Journal of Family Violence, 3,* 121–130.

Hastings, J. E., & Hamberger, L. K. (1988). Personality characteristics of spouse abusers: A controlled comparison. *Violence and Victims, 3,* 31–47.

Hathaway, S. R., & McKinley, J. C. (1967). *Minnesota Multiphasic Personality Inventory manual.* New York: Psychological Corporation.

Helmes, E., & Barilko, O. (1988). Comparison of three multiscale inventories in identifying the presence of psychopathological symptoms. *Journal of Personality Assessment, 52,* 74–80.

Hess, A. K. (1985). Review of Millon Clinical Multiaxial Inventory. In J. V. Mitchell, Jr. (Ed.), *Ninth mental measurement yearbook* (pp. 984–986). Lincoln, NB: Buros Institute.

Hibbard, S. (1989). Personality and object relational pathology in young adult children of alcoholics. *Psychotherapy, 26,* 504–509.

Hibbs, B. J., Kobos, J. C., & Gonzalez, J. C. (1979). Effects of ethnicity, sex and age on MMPI profiles. *Psychological Reports, 45,* 591–597.

Hippocrates. (1950). The sacred disease. In *The medical works of Hippocrates* (J. Chadwich & W. N. Mann, Trans.; pp. 179–193). Springfield, IL: Charles C Thomas.

Hirschfeld, R. M. A., & Klerman, G. L. (1979). Personality attributes and affective disorders. *American Journal of Psychiatry, 136,* 67–70.

Hirschfeld, R. M. A., Klerman, G. L., Clayton, P. J., Keller, M. P., McDonald-Scott, P., & Larkin, B. H. (1983). Assessing personality: Effects of the depressive state on trait measurement. *American Journal of Psychiatry, 140,* 195–699.

Hoffman, B., Choca, J., Gutmann, D., Shanley, L., & Van Denburg, E. (1989, August). *Personality changes with aging in male psychiatric patients.* Paper presented at the 97th Annual Convention of the American Psychological Association, New Orleans, LA.

Hogg, B., Jackson, H., Rudd, R., & Edwards, J. (1990). Diagnosing personality disorders in recent-onset schizophrenia. *Journal of Nervous and Mental Disease, 178,* 194–199.

Holcomb, W. R., & Adams, N. (1982). Racial influences on intelligence and personality measures of people who commit murder. *Journal of Clinical Psychology, 38,* 793–796.

Holliman, N. B., & Guthrie, P. C. (1989). A comparison of the Millon Clinical Multiaxial Inventory and the California Psychological Inventory in assessment of a nonclinical population. *Journal of Clinical Psychology, 45,* 373–382.

Hollingshead, A. (1975). *Four factor index of social status.* Unpublished manuscript.

Honigfeld, G. (1971). In defense of diagnosis. *Professional Psychology, 2,* 289–291.

Horowitz, M., Marmar, C., Krupnick, J., Wilner, N., Kaltreider, N., & Wallerstein, R. (1984). *Personality styles and brief psychotherapy.* New York: Basic Books.

Hyer, L., & Boudewyns, P. A. (1987). The 8-2 MCMI code in a PTSD typology. *Center for Stress Recovery Newsletters, 4,* 7–8.

Hyer, L., O'Leary, W. C., Saucer, R. T., Blount, J., Harrison, W. R., & Boudewyns, P. (1986). Inpatient diagnosis of posttraumatic stress disorder. *Journal of Consulting and Clinical Psychology, 54,* 698–702.

Hyer, L., Woods, M., Boudewyns, P., Harrison, W., & Tamkin, A. (1990). MCMI and 16PF with Vietnam veterans: Profiles and concurrent validation of the MCMI. *Journal of Personality Disorders, 4,* 391–401.

Hyer, L., Woods, M., Bruno, R., & Boudewyns, P. (1989). Treatment outcomes of Vietnam veterans with PTSD and the consistency of the MCMI. *Journal of Clinical Psychology, 45,* 547–552.

Ibsen, H. (1879). A doll's house. In *Eleven plays of Henrik Ibsen.* New York: Random House.

Jensen, A. R. (1980). *Bias in mental testing.* New York: Free Press.

Jaffe, L. T., & Archer, R. P. (1987). The prediction of drug use among college students from MMPI, MCMI, and Sensation Seeking Scales. *Journal of Personality Assessment, 51,* 243–253.

Joffe, R., & Regan, T. (1989a). Personality and response to tricyclic antidepressants in depressed patients. *Journal of Nervous and Mental Disease, 177,* 745–749.

Joffe, R., & Regan, J. (1989b). Personality and suicidal behavior in depressed patients. *Comprehensive Psychiatry, 30,* 157–160.

Julian, T., Metcalfe, M., & Coppen, A. (1969). Aspects of personality of depressive patients. *American Journal of Psychiatry, 115,* 587–589.

Jung, C. G. (1933). *Modern man in search of a soul.* New York: Harcourt, Brace.

Keane, T. M., Malloy, P. F., Fairbank, J. A. (1984). Empirical development of an MMPI subscale for the assessment of combat-related posttraumatic stress disorder. *Journal of Consulting and Clinical Psychology, 52,* 888–891.

Keane, T. M., Wolfe, J., & Taylor, K. L. (1987). Posttraumatic stress disorder:

Evidence for diagnostic validity and methods for psychological assessment. *Journal of Clinical Psychology, 43,* 32–43.

Kelly, G. (1969a). Ontological acceleration. In B. Maher (Ed.), *Clinical psychology and personality: The selected papers of George Kelly* (pp. 7–45). New York: Wiley.

Kelly, G. (1969b). The psychotherapeutic relationship. In B. Maher (Ed.), *Clinical psychology and personality: The selected papers of George Kelly* (pp. 66–93). New York: Wiley.

Kendell, R. E. (1983). DSM-III: A major advance in psychiatric nosology. In R. L. Spitzer, J. B. W. Williams, & A. E. Skodol (Eds.), *International perspectives on DSM-III* (pp. 55–68). Washington, DC: American Psychiatric Press.

Kendell, R. E., & DiScipio, W. J. (1968). Eysenck Personality Inventory scores of patients with depressive illness. *British Journal of Psychiatry, 114,* 767–770.

Kernberg, O. F. (1975). *Borderline conditions and pathological narcissism.* Northvale, NJ: Jason Aronson.

Kernberg, O. F. (1984). *Treatment of severe personality disorders: Psychotherapeutic strategies.* New Haven, CT: Yale University Press.

Kiesler, D. J. (1977). *Communications assessment of interview behavior of the obsessive personality.* Unpublished manuscript.

Kiesler, D. J. (1979). An interpersonal communication analysis of relationship in psychotherapy. *Psychiatry, 42,* 299–311.

Kiesler, D. J. (1982). Interpersonal theory for personality and psychotherapy. In J. Anchin & D. Kiesler (Eds.), *Handbook of interpersonal psychotherapy* (pp. 3–24). New York: Pergamon Press.

Kiesler, D. J. (1983). The interpersonal circle: A taxonomy for complementarity in human transactions. *Psychological Review, 90,* 184–214.

Kiesler, D. J. (1985). *The maladaptive transaction cycle.* Unpublished manuscript.

Kiesler, D. J. (1986a). The 1982 interpersonal circle: An analysis of DSM-III personality disorders. In T. Millon & G. Klerman (Eds.), *Contemporary issues in psychopathology* (pp. 1–23). New York: Guilford Press.

Kiesler, D. (1986b). Interpersonal methods of diagnosis and treatment. In R. Michels & J. Cavenar (Eds.), *Psychiatry* (pp. 571–597). Philadelphia: Lippincott.

Kiesler, D., Van Denburg, T., Sikes, V., Larus, J., & Goldston, C. (1990). Interpersonal behavior profiles of eight cases of DSM-III personality disorder. *Journal of Clinical Psychology, 46,* 440–453.

Klerman, G., Weissman, M., Rounsaville, B., & Chevron, E. (1984) *Interpersonal psychotherapy of depression.* New York: Basic Books.

Kohut, H. (1971). *The analysis of the self.* Madison, CT: International Universities Press.

Kohut, H. (1977). *The restoration of the self.* Madison, CT: International Universities Press.

Lachar, D. (1974). *The MMPI: Clinical assessment and automated interpretation.* Los Angeles: Western Psychological Services.

Lambert, N. M. (1981). Psychological evidence in *Larry P. v. Wilson Riles. American Psychologist, 36,* 937–952.

Langs, R. (1973). *The technique of psychoanalytic psychotherapy* (Vol. 1). Northvale, NJ: Jason Aronson.

Lanyon, R. I. (1984). Personality assessment. *Annual Review of Psychology, 35,* 667–701.

Lazare, A., & Klerman, G. L. (1968). Hysteria and depression: The frequency and significance of hysterical personality features in hospitalized depressed women. *American Journal of Psychiatry, 124,* 48–56.

Leaf, R. C., DiGiuseppe, R., Ellis, A., Mass, R., Backx, W., Wolfe, J., & Alington, D. E. (1990). "Healthy" correlates of MCMI scales 4, 5, 6, and 7. *Journal of Personality Disorders, 4,* 312–328.

Leary, T. (1957). *Interpersonal diagnosis of personality.* New York: Ronald Press.

Leary, T., & Coffey, H. (1955). Interpersonal diagnosis: Some problems of methodology and validation. *Journal of Abnormal and Social Psychology, 50,* 110–124.

Levine, J., Tischer, P., Antoni, M., Green, C., & Millon, T. (1985). Refining personality assessments by combining MCMI high-point profiles and MMPI codes, Part II: MMPI 27/72. *Journal of Personality Assessment, 49,* 501–507.

Levinson, D. J. (1978). *The seasons of a man's life.* New York: Knopf.

Levinson, D. J. (1980). Toward a conception of the adult life course. In N. J. Smelser & E. H. Erikson (Eds.), *Themes of work and love in adulthood* (pp. 265–290). Cambridge, MA: Harvard University Press.

Levy, S. (1987). Therapeutic strategy and psychoanalytic technique. *Journal of the American Psychoanalytic Association, 35,* 447–466.

Lewis, S., & Harder, D. (1990). Factor structure of the MCMI among personality disordered outpatients and in other populations. *Journal of Clinical Psychology, 46,* 613–617.

Libb, J. W., Stankovic, S., Freeman, A., Sokol, R., Switzer, P., & Houck, C. (1990). Personality disorders among depressed outpatients as identified by the MCMI. *Journal of Clinical Psychology, 46,* 277–284.

Lorr, M., Katz, M., & Rubinstein, E. (1958). The prediction of length of stay in psychotherapy. *Journal of Consulting Psychology, 22,* 321–327.

Lorr, M., Retzlaff, P. D., & Tarr, H. C. (1989). An analysis of the MCMI-I at the item level. *Journal of Clinical Psychology, 45,* 884–890.

Lorr, M., & Strack, S. (1990). Profile clusters of the MCMI-II personality disorder scales. *Journal of Clinical Psychology, 46,* 606–612.

Lorr, M., Strack, S., Campbell, L., & Lamnin, A. (1990). Personality and symptom dimensions of the MCMI-II: An item factor analysis. *Journal of Clinical Psychology, 46,* 749–754.

Lovitt, R. (1988). Current practice of psychological assessment: Response to Sweeney, Clarkin, and Fitzgibbon. *Professional Psychology: Research and Practice, 19,* 516–521.

Lumsden, E. A. (1986, March). *Internal structure validation of the MCMI: Correlations among unshared scale items.* Paper presented at the conference of the Millon Clinical Inventories, Miami, FL.

Lumsden, E. A. (1988). The impact of shared items on the internal structure validity of the MCMI. *Educational and Psychological Measurement, 49,* 669–678.

Luteijn, F. (1990). The MCMI in the Netherlands: First findings. *Journal of Personality Disorders, 4,* 297–302.

Machiavelli, N. (1931). *The prince* (W. Marriott, Trans.). London: J. M. Dent. (Original work published 1532)

Malan, D. (1976). *Frontiers of brief psychotherapy.* New York: Plenum Press.

Malec, J., Wolberg, W., Romsaas, E., Trump, D., & Tanner, M. (1988). Millon Clinical Multiaxial Inventory (MCMI) findings among breast clinic patients after initial evaluation and at 4- or 8-month follow-up. *Journal of Clinical Psychology, 44,* 175–180.

Mann, J. (1973). *Time limited psychotherapy.* Cambridge, MA: Harvard University Press.

Marsella, A. J., Sanaborn, K. O., Kameoka, V., Shizuru, L., & Brennan, J. (1975). Cross validation of self-report measures of depression among normal populations of Japanese, Chinese, and Caucasian ancestry. *Journal of Clinical Psychology, 31,* 281–287.

Marsh, D. T., Stile, S. A., Stoughton, N. L., & Trout-Landen, B. L. (1988). Psychopathology of opiate addiction: Comparative data from the MMPI and MCMI. *American Journal of Drug and Alcohol Abuse, 14,* 17–27.

Matarazzo, J. D. (1986). Computerized clinical psychological test interpretations: Unvalidated plus all mean and no sigma. *American Psychologist, 41,* 14–24.

Mayer, G. S., & Scott, K. J. (1988). An exploration of heterogeneity in an inpatient male alcoholic population. *Journal of Personality Disorders, 2,* 243–255.

McCann, J. T. (1989). MMPI personality disorder scales and the MCMI: Concurrent validity. *Journal of Clinical Psychology, 45,* 365–369.

McCann, J. T. (1990). A multitrait-multimethod analysis of the MCMI-II clinical syndrome scales. *Journal of Personality Assessment, 55,* 465–476.

McCann, J. T. (1991). Convergent and discriminant validity of the MCMI-II and MMPI personality disorder scales. *Psychological Assessment: A Journal of Consulting and Clinical Psychology, 3,* 9–18.

McCann, J., & Gergelis, R. (1990). Utility of the MCMI-II in assessing suicide risk. *Journal of Clinical Psychology, 46,* 764–770.

McCann, J., & Suess, J. (1988). Clinical applications of the MCMI: The 1-2-3-8 codetype. *Journal of Clinical Psychology, 44,* 181–186.

McCrae, R. R., & Costa, P. T. (1990). *Personality in adulthood.* New York: Guilford Press.

McCreary, C., & Padilla, E. (1977). MMPI differences among black, Mexican-American and white male offenders. *Journal of Clinical Psychology, 33,* 171–177.

McCullough, J. (1984). Cognitive-behavioral analysis system of psychotherapy: An interactional treatment approach for dysthymic disorder. *Psychiatry, 47,* 234–250.

McDermott, W. F. (1987). The diagnosis of post-traumatic stress disorder using the

Millon Clinical Multiaxial Inventory. In C. Green (Ed.), *Conference of the Millon Clinical Inventories (MCMI, MBHI, MAPI)* (pp. 257–262). Minneapolis, MN: National Computer Systems.

McGill, J. C. (1980). MMPI score differences among Anglo, black and Mexican American welfare recipients. *Journal of Consulting and Clinical Psychology, 36,* 147–171.

McMahon, R., Applegate, B., Kouzekanani, K., & Davidson, R. (1990, August). *Confirmatory factor analysis of the Millon Clinical Multiaxial Inventory.* Paper presented at the 98th Annual Convention of the American Psychological Association, Boston.

McMahon, R., & Davidson, R. (1985a). Transient versus enduring depression among alcoholics in inpatient treatment. *Journal of Psychopathology and Behavioral Assessment, 7,* 317–328.

McMahon, R., & Davidson, R. (1985b). An examination of the relationship between personality patterns and symptom/mood patterns. *Journal of Personality Assessment, 49,* 552–556.

McMahon, R., & Davidson, R. (1986a). Concurrent validity of the clinical symptom scales of the Millon Multiaxial Inventory. *Journal of Clinical Psychology, 42,* 908–912.

McMahon, R., & Davidson, R. (1986b). An examination of depressed vs. nondepressed alcoholics in inpatient treatment. *Journal of Clinical Psychology, 42,* 177–184.

McMahon, R. C., & Davidson, R. S. (1988, August). *Factor structure of the Millon Clinical Multiaxial Inventory in an alcohol abusing population.* Paper presented at the 96th Annual Convention of the American Psychological Association, Atlanta, GA.

McMahon, R., & Davidson, R. (1989, August). *A comparison of continuous and episodic drinkers using the MCMI, MMPI, and ALCEVAL-R.* Paper presented at the 97th Annual Convention of the American Psychological Association, New Orleans, LA.

McMahon, R. C., Davidson, R. S., & Flynn, P. M. (1986). Psychosocial correlates and treatment outcomes for high and low social functioning alcoholics. *International Journal of Addictions, 21,* 819–835.

McMahon, R. C., Flynn, P. M., & Davidson, R. S. (1985a). Stability of the personality and symptom scales of the Millon Clinical Multiaxial Inventory. *Journal of Personality Assessment, 49,* 231–234.

McMahon, R. C., Flynn, P. M., & Davidson, R. S. (1985b). The personality and symptoms scales of the Millon Clinical Multiaxial Inventory: Sensitivity to posttreatment outcomes. *Journal of Clinical Psychology, 41,* 862–866.

McMahon, R. C., Gersh, D. M., & Davidson, R. S. (1989a, August). *Factor structure and correlates of the Millon Clinical Multiaxial Inventory.* Paper presented at the 97th Annual Convention of the American Psychological Association, New Orleans, LA.

McMahon, R. C., Gersh, D., & Davidson, R. S. (1989b). Personality and symptom characteristics of continuous vs. episodic drinkers. *Journal of Clinical Psychology, 45,* 161–168.

McMahon, R., Kouzekanani, K., & Bustillo, S. (1991, August). *Factor structure of the Millon Clinical Multiaxial Inventory-II.* Paper presented at the 99th Annual Convention of the American Psychological Association, San Francisco, CA.

McMahon, R., & Tyson, D. (1989). *Transient versus enduring depression among alcoholic women.* Paper presented at the 97th Annual Convention of the American Psychological Association, New Orleans, LA.

McMahon, R., & Tyson, D. (1990). Personality factors in transient versus enduring depression among inpatient alcoholic women: A preliminary analysis. *Journal of Personality Disorders, 4,* 150–160.

McNiel, K., & Meyer, R. (1990). Detection of deception on the Millon Clinical Multiaxial Inventory (MCMI). *Journal of Clinical Psychology, 46,* 755–764.

Meehl, P. (1960). The cognitive activity of the clinician. *American Psychologist, 15,* 19–27.

Meehl, P. (1973). *Psychodiagnosis: Selected papers.* New York: Norton.

Meehl, P. E., & Rosen, A. (1955). Antecedent probability and the efficiency of psychometric signs, patterns, or cutting scores. *Psychological Bulletin, 52,* 194–216.

Merbaum, M., & Butcher, J. (1982). Therapists' liking of their psychotherapy patients: Some issues related to severity of disorder and treatability. *Psychotherapy: Theory, Research and Practice, 19,* 69–76.

Miller, C., Knapp, S., & Daniels, C. (1968). MMPI study of Negro mental hygiene clinic patients. *Journal of Abnormal Psychology, 73,* 168–173.

Miller, C., Wertz, C., & Counts, S. (1961). Racial differences on the MMPI. *Journal of Clinical Psychology, 17,* 159–160.

Miller, H. R., & Streiner, D. L. (1990). Using the Millon Clinical Multiaxial Inventory's Scale B and the MacAndrew Alcoholism Scale to identify alcoholics with concurrent psychiatric diagnoses. *Journal of Personality Assessment, 54,* 736–746.

Millon, T. (1969). *Modern psychopathology: A biosocial approach to maladaptive learning and functioning.* Philadelphia: Saunders.

Millon, T. (1973). A biosocial-learning approach. In T. Millon (Ed.), *Theories of psychopathology and personality* (pp. 492–502). Philadelphia: Saunders.

Millon, T. (1974). *MCMI manual.* Unpublished manuscript.

Millon, T. (1977). *Millon Clinical Multiaxial Inventory.* Minneapolis, MN: National Computer Systems.

Millon, T. (1981). *Disorders of personality: DSM-III Axis II.* New York: Wiley.

Millon, T. (1982). *Millon Clinical Multiaxial Inventory manual* (2nd ed.) Minneapolis, MN: National Computer Systems.

Millon, T. (1983). *Millon Clinical Multiaxial Inventory manual* (3rd ed.). Minneapolis, MN: National Computer Systems.

Millon, T. (1985). The MCMI provides a good assessment of DSM-III disorders:

The MCMI-II will prove even better. *Journal of Personality Assessment, 49,* 379–391.

Millon, T. (1986). The MCMI and DSM-III: Further commentaries. *Journal of Personality Assessment, 50,* 205–207.

Millon, T. (1987). *Manual for the MCMI-II* (2nd ed.). Minneapolis, MN: National Computer Systems.

Millon, T. (1988). Personologic psychotherapy: Ten commandments for a posteclectic approach to integrative treatment. *Psychotherapy, 25,* 209–219.

Millon, T. (1990). *Toward a new personology: An evolutionary model.* New York: Wiley.

Mischel, W. (1968). *Personality assessment.* New York: Wiley.

Mischel, W. (1973). Toward a cognitive social learning reconceptualization of personality. *Psychological Review, 80,* 252–283.

Moreland, K. L., & Onstad, J. A. (1987). Validity of Millon's computerized interpretation system for the MCMI: A controlled study. *Journal of Consulting and Clinical Psychology, 55,* 113–114.

Moreland, K. L., & Onstad, J. A. (1989). Yes, our study could have been better: Reply to Cash, Mikulka, and Brown. *Journal of Consulting and Clinical Psychology, 57,* 313–314.

Morey, L. C. (1985). An empirical comparison of interpersonal and DSM-III approaches to classification of personality disorders. *Psychiatry, 48,* 358–364.

Morey, L. C. (1986). A comparison of three personality disorder assessment approaches. *Journal of Psychopathology and Behavioral Assessment, 8,* 25–30.

Morey, L. C., Blashfield, R. K., Webb, W. W., & Jewell, J. (1988). MMPI scales for the DSM-III personality disorders: A preliminary validation study. *Journal of Clinical Psychology, 44,* 47–50.

Morey, L. C., Waugh, M. H., & Blashfield, R. K. (1985). MMPI scales for the DSM-III personality disorders: Their derivation and correlates. *Journal of Personality Assessment, 49,* 245–251.

Mortimer, R., & Smith, W. (1983). The use of the psychological test report in setting the focus of psychotherapy. *Journal of Personality Assessment, 47,* 134–138.

Murray, L. G., & Blackburn, I. M. (1974). Personality differences in patients with depressive illness and anxiety neurosis. *Acta Psychiatrica Scandinavica, 50,* 183–191.

Neimeyer, G. (1987). Personal construct assessment, strategy, and technique. In R. Neimeyer & G. Neimeyer (Eds.), *Personal construct therapy casebook* (pp. 20–36). New York: Springer.

Nerviano, V., & Gross, W. (1983). Personality types of alcoholics in objective inventories. *Journal of Studies on Alcohol, 44,* 837–851.

Neugarten, B. L. (1975). The awareness of middle age. In B. L. Neugarten (Ed.), *Middle age and aging* (pp. 93–98). Chicago: Chicago University Press.

Norcross, J., & Prochaska, J. (1982). A national survey of clinical psychologists: Characteristics and activities. *Clinical Psychologist, 35,* 1–8.

Nystrom, S., & Lindegard, B. (1975). Predisposition for mental syndromes: A study comparing predisposition for depression, neurasthenia and anxiety state. *Acta Psychiatrica Scandinavica, 51,* 69–76.

Overholser, J. C. (August, 1989). *Temporal stability of the MCMI personality disorder scales.* Paper presented at the 97th Annual Convention of the American Psychological Association, New Orleans, LA.

Overholser, J. C., Kabakoff, R., & Norman, W. H. (1989). The assessment of personality characteristics in depressed and dependent psychiatric inpatients. *Journal of Personality Assessment, 53,* 40–50.

Ownby, R. L., Wallbrown, F., Carmin, C., & Barnett, R. W. (1990). A combined factor analysis of the Millon Clinical Multiaxial Inventory and the MMPI in an offender population. *Journal of Clinical Psychology, 46,* 89–96.

Ownby, R. L., Wallbrown, F. H., Carmin, C., & Barnett, R. (1991). A canonical analysis of the Millon Clinical Multiaxial Inventory and the MMPI for an offender population. *Journal of Personality Disorders, 5,* 15–24.

Page, R. D., & Bozlee, S. (1982). A cross-cultural MMPI comparison of alcoholics. *Psychological Reports, 50,* 639–646.

Palmer, C. (1975). Characteristics of effective counselor-trainees. *Dissertation Abstracts International, 36A,* 2031.

Palmer, H. D., & Sherman, S. H. (1938). Involutional melancholia process. *Archives of Neurology and Psychiatry, 40,* 762–788.

Pancoast, D. L., Archer, R. P., & Gordon, R. A. (1988). The MMPI and clinical diagnosis: A comparison of classification system outcomes with discharge diagnoses. *Journal of Personality Assessment, 52,* 81–90.

Patrick, J. (1988). Concordance of the MCMI and the MMPI in the diagnosis of three DSM-III Axis I disorders. *Journal of Clinical Psychology, 44,* 186–191.

Peniston, E. G., & Kulkosky, P. J. (1990). Alcoholic personality and alpha-theta brainwave training. *Medical Psychotherapy, 3,* 37–45.

Perris, C. (1966). A study of bipolar (manic-depressive) and unipolar recurrent depressive psychosis: A multidimensional study of personality traits. *Acta Psychiatrica Scandinavica Supplement, 194,* 68–82.

Perris, C. (1971). Personality patterns in patients with affective disorders. *Acta Psychiatrica Scandinavica Supplement, 221,* 43–51.

Piersma, H. L. (1986a). The stability of the Millon Clinical Multiaxial Inventory for psychiatric inpatients. *Journal of Personality Assessment, 50,* 193–197.

Piersma, H. L. (1986b). The factor structure of the Millon Clinical Multiaxial Inventory (MCMI) for psychiatric inpatients. *Journal of Personality Assessment, 50,* 578–584.

Piersma, H. L. (1986c). The Millon Clinical Multiaxial Inventory (MCMI) as a treatment outcome measure for psychiatric inpatients. *Journal of Clinical Psychology, 42,* 493–499.

Piersma, H. L. (1986d, August). *Computer-generated diagnoses: How do they compare to clinical judgment?* Paper presented at the 94th Annual Convention of the American Psychological Association, Washington, DC.

Piersma, H. L. (1987). The MCMI as a measure of DSM-III Axis II diagnoses: An empirical comparison. *Journal of Clinical Psychology, 43,* 478–483.

Piersma, H. L. (1989). The stability of the MCMI-II for psychiatric inpatients. *Journal of Clinical Psychology, 45,* 781–785.

Piersma, H. L. (1991). The MCMI-II depression scales: Do they assist in the differential prediction of depressive disorders? *Journal of Personality Assessment, 56,* 478–486.

Pincus, A. L., & Wiggins, J. S. (1990). Interpersonal problems and conceptions of personality disorders. *Journal of Personality Disorders, 4,* 342–352.

Piotrowski, C., & Keller, J. W. (1989). Psychological testing in outpatient mental health facilities: A national study. *Professional Psychology: Research and Practice, 20,* 423–425.

Piotrowski, C., & Lubin, B. (1989). Assessment practices of Division 38 practitioners. *Health Psychologist, 11,* 1.

Piotrowski, C., & Lubin, B. (1990). Assessment practices of health psychologists: Survey of APA Division 38 clinicians. *Professional Psychology: Research and Practice, 21,* 99–106.

Plemons, G. (1977). A comparison of the MMPI scores of Anglo and Mexican-American psychiatry patients. *Journal of Consulting and Clinical Psychology, 45,* 149–150.

Pochyly, J. M., Greenblatt, R. L., & Davis, W. E. (1989, August). *The effect of race on MCMI clinical scales.* Paper presented at the 97th Annual Convention of the American Psychological Association, New Orleans, LA.

Pollack, D., & Shore, J. H. (1980). Validity of the MMPI with Native Americans. *American Journal of Psychiatry, 137,* 946–950.

Prifitera, A., & Ryan, J. J. (1984). Validity of the Narcissistic Personality Inventory (NPI) in a psychiatric sample. *Journal of Clinical Psychology, 40,* 140–142.

Pritchard, D. A., & Rosenblatt, A. (1980). Racial bias in the MMPI: A methodological review. *Journal of Consulting and Clinical Psychology, 48,* 263–267.

Raskin, R. N., & Hall, C. S. (1979). A narcissistic personality inventory. *Psychological Reports, 45,* 590.

Reich, J. (1985). Measurement of DSM-III Axis II. *Comprehensive Psychiatry, 26,* 352–363.

Reich, J. (1989). Update on instruments to measure DSM III and DSM-III-R personality disorders. *Journal of Nervous and Mental Disease, 177,* 366–370.

Reich, J., & Troughton, E. (1988). Comparison of DSM-III personality disorders in recovered depressed and panic disorder patients. *Journal of Nervous and Mental Disease, 176,* 300–304.

Reich, W. (1949). *Character analysis.* New York: Noonday Press.

Repko, G. R., & Cooper, R. (1985). The diagnosis of personality disorder: A comparison of MMPI profile, Millon inventory, and clinical judgment in a workers' compensation population. *Journal of Clinical Psychology, 41,* 867–881.

Retzlaff, P., & Gibertini, M. (1987). Factor structure of the MCMI basic personality scales and common item artifact. *Journal of Personality Assessment, 51,* 588–594.

Retzlaff, P. D., & Gibertini, M. (1990). Factor based special scales for the MCMI. *Journal of Clinical Psychology, 46,* 47–52.

Retzlaff, P., Lorr, M., & Hyer, L. (1989). *An MCMI-II item-level component analysis: Personality and clinical factors.* Unpublished manuscript.

Retzlaff, P. D., Sheehan, E. P., & Fiel, A. (1991). MCMI-II report style and bias: Profile and validity scales analysis. *Journal of Personality Assessment, 56,* 478–486.

Retzlaff, P. D., Sheehan, E. P., & Lorr, M. (in press). MCMI-II scoring: Weighted and unweighted algorithms. *Journal of Personality Assessment.*

Reynolds, C. R. (1982). The problem of bias in psychological assessment. In C. R. Reynolds & T. B. Gutkin (Eds.), *The handbook of school psychology* (pp. 178–208). New York: Wiley.

Reynolds, C. R. (1983). Test bias: In God we trust; all others must have data. *Journal of Special Education, 17,* 241–260.

Robert, J. A., Ryan, J. J., McEntyre, W. L., McFarland, R. S., Lips, O. J., & Rosenberg, S. (1985). MCMI characteristics of DSM-III: Posttraumatic stress disorder in Vietnam veterans. *Journal of Personality Assessment, 49,* 226–230.

Rogers, C. (1951). *Client centered therapy.* Cambridge, MA: Riverside Press.

Rosenthal, S. H., & Gudeman, J. E. (1967). The endogenous depressive pattern: An empirical investigation. *Archives of General Psychiatry, 16,* 241.

Sabshin, M. (1989). Normality and the boundaries of psychopathology. *Journal of Personality Disorders, 3,* 259–273.

Schectman, F. (1989). Countertransference dilemmas with borderline patients. *Bulletin of the Menninger Clinic, 53,* 310–318.

Schwartz, M. A., Wiggins, O. P., & Norko, M. A. (1989). Prototypes, ideal types and personality disorders: The return to classical psychiatry. *Journal of Personality Disorders, 3,* 1–9.

Sexton, D. L., McIlwraith, R., Barnes, G., & Dunn, R. (1987). Comparison of the MCMI and the MMPI-168 as psychiatric inpatient screening inventories. *Journal of Personality Assessment, 51,* 388–398.

Shapiro, D. (1989). *Psychotherapy of neurotic character.* New York: Basic Books.

Shapiro, T. (1988). *Structure and psychoanalysis.* Madison, CT: International Universities Press.

Shapiro, T. (1989). Psychoanalytic classification and empiricism with borderline personality disorder as a model. *Journal of Consulting and Clinical Psychology, 57,* 187–194.

Shaughnessy, R., Dorus, E., Pandey, G. N., & Davis, J. M. (1980). Personality correlates of platelet monoamine oxidase activity and red blood cell lithium transport. *Psychiatric Research, 2,* 63–74.

Shure, G. H., & Rogers, M. S. (1965). Note of caution on the factor analysis of the MMPI. *Psychological Bulletin, 63,* 14–18.

Sifneos, P. (1972). *Short-term psychotherapy and emotional crisis*. Cambridge, MA: Harvard University Press.

Silverman, J. T. (1979). *The effect of personality variables on the patient-therapist relationship in psychotherapy*. Unpublished doctoral dissertation, Boston College.

Sim, J. P., & Romney, D. M. (1990). The relationship between a circumplex model of interpersonal behaviors and personality disorders. *Journal of Personality Disorders, 4*, 329–341.

Simonsen, E., & Mortensen, E. L. (1990). Difficulties in translation of personality scales. *Journal of Personality Disorders, 4*, 290–296.

Smith, D., Carroll, J., & Fuller, G. (1988). The Millon Clinical Multiaxial Inventory and the MMPI in a private outpatient mental health clinic population. *Journal of Clinical Psychology, 44*, 165–174.

Stone, M. H. (1980). *The borderline syndromes*. New York: McGraw-Hill.

Strack, S., Lorr, M., & Campbell, L. (August, 1989). *Similarities in Millon personality styles among normals and psychiatric patients*. Paper presented at the 97th Annual Convention of the American Psychological Association, New Orleans, LA.

Strack, S., Lorr, M., & Campbell, L. (1990). An evaluation of Millon's circular model of personality disorders. *Journal of Personality Disorders, 4*, 353–361.

Strack, S., Lorr, M., Campbell, L., & Lamnin, A. (in press). Personality disorders and clinical syndrome factors of the MCMI-II scales. *Journal of Personality Disorders*.

Strandman, E. (1978). "Psychogenic needs" in patients with affective disorders. *Acta Psychiatrica Scandinavica, 58*, 16–29.

Strassberg, D., Cooper, L., & Marks, P. (1987). *The Marks Adult MMPI Report. Version 2.1: The MMPI Scoring Program II*. Wakefield, RI: Applied Innovations.

Streiner, D. L., & Miller, H. R. (1989). The MCMI-II: How much better than the MCMI? *Journal of Personality Assessment, 53*, 81–84.

Strupp, H., & Binder, J. (1984) *Psychotherapy in a new key*. New York: Basic Books.

Sullivan, H. S. (1953). *The interpersonal theory of psychiatry*. New York: Norton.

Sweeney, J. A., Clarkin, J. F., & Fitzgibbon, M. L. (1987). Current practice of psychological assessment. *Professional Psychology: Research and Practice, 18*, 377–380.

Symonds, M. (1978). The psychodynamics of violence-prone marriages. *American Journal of Psychoanalysis, 38*, 213–222.

Terry, C. (1990, December 30). Vaclav Havel's new role. *Chicago Tribune*, Section 13, p. 3.

Tisdale, M. J., Pendleton, L., & Marler, M. (1990). MCMI characteristics of DSM-III-R bulimics. *Journal of Personality Assessment, 55*, 477–483.

Torgersen, S., & Alnaes, R. (1990). The relationship between the MCMI personality scales and the DSM-III Axis II. *Journal of Personality Assessment, 55*, 698–707.

Trimboli, F. (1979). *MMPI interpretation and treatment implications*. Unpublished manuscript.

Trimboli, F., & Kilgore, R. (1983). A psychodynamic approach to MMPI interpretation. *Journal of Personality Assessment, 47,* 614–626.

Turkat, I. (1988). Issues in the relationship between assessment and treatment. *Journal of Psychopathology and Behavioral Assessment, 10,* 185–197.

Turkat, I. (1990). *The personality disorders: A psychosocial approach to clinical management.* Elmsford, NY: Pergamon Press.

Turkat, I., & Maisto, S. (1985). Application of the experimental method to the formulation and modification of personality disorders. In D. H. Barlow (Ed.), *Clinical handbook of psychological disorders* (pp. 503–570). New York: Guilford Press.

Uomoto, J. M., Turner, J. A., & Herron, L. D. (1988). Use of the MMPI and the MCMI in predicting outcome of lumbar laminectomy. *Journal of Clinical Psychology, 44,* 191–197.

Vaglum, P., Friis, S., Irion, T., Johns, S., Karterud, S., Larsen, F., & Vaglum, S. (1990). Treatment response of severe and nonsevere personality disorders in a therapeutic community day unit. *Journal of Personality Disorders, 4,* 161–172.

Van Denburg, T. (1987). *Stage process model of psychotherapy: Passive-dependent personality disorder.* Unpublished manuscript.

Van Gorp, W. G., & Meyer, R. G. (1986). The detection of faking on the Millon Clinical Multiaxial Inventory (MCMI). *Journal of Clinical Psychology, 42,* 742–747.

van Reken, M. (1981). Psychological assessment and report writing. In C. E. Walker (Ed.), *Clinical practice of psychology.* New York: Pergamon Press.

von Zerssen, D. (1982). Personality and affective disorders. In E. S. Paykel (Ed.), *Handbook of affective disorders* (pp. 212–228). New York: Guilford Press.

Wade, T., & Baker, T. (1977). Opinions and use of psychological tests: A survey of clinical psychologists. *American Psychologist, 31,* 874–882.

Walker, J. (1974). The word association sentence method as a predictor of psychotherapeutic outcome. *British Journal of Social and Clinical Psychology, 77,* 219–221.

Webb, J. T., Miller, M. L., & Fowler, R. D. (1970). Extending professional time: A computerized MMPI interpretation service. *Journal of Clinical Psychology, 26,* 210–214.

Weiner, I. (1972). Does psychodiagnosis have a future? *Journal of Personality Assessment, 36,* 534–546.

Werman, D. (1984). *The practice of supportive psychotherapy.* New York: Brunner/Mazel.

Wetzler, S. (1990). The Millon Clinical Multiaxial Inventory (MCMI): A review. *Journal of Personality Assessment, 55,* 445–464.

Wetzler, S., & Dubro, A. (1990). Diagnosis of personality disorders by the Millon Clinical Multiaxial Inventory. *Journal of Nervous and Mental Disease, 178,* 261–263.

Wetzler, S., Kahn, R. S., Cahn, W., van Praag, H. M., & Asnis, G. M. (1990). Psychological test characteristics of depressed and panic patients. *Psychiatry Research, 31,* 179–192.

Wetzler, S., Kahn, R., Strauman, T., & Dubro, A. (1989). Diagnosis of major depression by self-report. *Journal of Personality Assessment, 53,* 22–30.

Wetzler, S., & Marlowe, D. (1990). "Faking bad" on the MMPI, MMPI-2 and Millon-II. *Psychological Reports, 67,* 1117–1118.

Widiger, T. A. (1985). Review of Millon Clinical Multiaxial Inventory. In J. V. Mitchell, Jr. (Ed.), *Ninth mental measurement yearbook* (pp. 986–988). Lincoln, NB: Buros Institute.

Widiger, T. A. (1989). The categorical distinction between personality and affective disorders. *Journal of Personality Disorders, 3,* 77–91.

Widiger, T. A., & Frances, A. (1987). Interviews and inventories for the measurement of personality disorders. *Clinical Psychology Review, 7,* 49–74.

Widiger, T. A., Frances, A., Spitzer, R. L., & Williams, J. B. (1988). The DSM-III-R personality disorders: An overview. *American Journal of Psychiatry, 145,* 786–795.

Widiger, T. A., Hurt, S. W., Frances, A., Clarkin, J. F., & Gilmore, M. (1984). Diagnostic efficiency and the DSM III. *Archives of General Psychiatry, 41,* 1005–1012.

Widiger, T. A., & Kelso, K. (1983). Psychodiagnosis of Axis II. *Clinical Psychology Review, 3,* 491–510.

Widiger, T. A., & Sanderson, C. (1987). The convergent and discriminant validity of the MCMI as a measure of the DSM-III personality disorders. *Journal of Personality Assessment, 51,* 228–242.

Widiger, T. A., Williams, J. B. W., Spitzer, R. L., & Frances, A. (1985). The MCMI as a measure of DSM-III. *Journal of Personality Assessment, 49,* 366–378.

Widiger, T. A., Williams, J. B. W., Spitzer, R. L., & Frances, A. (1986). The MCMI and DSM-III: A brief rejoinder to Millon. *Journal of Personality Assessment, 50,* 198–204.

Wiggins, J. S. (1982). Circumplex models of interpersonal behavior in clinical psychology. In P. C. Kendall & J. N. Butcher (Eds.), *Handbook of research methods in clinical psychology* (pp. 183–222). New York: Wiley.

Winston, A., Pinsker, H., & McCullough, L. (1986). A review of supportive psychotherapy. *Hospital and Community Psychiatry, 37,* 1105–1114.

Wright, W. (1975). Counselor dogmatism: Willingness to disclose and client's empathy ratings. *Journal of Counseling Psychology, 22,* 390–394.

Young, D., & Beier, E. (1982). Being asocial in social places: Giving the client a new experience. In J. Anchin & D. Kiesler (Eds.), *Handbook of interpersonal psychotherapy* (pp. 262–273). New York: Pergamon Press.

Author and Subject Index